SHANGHAI LAWYER

The Memoirs of America's China
Spymaster

Norwood F. Allman

With annotations, illustrations and embellishments
by Douglas Clark

Shanghai Lawyer

By Norwood F. Allman

ISBN-13: 978-988-8422-20-3

Introduction, epilogue, index, annotations
and selection of materials ©2017 Douglas Clark
Layout and typesetting ©2017 Earnshaw Books

This book has been reset in 10pt Book Antiqua. Spellings and punctuations are left as in
the original edition.

HISTORY / Asia / China

EB081

Published by Earnshaw Books Ltd. (Hong Kong)

FOREWORD
by Douglas Clark

Lawyer, judge, consul, businessman, newspaper publisher, politician, spy and spymaster. These are just few of the jobs that Norwood Allman held over the years — many at the same time.

In *Shanghai Lawyer*, first published in 1943, Allman tells the story of his amazing life in the China — a country which along with its people and its language he loved deeply. Allman came to China in his early twenties and left — other than a brief gap during World War II — only in the 1950s when forced to by the Chinese Communist Revolution.

Allman first arrived in Shanghai as a young man in the year 1916. He had passed the United States Foreign Service examination and was bound for Peking to study Chinese. In those days, the United States, following the British example, trained a corps of foreign service officers in Chinese with the intention that they would serve their entire careers in China. They had to learn the language because America, like other foreign powers in China, had special rights that meant Americans were not subject to Chinese law. Consuls had to represent the interests of American citizens around the country, and this required constant contact with Chinese officials, very few of whom spoke English.

Allman excelled at his Chinese studies, despite (or perhaps because of) the very hard work it required. Outside his studies, he recounts the whirlwind life of young men exploring early 20th century Beijing; the quirky personalities of his various bosses;

and the tedium of diplomatic life for one on the bottom rung of protocol—all stories told with humour.

Only a few years after his arrival, Allman was serving as American consul in numerous far-flung cities in China. His first posting was to Andong in Manchuria on the border with then Japanese-controlled Korea. He was next posted to war-torn Shandong Province where on many occasions he had to travel between the front lines of warring factions. He also had responsibility for the port city of Qingdao which the Japanese had taken over from Germany—with help from the British—at the beginning of World War I. After brief postings in Tianjin and Nanjing, he was sent to Chongqing far upriver on the Yangtze as Acting Consul before finally receiving a longer term posting in Shanghai.

Having already qualified as a lawyer—and briefly serving as Deputy Clerk to the United States Court for China—while based in Tianjin, Allman was appointed an assessor of the International Mixed Court in Shanghai. The Mixed Court, established in the 1860s, tried cases against all Chinese as well as against foreigners without treaty rights. Originally run by the Chinese government with foreign assessors sitting to observe, following the fall of the Qing Dynasty in 1911-12, the Shanghai Municipal Council had taken over the running of the court and the foreign assessors were effectively co-judges. Allman sat for four years hearing cases in Chinese with the Chinese magistrates. He recalls many tales of perfidy from this fascinating time.

In 1924, Allman resigned from the consular service to practice as a lawyer in Shanghai. As an attorney enrolled with the United States Court for China, Allman was, by courtesy, allowed to practice before all other foreign and Chinese courts in Shanghai. He regularly appeared before the Chinese courts trying cases in Chinese. He also reprised his role as a judge when he was appointed honourary Mexican consul, making him, also, the judge of the Mexican consular court.

Allman practiced very successfully as a lawyer, first in partnership with William Fleming and Cornell Franklin and from 1930, following Fleming's death, in his own firm. His clients included large American multinationals, local Chinese and many local Shanghai celebrities. He also acted for Russians and Americans accused of espionage and even the "wastrel brother" of an American movie tycoon. Allman also, like many lawyers, branched out into other businesses, sometimes as the request of clients, other times, seeing a chance for a profit. The business that put him on a Japanese black list and brought genuine threats to his life was as owner and editor of the Chinese language newspaper, the *Shun Pao*, which he took over after its editor Shi Liangcai was assassinated.

Allman, an avid horseman and polo player, was also a member and, later commander, of the American troop of the Shanghai Volunteer Corps ("SVC"). This saw him defending the International Settlement in 1932 and 1937 when Japanese troops fought the Chinese army in and around Shanghai. The book begins and ends with Allman's story of the battle for Hong Kong against the invading Japanese army in December 1941 and his internment by the Japanese in Stanley Internment Camp.

With war raging with Japan, Allman—already head of Far Eastern counter intelligence in the Office of Strategic Services— clearly intended *Shanghai Lawyer* to be anti-Japanese and pro-Chinese propaganda. This is made clear by his dedication of the book to Madame and General Chiang Kai-shek, whom Allman knew personally (his wife was at university with Madame Chiang and they both attended the Chiangs' wedding). As a result, Allman underplays the many problems with the Kuomintang rule—he does not mention that Chiang, upset with the *Shun Pao's*

editorial policy, had ordered the assassination of Shi Liangcai—
and overplays the evil of the Japanese, suggesting sometimes that
the Japanese were responsible for atrocities when they were not.

Nevertheless, *Shanghai Lawyer* is a fascinating insight into a
very important time in Chinese history. Most foreigners are only
faintly aware of the period in living history when America and
other foreign powers based their navies and armies in China,
had their nationals sit as judges in foreign and Chinese courts
and fought battles with the Chinese as each foreign power
sought to protect their slice of the China cake. The "Century of
Humiliation", as Chinese propaganda now calls it, has not been
forgotten in China. It is a fundamental part of the Communist
Party's world view and its hold on power. The message to
Chinese people is clear: foreigners are constantly seeking to
split China and return it to a semi-colonial status, and only the
Communist Party can save China from this fate. As China has
come to assert itself on the world stage, we must all understand
how it sees and interprets its own history.

Political, diplomatic and legal considerations compelled
Allman to use pseudonyms for many people mentioned in the
book and to change other details. As far as possible, by research
through public and personal archives, I have annotated the book
with the true names of people and the actual details of events.
Where Allman's recollections are, perhaps, misleading I have
added notes making the story clear. As far as possible, I have also
illustrated the book with contemporaneous pictures, documents
and newspaper clippings to help bring Allman's story to life. In
a new epilogue, I briefly tell the story of Allman's later life as a
spymaster in the OSS and CIA. During the war, he ran operations
in China and after the war recently de-classified documents show
he was working with the CIA while running his law practice in
Shanghai. After his return to the US, he worked with the CIA and

was part of a team that organized a coup in Guatemala.

World War II was not the beginning of Allman's life as a spy. As a consul, he was clearly involved in gathering intelligence. In the book, he details his successful efforts to get access to the closed German consulate in Jinan during World War I. He was posted to Qingdao to keep an eye on Japanese navy and troop movements. He regularly crossed front lines in Shandong, and surely was watching battlefield dispositions closely. In later years, Allman represented Russians and Americans accused of espionage. Later while a member of the SVC, he recounts going behind the Japanese lines to locate Japanese artillery placements. Allman was a close friend of American Cornelius Starr, the founder of AIG, who used his insurance companies and agents to spy for the British in China. In Allman's personal archive, there are notes of de-briefings he conducted in the 1930s. It is not, however, clear for whom these were prepared; the OSS was America's first formal intelligence service and only established during World War II. Perhaps, like Starr, he had also been working with the British.

One striking thing throughout the book is Allman's almost blasé disregard for his own personal safety and totally disengaged attitude to death. He recounts military battles, assassinations and personal threats to his safety with a complete air of detachment. There is no doubt he was personally very brave; perhaps there was an element of belief in himself as an almost supernatural being.

Norwood Allman was, truly, an extraordinary man. He was a multi-talented multi-lingual polymath with a superb head for business. He clearly loved China very much and would have lived out his life there if the Communists had not expelled all foreigners. *Shanghai Lawyer* is not the memoir of some ivory tower foreigner who lived in an expatriate bubble. These are the memoirs of someone who spoke the language, worked in, lived

in and travelled all over the country negotiating with, doing
business with and engaging directly with the Chinese people.
His truly remarkable story remains relevant to this day.

Douglas Clark
Shanghai
October 2016

SHANGHAI LAWYER

Norwood F. Allman

ACKNOWLEDGEMENT

I wish to thank Frances Russell Kay for her collaboration; without her assistance this book could not have been written.[1]

1   Frances Russell had been women's editor of the *North China Daily News* in Shanghai in the 1930s. She returned to the United States in 1938 and continued to work as a journalist into the 1970s.

SHANGHAI LAWYER

NORWOOD F. ALLMAN

To *the*

GENERALISSIMO[1] *and* MADAME CHIANG KAI-SHEK

The Two Outstanding People of History

---

1   Chiang Kai-Shek (蔣介石 Jiang Jieshi) (1887-1975) was the leader of the Chinese
    Kuomintang from 1925 following the death of its founder, Sun Yat-sen. Chiang had
    been commandant of the Whampoa Military Academy. See Chapter 11 footnote 1 for
    details of Sun and Chapter 10 footnote 6 for details of Madam Chiang.

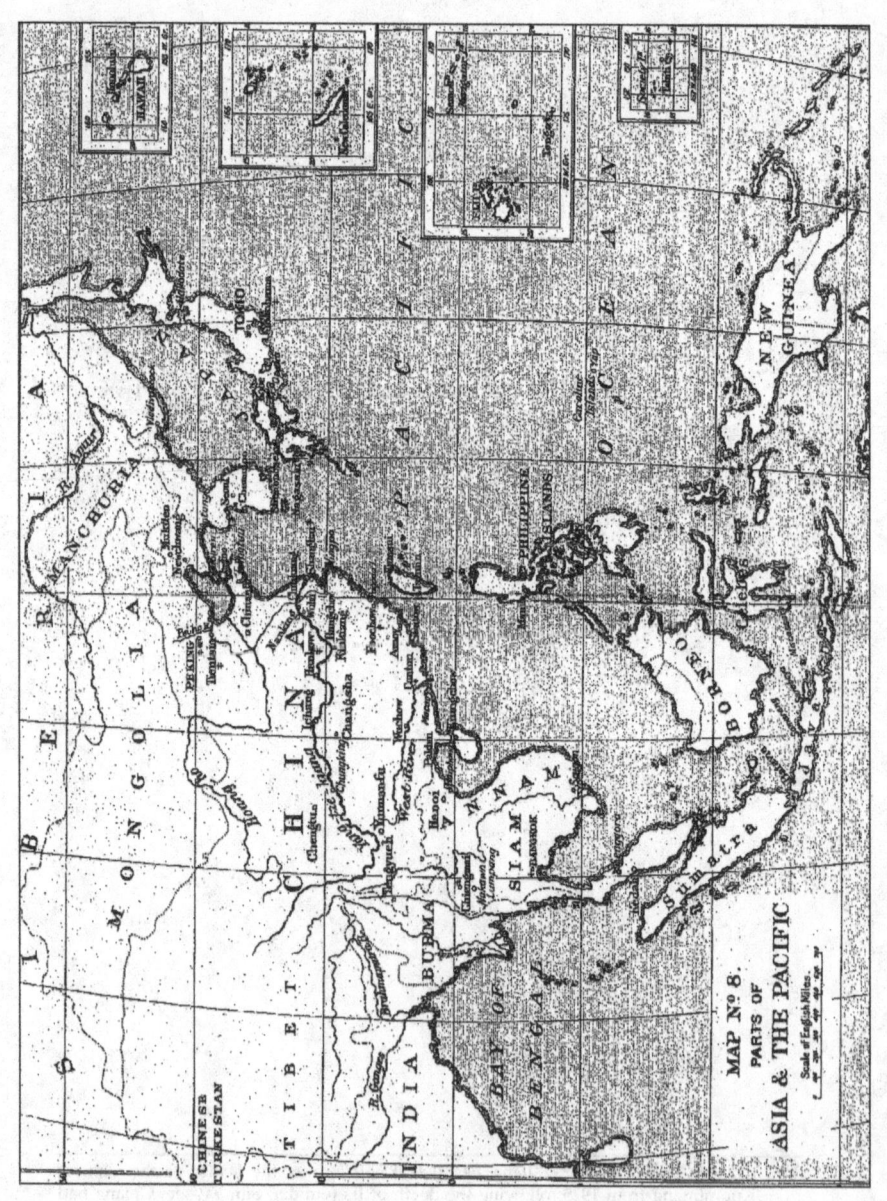

MAP No 8.
PARTS OF
ASIA & THE PACIFIC
Scale of English Miles.

Contents

I

A Prisoner Of The Japs

Of all the twenty-six eventful years I spent in China as an American consul, as assessor (or judge) on the International Mixed Court, and finally as a practicing American attorney in Shanghai, the last six months in that war-torn country were without question the most memorable and the ones I would least like to live over again. For that was the period I spent behind barbed wire in Stanley Prison as an involuntary "guest" of the ruthless Jap invaders. I can still break out in a cold sweat remembering the dark night when a scream rang out through the silent prison grounds and a group of us rushed over to the eight by four foot room occupied by two American girls, to find a drunken, heavily armed Japanese guard leaning over the bed of one of them.

And I remember another night when I stood guard at a hole we had made under the barbed wire, expecting any moment to be apprehended and shot at by the Jap guards, while fellow prisoners Paul Dietz[1] and Gordon Frisque[2] wormed their way outside and down a cliff to get a pail of sea water, so that we might have some precious and forbidden salt to flavor our meager ration of rice.

And the bitter February morning when some three thousand thinly clad and ragged prisoners—American, British, and Dutch

---

1   Paul Dietz (born 1903), an American, was the Shanghai-based China Manager of the Goodrich Rubber Company.
2   Gordon E. Frisque (1904-2006), an American, was the Manager of Kodak in Hong Kong. He returned to Hong Kong after the war.

Paul Dietz *Gordon Frisque*

men, women, and children—were ordered out of their quarters (built to house a few hundred) and made to stand around for hours in a freezing rain, surrounded by a ring of Jap machine guns, while patrols of Japanese and Indian "inspectors" systematically looted their rooms and persons of precious food and the few remaining possessions they had previously been allowed to keep. Now that I am safely back in America, it is often difficult for me to realize that these months in prison ended an important chapter of my life—that my successful law business in Shanghai has been destroyed, my offices and extensive law library looted, and my partners and staff scattered or imprisoned. But I look upon it not as the beginning of the end for me, but rather as the beginning of a new chapter.

For I am going back after the war is ended and start over. The switch from an officer of the law to a prisoner of the lawless was quite a jump for a respectable, hard-working lawyer to take in middle life; but it was a case of take it "or else" when late on the evening of January 4, 1942, the following order was posted around Hong Kong:

ORDER

All enemy aliens shall assemble at the Murray Parade Ground, Victoria, Hong Kong, from 10 a. m. to 12 noon on the 5th of January, 1942.

Personal effects are allowed to be carried.

Enemy subjects in this order include British, American, Dutch, and other nationals whose countries are at war with Japan, exempting Chinese and Indian.

Signed — Lt. Colonel Noma[3],

Commander of the Imperial Japanese

Gendarmerie, Hong Kong.

I had survived the siege of Hong Kong, where I had been trapped on a business trip, and was contemplating how I might escape the Japs and get back to my family in Shanghai, when the order was issued which resulted in my internment next day, along with other "enemy aliens" who, like myself, had been caught by the Jap invaders.

There were 316 Americans, 2481 British, and 70 Dutch nationals in the original group, herded together in a barbed-wire enclosure approximately one-fourth mile wide by one-third mile long on Stanley Peninsula, a neck of land jutting out into the bay from Hong Kong Island. This was to be known as the Stanley internment camp and was to be our unhappy home for the next six months.

The peninsula had been the scene of some of the hardest fighting during the siege of Hong Kong. As a result the twenty buildings included in the camp area had been badly battered.

---

3   Colonel Kennosuke Noma (野間憲之助) (1896-1947), who was in charge of the Japanese Kempeitai in Hong Kong from 25 December 1941 to 18 January 1945. Noma was tried as a war criminal in Hong Kong after the war, found guilty, and executed at Stanley Prison on 27 May 1947.

Stanley Intermnent Camp, Hong Kong, where Allman was interned for 6 months

The Americans were assigned to a group of four buildings which formerly had been part of the warders' quarters for Stanley Prison, a British prison operated by the Colonial government. The British were put in some fifteen buildings of St. Stephen's college and preparatory school, and the Dutch in one building which had been a part of the warders' club. In all, 3,000 internees were packed into quarters which had housed some 250 warders.[4]

A small working group had been sent in ahead to clean up the camp, but they hadn't had time to do much toward piling up the rubble, propping up walls, and patching up the windows, almost all of which had been shattered by shell fire. Since unbroken glass was not obtainable from the Japs, many internees had to sleep in rooms that were open to the elements. This caused no little hardship for those who lacked warm clothes and bedding during the many cold nights.

In spite of the handicaps, however, the energetic American working party had a cookstove going—a stove which a Seventh

---

4   For more details of life in Stanley Internment camp, see G. Emerson, Hong Kong Internment, 1942-1945: Life in the Japanese Civilian Camp at Stanley.

Day Adventist missionary and a Maryknoll father helped them build—and had boiled water and hot food ready for their fellow internees when they arrived.

The Japs informed us that we could govern ourselves, but threatened that if we didn't, they would. Our first job was to arrange for billeting. We agreed that families and married couples should be kept together as much as possible. The American task was fairly simple, because of our smaller number. The British, on the other hand, because of their greater numbers, were billeted with an utter disregard for family privacy.

Sanitary facilities were primitive at best, and bathing (what there was of it) was done in two small community bathrooms, later augmented by two other small rooms which had been kitchens. There was little privacy anywhere.

We established a community mess hall in what had been the prison garage. The Americans, without permission from the Japs, named the walk which ran from their quarters to the mess Roosevelt Avenue. It was the main and most popular thoroughfare of the camp.

As soon as the housing problem was attended to, the American group met together in a mass meeting to elect, in true democratic manner, their community government. The British and Dutch likewise went about selecting their governing groups. I presided at the American meeting, and we elected a communal governing committee made up of William P. Hunt[5], chairman;

---

5   William Peter Hunt (1901-1966), the owner of William P. Hunt & Co. a large shipping company in China was a former US Consular Officer. He had come to Hong Kong from Shanghai on his way to Chungking. His business continued after the war with offices all over Asia. Hunt had even before the formal internment been making arrangements for Americans and "was able to secure better quarters for the Americans than were allotted to the British and the circumstance that one of the puppet supervisors had been employed by Mr. Hunt made the latter's work easier." Hunt was accused of being autocratic in his management.

Father J.J. Toomey   *William P Hunt*

A. W. Bourne[6], vice-chairman; Father J. J. Toomey[7], treasurer; Dr. William H. Taylor[8], secretary, and seven others[9]. In addition to the council, permanent committees such as the following were selected: finance, audit and control, water-boiling, food, quarters, sanitation, gardening, maintenance and repair, firewood and fuel, medical, educational, recreation.

Every man, woman, and child was given some definite duty to perform. One of the first and most disagreeable for the men was the burying of the dead bodies, left where they had fallen in battle. There were only a few persons who refused to work, on the theory

6   Bourne was the General Manager of the Standard Vacuum Company in Hong Kong.

7   John Joseph Toomey (1890-1963) was a Jesuit priest from New Bedford Massachusetts. In 1941 he was appointed Procurator and Local Superior of the Maryknoll house at Stanley. He was released with the other Maryknollers on September 12, 1942, and eventually made his way to India and then the United States. He returned to China after the war and was expelled by the communist government in 1952.

8   William Henry Taylor (1906-1965) was an employee of the US Treasury who was in China to advise the Chinese Currency Stabilization Fund. He served as an alternate member to A. Manuel Fox. Taylor later worked for the IMF and was accused of been a Soviet spy and a member of the Communist Party of the United States. Taylor denied this. See Chapter 18 for a photo.

9   Four of the others were Mr. Kelly; T.B. Wilson, American President Lines; T.B. Williams, Standard Oil Co.; and, Dr. Frank, Lingnan University. Report by F. W. Wright, (BAAG codename SHINAH), who escaped from Stanley on the 18th March, 1942. Submitted to BAAG in Kukong, 14th June 1942.

that they had never done any physical work before in their lives and felt that they were too old to begin at this point. One man was all of thirty. The camp committee took the stand, "No wanchee workee, no wanchee eatee." The rebels held out about twenty-four hours. Then one of them, a fastidious young intellectual, was given the job of cleaning out a particularly evil-smelling social hall in the former warders' quarters, which the Japs, true to form, had used as a latrine instead of the regular lavatory next door.

Addison Southard US Consul-General in HK

I was elected legal adviser for the American group and for want of a better title was called provost-marshal. Our internment had been sudden, and few of us had made adequate preparation for it when we were assembled on the Murray Parade Ground and told that we would not be permitted to return to our homes or hotels. Many were short of clothing and money. Some had been robbed on their way to the assembly place; others had left passports and other personal papers in strongboxes at home or bank. A number were in desperate need of odds and ends of legal advice.

To provide those without passports with documents that would tend to establish their American citizenship, I prepared a number of affidavits, in which the affiants set forth such details as when and where they were born, who their parents were, when and where their passports were lost, and so forth.

Ordinarily such details would be handled by the American consul-general in Hong Kong, A. E. Southard[10]; but that gentleman

---

10   Addison E. Southard (1884-1970) was a career foreign service officer. He had served as American Minister/Resident in Ethiopia from 1928 to 1932 and then as consul general in Paris. He had arrived in Hong Kong in 1938.

and his entire staff were interned and held incommunicado in a building just outside our barbed-wire enclosure.[11]

My first Stanley client was Mrs. Robert Rogers[12], a soft-spoken, courageous widow who needed legal documents to protect insurance and property claims arising from the death of her husband. Mr. Rogers, a former broker, had been killed fighting with the Hong Kong Volunteer Corps.

Mrs. Rogers wanted to pay me for my services, which I of course refused; but to jolly her a bit I suggested, "Why not invite me to a meal some day?" That, I thought, was about as far-fetched an idea as I could conceive. But I didn't know Mrs. Rogers! A day or two later she invited me to lunch. Somehow or other she had found a little flour — whether she had begged or borrowed it, I was too polite to ask — and she generously shared with me her last two teaspoons of coffee. That meal, consisting of two pancakes and a cup of coffee each, was more welcome than any banquet I can recall or any fee I ever collected.

Alice Dobbs had lost her passport and needed proof of American citizenship. I had firsthand knowledge of her nationality and also of her husband's death. She was a young American I had known since her childhood in Tientsin. Her British husband was an employee of the Chinese American Stabilization Board in Hong Kong. Alice had been in Kunming with her two children and had left them there while she went to visit her husband in Hong Kong just before hostilities broke out. The couple were living with me in the Hong Kong Hotel the day Dobbs went out to establish a food center near the Happy Valley Race Course, where there had been heavy shelling. When he didn't return, I went looking for him and

---

11   The American consular staff were interned on two houses on the Peak and then moved to Stanley but in a separate building that was heavily guarded. Southard and the consular staff were repatriated in 1942. Upon his return to the United States, Southard said "To stop the Japs, you've got to kill them — that's what we've got to do and that's what we must begin to realize." *New York Herald Tribune*, Aug 26, 1942, p10
12   Mary Rogers.

two days later found his burned and shell-torn body.[13]

It was not necessary to rely on records, either, for the facts of Madeline Jeanette Owens's[14] birth. I was right at hand when it happened. I helped build her crib out of a packing box. Baby Madeline was born in Stanley internment camp of an American father and a British mother. Her birth was a camp event. Everybody joined in the attempt to make Madeline's entrance into this world as pleasant as possible. The parents were quartered in a twelve-by-ten room with two other couples, one of which was Dr. Gourdin[15], the only American doctor in camp, and his wife. As the mother's accouchement approached, several of us pitched in and cleaned out a small, debris-filled room that had once been a kitchen. Two weeks before the baby came, the Owenses moved in. At least they were assured of some privacy and a little comfort. According to prevailing camp standards the room was downright luxurious, with two cots, a chair, and the baby's homemade bed. Madeline Jeanette was born early one April morning in what we called the Tweed Bay Hospital[16], rigged up in one of the prison buildings by the combined efforts of the British, American, and Dutch internees. Equipment was inadequate, but the baby did not lack for medical attention. We usually had more British doctors and nurses on hand than patients.

My first job as legal adviser to the camp council was to analyze the Geneva Prisoners of War Convention of 1929 and find out

---

13   F.E.L Dobbs was an inspector with the Chinese Salt Gabelle. The British record of his death states he was killed in a boiler explosion. Alice was the former Ms. Alice Gibb. She had been born in Peking in 1909. They had three children. Alice was repatriated in 1942.

14   Born 14 April 1942 weighing 7.5 pounds to Mr. and Mrs. Reginald Owens. She was repatriated in 1942.

15   Dr. Allston Gourdin (died 1973) had been born in Hong Kong. He commenced practice in 1929 after graduating from the University of Hong Kong. He returned to Hong Kong after the war and resumed practice in 1947. He died in Lisbon in 1973.

16   The staff and patients of Queen Mary Hospital had all been moved to Stanley on January 19, 1942. The hospital was in the old Indian Single Warders' Quarters which had served as an emergency medical centre during the war.

what our rights were. This Convention laid down regulations for the humane treatment of prisoners of war in addition to those already in effect, and, while it referred specifically to members of armed forces and their auxiliaries, I felt we could make a case for an analogous treatment of civilian prisoners.

I listed a few of the Japs' most glaring violations of the terms of the Geneva Convention, but when they were presented to the camp commandant, he sent back word that it was all damned nonsense and that he'd never heard of the Geneva Convention.

Our number one complaint, then and throughout our internment, was lack of food. When we arrived at Stanley, there were three good-sized godowns (warehouses) on the Peninsula, filled with enough assorted food to feed the entire camp for a year. These, however, were soon cleaned out by the military, and from the first we were faced with a serious food shortage. Later on the camp population was actually hungry all the time.

Before a month was out, the food ration per head per day was down to one-half pound of rice, one-fortieth pound of sugar, one-fiftieth pound of salt, one-fiftieth pound of oil, and one-tenth pound of beans, with the addition on occasion of a small ration of fish and half an eight-ounce tin of milk for children up to three years of age.

On February 15, the day following the Japanese gendarmerie's "inspection" (looting) of the camp, soybeans were cut off; on February 22 salt was deleted; sugar disappeared on February 24, and rice, our main food, was rationed on February 26. Flour ended on February 27 and peanut oil on the twenty-ninth. Milk for the babies was withdrawn after March 5. Occasionally, however, these items were restored for brief periods. Up to this time, our ration had amounted to approximately 1,350 calories a day. After March 5, it dropped as low as 870 calories, of which 830 were carbohydrates — a diet that could lead only to slow starvation.

Our supplies, brought in by motor truck, were unprotected from flies, rain, or dirt. They were dumped on the ground to be divided pro rata among the various national groups. We had a garden of sorts within the compound, made up of a patch of alfalfa, already there, and a patch of tomatoes for which we found seeds. We cooked the alfalfa and ate it with relish, and almost everyone in camp got at least one tomato during the season. In order that no one should get more than his share, we posted a guard over the garden. Two teen-age girls were the only culprits ever caught by the garden guard. They almost got away with a tomato apiece. They were brought before me for punishment, but I had not the heart to do anything except wish I had more to give them.

In addition to the garden, some internees were able to augment their meager food ration through the canteen. Under terms of the Geneva Convention, prisoners of war are entitled to a canteen. We asked for one the first thing. Three months later our request was granted.

We appointed a canteen committee of British, American, and Dutch prisoners. At irregular intervals the Japs sent in limited supplies of canned goods to be sold at exorbitant prices. It was possible for an internee with plenty of money and some luck to buy a twelve-ounce, seventy-cent (Hong Kong currency) can of Australian butter for seven dollars, Hong Kong (or a dollar and seventy-five cents, as one Hong Kong dollar was worth twenty-five American cents); or a thirty-cent can of sardines for three dollars and fifty cents. Quantities were so low that prospective purchasers formed queues immediately after curfew was lifted at 8 a.m. and waited in line all day for the canteen to open at 2 p.m. Only the first third ever had the slightest chance of buying anything.

The canteen had been open a little more than a week when the operating committee discovered that it was being robbed, obviously by one of the internees.

In Stanley there was always a minor crisis of one kind or another. When you think of several hundred Americans of all types and backgrounds, jammed together without sufficient food, clothing, or privacy, and with nothing to do except dwell on their misfortunes, it is remarkable that more of us didn't go berserk. We could forgive almost anything but stealing our precious food.

Circumstantial evidence pointed to two American seamen as the culprits. There was also reason to believe that these men were stealing not because of hunger, but because they wanted food to sell at black-market prices.

A trap was set to catch the thieves. Two internees whose reputations were above suspicion were chosen to sleep in the canteen at night. Nothing happened for several nights, except that the guards were nearly eaten alive by the ferocious mosquitoes infesting the area. Obviously the thieves were aware that the canteen was guarded. One day the canteen committee made a great show of dismissing the guards, then quietly slipped them back. Three nights later the men were caught red-handed, taking chocolate and two cans of bully beef. They admitted their guilt, and their confession was reported to me for appropriate action. I recommended to the camp committee that, rather than report them to the Jap authorities and possibly subject the whole camp to punishment, we hold a kangaroo court and deal with the culprits ourselves.

We agreed on the latter method. I was to sit as judge and pass sentence. Attorneys were appointed for the defense. In order to prevent the whole camp from turning out and drawing unwelcome Jap attention, we held the first and only American trial in Stanley internment camp before a handful of spectators and the governing council. The trial was held with as much realism and dignity as was possible in a ten-by-twelve-foot room that had had its windows blown out.

The defense counsel waived formal arraignment, pleaded guilty, and offered, in mitigation of the defendants' offense, hunger. I could take judicial cognizance of the fact that they were hungry — We all were!

And what were the sentences? Solitary confinement? Not on your life! I profited by Sir Athol MacGregor's[17] mistake. As judge of the British camp court he had

Athol MacGregor, Chief Justice of Hong Kong, interned with Allman.

sentenced the first man found guilty of an offense to thirty days' solitary confinement. Since privacy was at a great premium, the sentence turned out to be a reward for the prisoner and a punishment for his guards, who, after dreary eight-hour shifts, returned to a ten-by twelve-foot cubicle shared with eight roommates. Several internees had been put out of a room and packed in with others to make way for the prisoner.

I sentenced our two prisoners to be confined in different buildings, where they were to engage in certain designated heavy work for a period of twenty days.

In addition to my duties as lawyer and judge I also acted as chief of police, arranging for twenty-four-hour voluntary guard duty by our own men. This was necessary, we felt, to protect our women and children from the Jap guards, who frequently

---

17 Sir Alasdair Duncan Athol MacGregor, KC (1883-1945). Sir Athol was the Chief Justice of Hong Kong having been appointed in 1933. He survived internment but contracted beriberi in the camp. He was put on the first hospital ship out of Hong Kong after the Japanese surrender, but died at sea. His last official act was to swear Frank Grimson in as acting Governor in August 1945. He had from time to time sat as a judge of the Full Court of the British Supreme Court for China in Shanghai. See Gunboat Justice, Vol 3.

wandered into our quarters at all hours of the day and night.[18]

On the occasion when one of our young women woke one night to find a drunken Jap guard leaning over her bed, our own guards rushed over in answer to her screams and surrounded the Jap. He was so befuddled and startled at the nerve of a group of unarmed men trying to face him down, that he didn't shoot, but was content to strut around for several minutes, threatening violence and slapping faces.

Another time, a group of three drunken Jap officials broke into a young woman's room in the British section. Their guards called for help, and we rushed over and again surrounded the Japs. This time they got really nasty, drawing out revolvers and forcing two of the British guards to their knees, with guns at their temples. This was too much for two former British police officials, who waded in and dis-armed the Japs with a jujitsu trick.

We protested these acts of the Japs vigorously, but nothing was done about it; and until the day of our repatriation, we continued to have similar unprovoked attacks.

As our plight steadily worsened, it was inevitable that there would be attempts to escape from the camp. The first and only successful one occurred on the night of March 17, and by a strange coincidence those who escaped were in two parties, neither of which was aware of the other's plans.

The larger group, made up of one British and three American men and a British woman, was led by the latter, tall, blond Elsie

---

18 One report on conditions in the camp stated the reason for the 24-hour guard to be that "impelled by misery and hunger, looting and petty theft were the order of the day through every section of the community. Thus from starting by taking anything that was regarded as "abandoned property", people proceeded to take anything that they could lay hands on. The Japanese issued an order that no doors were to be locked. It therefore became necessary not only for each room or flat to have one person always on guard, but for each community to organise its own guards. Those guards operated day and night. The Americans were concentrated in two blocks of buildings, so their problem was comparatively simple. There were always four guards on duty who patrolled the road in front of the buildings in the day, but remained inside the gates at night." F.W. Wright, cited above.

Elsie Fairfax-Cholmeley with Israel   *Gwen Priestwood*
Epstein in 1946

Chumley[19]. She was a striking young woman of about thirty, who was generally credited with being a British secret agent. She had discovered a small boat in the weeds near a bathing beach just outside our barbed wire and had arranged through friends on the outside to have a junk meet her party off Stanley Peninsula. I saw her about ten o'clock that night and noted that she was in a high state of excitement, but I didn't reveal that I knew an escape attempt was afoot and went on about my nightly tour of inspection. They made the break at midnight.

At almost the same time, another young British woman, Gwen Priestwood[20], and Thompson[21], a former British police official, crawled under the barbed wire and escaped to the hills

---

19   Elsie Fairfax-Cholmeley (1905-1984) (which is pronounced Chumley) was the daughter of a Yorkshire squire. She later married Israel Epstein. After the Communist Revolution, they moved to China. Epstein edited the propaganda magazine *China Today*. During the Cultural Revolution she took part in the sacking of the British Embassy in Beijing. She and her husband were imprisoned from 1968 to 1973.

20   Gwen Priestwood (nee Fullbrook) (1916?-2000) was the estranged wife of the penultimate British Crown Advocate in Shanghai, Victor Priestwood. Gwen had moved to Hong Kong in 1940 to live with her mother. She and W.P. Thompson made it to Chungking in Free China. She then went on a speaking tour in America and the UK to drum up support for the war. She wrote a story of her escape: *Through Japanese Barbed Wire*.

21   Police Superintendent W.P. Thompson. Thompson continued to operate behind Japanese lines after his escape.

overlooking the camp, where they hid all the next day.

The few of us who knew about their plans were on edge for some time, wondering if they would be caught. But they never were. When the Japs discovered the break next morning, there was hell to pay. Nobody told the names of those who had escaped, but a roll call quickly revealed all the names except that of Elsie Chumley. Her roommate had reported her in the hospital, and the Japs didn't discover the ruse until they searched the British quarters and found in her confederate's room a suitcase that contained Elsie's photograph.

The entire camp was punished for this escape. We were put on shorter rations, visiting was banned between 8 p.m. and 8 a.m., and everyone had to be in bed by ten o'clock at night. Electric lights were strung around the barbed wire, and guards were increased.

A month later four ex-members of the British Hong Kong police force[22] made a break and got as far as the city, where they were caught when one of them attempted to visit a sweetheart whose home was being watched by the Jap police. They eventually were returned to camp in a badly battered and beaten-up state. When we left Hong Kong these four men were still sick and were still being punished by being kept in solitary confinement in Stanley Prison.

Aside from the few breaks for freedom and an occasional clash with Jap guards, there was little excitement in camp to relieve the monotony of imprisonment. We had some entertainment, engineered by an international committee which arranged for the exchange and combining of talent.

On several Saturday nights we had a community sing fest in

---

22 Kevin Smythe, Brian Fay, Vincent Morrison and Vic Randall. Only Morrison was a former policeman. They were caught when, according to Morrison, they tried to get in touch with a Chinese contact to get a boat. They, were tried on June 20, 1942 in the Hong Kong Supreme Court and sentenced to two years solitary confinement in Stanley Prison. For more details see: George Wright-Nooth , *Prisoner of the Turnip Heads: Horror, Hunger and Humour in Hong Kong 1941-1945*, Chapter 5.

one of the American buildings. A four-piece orchestra of British-American internees supplied the music for an occasional dance, for which we were seldom given permission. In the early days, there frequently was a softball game in progress in the American section, and the British set up a bowling green. But as time went on, the lack of food kept most of us so weak that we didn't feel up to any athletic activity.

There was a school for the three or four hundred children in camp. It was pitiful to watch them sitting in cold, bleak rooms in tattered clothes and soleless shoes, trying to work without the books, paper, pencils, blackboards, and other paraphernalia usually thought necessary for a successful schoolroom. I taught a class in written Chinese. There were other classes for adults in languages and stenography. We had smuggled in books from the American Club. A few of political character were kept carefully hidden from our warders.

The only correspondence we had with the outside during our entire internment was through the medium of a few letters smuggled in and out by bribed guards. All pencils, pens, writing paper, and typewriters were forbidden us, but a few of us managed to smuggle in such equipment at the time of our entrance.

I had received no word from my wife and son, John, in Shanghai all during my internment, nor had I been able to get any direct word to them about my situation and state of health. I was, to say the least, greatly concerned about them and also my older son and daughter, at school in America; for I had not been able to send them funds for many months. I kept hoping fervently that the Shanghai members of my family would be repatriated.

During almost the entire six months of our internment the Japanese had spread frequent rumors through the camp to the effect that Americans were to be repatriated. They kept our hopes alternately at the peak and in the depths for month after month, until finally they posted a notice that we were to go on June 15. By this time we had grown pretty skeptical about this "war of nerves," but all of us packed our baggage in preparation for departure. When the day came, we were again plunged into depths of despair by the announcement that the sailing had been postponed. Almost two weeks went by. Then, on June 29, the Jap passenger liner appeared and dropped anchor about three miles off our camp. We really believed, then, that deliverance was at hand, and on the following day we bade our British and Dutch friends good-by and were ferried out to the ship, *Asama*.

Once on board, I heard that some American residents of Shanghai had been shipped out at about the same time on the Italian liner, *Conte Verde*, and for the next week, could hardly sleep a wink, hoping and praying that my wife and son would be on it. Not until the two ships docked in Singapore did I learn that they actually were among the passengers. I found later that they had known I was on the *Asama*, but the Japanese had permitted no communication between the groups. At the end of two more weeks, we both arrived at Lourenco Marques in Portugese East Africa[23]; and there, after nearly seven terrible months, we were happily reunited on the *Gripsholm*[24], which was to return us to America.

---

23 Now Maputo in Mozambique
24 The judges and staff of the United States Court for China were also on board the *Gripsholm*, which reached New York in late August 1942. The judge of the court, Milton Helmick, kept spirits up by arranging a party for all those who had been interned in China. See *Gunboat Justice* Vol 3, pp179-180.

Asama Maru and MS Gripsholm that took Allman home

II
A STUDENT'S PEKING PICNIC

IT WAS IN VERA CRUZ, Mexico, in the year 1915 that I made the wonderful discovery that eventually led to my career as an American lawyer in China. A green hillbilly, I had ventured down from the Blue Ridge Mountains of Virginia to find a job. I had chosen Mexico because, to my twenty-year-old way of thinking, it was replete with riches.

My one year at the University of Virginia made me yearn for further formal education, but the family farm couldn't see me through and support seven younger brothers and one sister as well.[1] It was up to me to earn my own way.

Back home in Union Hall, Virginia, it had seemed simple. My plan was to get a job with the United Fruit Company or one of the big oil companies, work a year or so, and earn an enormous salary out of which I'd save enough to complete my university course.

It wasn't working out that way. Perhaps my youth and gawkiness had something to do with it; perhaps it was my unpressed appearance, undoubtedly worse then than

Allman at University of Virginia

---

1   Allman was born on July 24, 1893 in Union Hall, Virginia, to John Isaac and Nannie Kate (English) Allman.

now. The big companies just weren't interested in me. Finally a friendly Mexican suggested I consult the American consul. Until that moment I had never heard of such a person, nor, in those dark days, had many other Americans.

I presented myself at the nearest American consulate and was ushered into the consul's presence. Bluntly I asked him about American companies. What I wanted was the inside stuff. The consul let me finish, then, sedately, gave me forty-seven different reasons why he couldn't supply the answers. From his story I gathered that he was willing to help in every way except tell me what I wanted to know.

With the know-it-allness of youth, I proceeded to question the consul about his business and asked how he had wangled what looked to me like an easy job. I intimated that I thought his racket, or whatever the term for racket was in that year, a good one to get into. That closed the interview. Indignantly he showed me the door and, figuratively, I went out on my face. No doubt he wrote the State Department to keep other brash young hillbillies out of Mexico; they were detrimental to what was then the equivalent of a good-neighbor policy.

Home again and dissatisfied with my low-wage job as a powder monkey for the du Ponts at Carney's Point[2], New Jersey, I decided to pursue the inquiry further. The State Department informed me that although my services were not needed at the top my application for consular assistant, student interpreter, or some other lowly office would be considered. I filled out numerous forms and, much to my surprise, was notified to take the consular service entrance examinations.

In those days a college or university degree was not necessary

---

2   A powder monkey is a person who works with explosives. Du Pont manufactured explosives as its factory at Carney's Point, New Jersey on the Eastern shore of the Delaware River.

DuPont's Carney's Point factory where Allman worked as a powder monkey

for entrance into the consular service. Any ambitious youth who could pass the entrance examinations had a chance. I chose to be a student interpreter rather than a consular clerk. In this way I would have a chance to see the world and to study a foreign language and the customs — and history of the country at first hand — all at government expense. Like most young Southerners, I wanted to continue the study of law, and I could do this too. The immediate serious question was: where to go? There were three places, Constantinople, Tokyo, and Peking (now Peiping[3]), where student interpreters were sent for their courses of study.[4] Equally ignorant of all, I decided to take the one with the largest population. The World Almanac indicated Peking.

3   At the time Allman was writing, Beijing was referred to as Peiping (or Beiping in pinyin). "Bei" or "Pei" means north. "Jing" (or "King") means capital in Chinese. "Ping" means peace. The Nationalist Government had moved the capital to Nanjing (Nanking) in the 1930s and changed the name of Beijing to Beiping.

4   A student interpreter was an entry-level position in the British and American diplomatic and consular service, principally in China, Japan, Siam and, in the case of the United States, Constantinople. The United States Department of State made provision for 10 student interpreters in Peking, 6 in Tokyo and 10 in Turkey. They were required to study the language of the country with a view to becoming interpreters to American diplomats and consular officials. Only unmarried male United States citizens between the ages of 19 and 26 were eligible to apply. Those who passed the exam were required to serve at least 5 years and were eligible for appointment to diplomatic and consular roles.

After a somewhat formal correspondence with the State Department, I faced the examiners and had the wits properly scared out of me. I don't know yet how I managed to pass, unless it was because I misled one of my examiners into thinking I was hot stuff in Spanish by sprinkling in a few choice Mexican slang and cuss words new to him.

The oral examination was set for a few days later but, ignorant of procedure, I barged in to see the chief of the examining board. I explained that I couldn't wait around Washington. I had a job that was real, and even if I passed their rigorous examination, I couldn't be sure of getting a job in the State Department.

My temerity must have disconcerted this austere gentleman, for he arranged my oral examination at once. Again, to my surprise, I passed and subsequently was appointed student interpreter to the American legation[5] at Peking. Needless to say I was excited.

About forty of us gathered in Washington for instructions before going into the field. This lasted about six weeks. We were handed the *Book of Words*, otherwise known as the *Consular Regulations*, and cautioned to follow them. Now I knew why my consul in Mexico had been so cagey about giving direct answers to my blunt questions. Our instructor, however, gave us one rule which I've always followed to good advantage: "Always send a cable or telegram as if the receiver were a damned fool. Leave nothing unexplained."

The upshot of the whole business was that almost before I knew it, I found myself on the way to Peking with some half a dozen other lads. We discovered that our traveling expenses were paid on the basis of five cents per mile traveled.

---

5   A legation is one rung below an embassy. Before WWII, embassies, headed by an ambassador, were only established in countries considered very important for diplomatic relations. Legations, headed, by a minister were established in other countries.

As all of us were short of cash we studied geography to find the longest way to Peking. The best we could do was from Washington to New Orleans to San Francisco to Honolulu to Yokohama to Shanghai, thence to Peking. I recommend this route to all traveling on the same basis.

When the good ship *Siberia Maru*, long since gone into scrap and Japanese armament, docked in Shanghai, good natured Sam Sokobin[6], who had passed through the student interpreter mill and was attached to the consulate-general in Shanghai, was there to meet us and escort us to an audience with Thomas E. Sammons[7], an old-type consul-general, a lovable character, albeit a bit pompous.

"Tommy" was noted for the numerous words he used in dispatches to explain how busy he was. One of the dispatches carried the date line, "In bed, Shanghai, 6:30 a.m. Sunday, July ..." Nevertheless everybody loved "Tommy."

Sam Sokobin who greeted Allman in Shanghai

Thomas Sammons (right), US Consul General in Shanghai, handing a cheque to Edward Ezra in payment for the American government site in Shanghai

---

6   Samuel Sokobin (1893-1986) was a career US China consular service officer. He stayed in China until 1941 and was interned for some time in Manila during WWII. From 1944, he served in the US consulate in Birmingham, England.

7   Thomas Sammons (1863-1935) joined the consular service in 1905 and served first in Seoul and Tokyo before serving as consul general in Shanghai until 1919 when he was transferred to serve as Consul-General in Melbourne, Australia. He retired due to ill-health in 1923.

NORWOOD F. ALLMAN

The six of us stayed in Shanghai several days, just long enough to spend about one month of Sam's salary; we hadn't yet drawn our transportation allowances. Sam and others warned us against eating practically anything and everything edible, and on the three-day train trip to Peking we had to choose between caution and hunger. To the horror of my companions, I bought pears in Tsinan and boiled sweet

Allman as a Student Interpreter. Courtesy Neal Burnham

potatoes in Tientsin. My colleagues gave me up for gone, but the truth is they all left China sick and early, and I left twenty-six years afterward, and then only at the point of a Japanese bayonet.

A delegation of "old" student interpreters and another half dozen in various stages of preparation met us at the Peking station. Dressed to the nines in top hats and morning coats, they tossed their peculiar brands of the Chinese language around to impress us; even the Chinese seemed to understand some of it. This welcoming committee included Joseph E. Jacobs, Clarence J. Spiker, Gene Lamb, Andrew Jackson Brewer, Ernest B. Price, and A. C. Chapin. Two of these men are now high-ranking and able officers in the Foreign Service. The others, including myself,

The American legation in Peking

Allman's Fellow Student Interpreters

	**Joseph Earle Jacobs** (1893-1971) was born in Johnston, South Carolina. He came to China as a student interpreter in 1915 and sat as an assessor on the International Mixed Court from 1918 to 1925. He remained in China until 1930 when he transferred to Washington in the Far Eastern Division of the State Department. His last position was Ambassador to Poland from 1955 to 1957.
	**Clarence J. Spiker** (1888-1970) was born in Washington, D.C.. He had been appointed a student interpreter in 1914. He served in the consular service in China for many years before serving in other countries, including as consul-general in Australia. He served as consul-general in Qingdao and Hong Kong after WWII and retired in 1948.
	**Eugene (Gene) M. Lamb** (1894-1948) was born in Washington D.C.. He had been a appointed a student interpreter in 1914 and resigned at the end of 1916. He later became a famous explorer, most notably in Tibet and Mongolia.
	**Ernest B. Price** (1890-1973) was born in Henzada, Burma of American parents. He was appointed a student interpreter in 1913 and served as a consular office until 1929. He left the service to become president of China Airways. He joined the OSS during WWII.
	**Andrew Jackson Brewer** (born 1894) was born in Magnolia, Arkansas. He was appointed a student interpreter in 1915 and served in a number of consular positions until 1920. He cannot be traced after that.
	**Albert Clark Chapin** (1892-1950) was born in Richmond Hill New York. He was appointed a student interpreter in 1915. He left the foreign service in 1919 to become President of the Manchuria Products Co. in Mukden (Shenyang).

British student interpreters' quarters

parted from the Foreign Service voluntarily or by polite request.[8]

I was awed by the formality of our reception and amazed at the grandeur of the students' mess. Our quarters consisted of a series of rooms arranged around Chinese courtyards which one entered through artistic moon gates. The ceiling of the communal dining hall was noted throughout China for its beauty. The older students jabbered in Chinese to coolies and houseboys with a deceptive ease. That night before dropping off to sleep, I said to myself, "This is it, Allman. This is the life."

We didn't waste time in getting down to work. Ray Tenney[9], who had just been graduated from the student interpreter corps, took us in hand and introduced us to his father, Charles E.

8   The two who succeeded in the consular service were Jacobs and Spiker.
9   Raymond Parker Tenney (1887-1963) was born in Tientsin and served in the consular service in China for many years. He sat for a time as American assessor on the Mixed Court in Shanghai. He then worked for the State Department in Washington. In 1934 he accepted an appointment to the Chinese government's salt gabelle. He returned to America at the outbreak of WWII and helped to decode Japanese messages for the State Department.

Charles Tenney

Ray Tenney

Tenney[10], Chinese secretary of the legation and a charming old gentleman who was to guide and examine us in our Chinese studies. "Ting Lao Yeh" (Old Gentleman Ding), as he was familiarly known, believed in efficiency. He thought that his students had come out to Peking because they wanted to study the Chinese language.

That first workday each one of us was given an individual Chinese teacher. These gentlemen, well versed in the Chinese language, were just as ignorant of teaching methods as we were of their language. Their method was to read these strange sounds to us, hand us the book and tell us to read the sounds back to them. This would go on for hours. We soon got this method down to a point where the teacher read while the student slept and vice versa. By perseverance and countless repetition we managed to grasp and hold on to a few of these weird sounds. It was a red-letter day for me when I overheard one Chinese say to another, "Listen to what that foreigner is saying. Sounds almost like Chinese." Little did he realize how hard I had worked, between naps, to make those sounds.

We didn't learn all our Chinese from the teachers assigned to us. One day Ting Lao Yeh called us up to the chancellery to lecture us on the seriousness and dignity of our duties. He warned us against the frivolities of Peking. "Don't go Chien Men Wai T'ou" (outside the Chin Mien Gate). The doctor was not so familiar

---

10   Dr Charles Daniel Tenney (1858-1930) came to China in 1882 as a missionary. In 1886 he established and served as principal of the Anglo-Chinese school in Tientsin. He also tutored Chinese statesman Li Hongzhang's children. From 1895-1906, he was president of the Imperial Chinese University (or Beiyang University) in Tientsin. In 1908 he was appointed Chinese Secretary of the American Legation in Peking and in 1921 served as Charge D'Affaires immediately prior to his retirement.

with the singsong girls outside the wall as we later became. It would have shocked him to know that we considered them far better teachers than the male drones he had put us under.

Dr. Tenney was a great Sinologue and had convinced himself that Chinese, both written and spoken, was easy. He loved to explain to his students that mechanically the entire Chinese language consisted of only nine strokes.

True, the doctor neglected to explain how many variations, by process of combinations and permutations, can be devised from nine simple strokes. Actually there are between forty thousand and fifty thousand characters or ideographs in the Chinese language. There are few, if any, non-Chinese who can write a decent Chinese hand. The Chinese themselves pay great attention to and admire beautiful calligraphy. There are many foreigners who learn to recognize and write Chinese characters, but it would be a bold one indeed who would undertake to write even a simple letter in longhand. Chinese typewriters are too cumbersome to have come into common use.

The student interpreter's greatest difficulty in learning spoken Chinese is starting so late in life, usually after his twenty-first birthday. Actually, spoken Chinese is simple. One merely says "Want bread," instead of " I want a piece of bread." Because of the economy of words and its simplicity, children learn to speak Chinese quickly and fluently.

Shortly after our arrival, the American Minister's wife[11] pridefully called our attention to her small children's ability to speak Chinese. They had picked up the coolie vernacular, which, as we learned later, includes much vulgarity. It most certainly would have shocked the good lady had anyone translated her little darlings' language for her.

---

11   Alma Marie Reinsch (nee Moser), the wife of Paul Reinsch. The Reinsches had married in 1900 and had three children, Paul, Claire and Pauline.

Swearing is a favorite coolie pastime, but it is all vulgarity rather than profanity. Coolie cussing is an art and goes into subtle allusions as well as aspersions upon one's ancestors and implications and improper personal relations. I soon mastered this art and on numerous occasions found coolie-style cussing a big help.

Probably my most embarrassing moment as a language student occurred after three months of study, when Dr. Tenney called us up for our first examination. He asked me to tell him in Chinese what I had eaten for dinner. I pondered a moment and replied, "Mienpao." That was all I could think of.

After moments of silence he prodded, "What else?"

My mind was a blank. In English I said, "That's all."

"Well," commented the old gentleman, "you are either a light eater or mighty hungry by this time if all you had for dinner was bread."

We devised numerous ways to memorize difficult Chinese passages. The story goes that when Nelson T. Johnson[12], later United States Ambassador to China and now United States Minister to Australia, was a timid young language student, he was called on to recite twenty-five lines from the *San Tze Ching*,[13] or *Trimetrical Classic*, a poem on which all Chinese students cut their eyeteeth in the old

Nelson T. Johnson on the cover of Time Magazine

---

12   Nelson Trusler Johnson (1887-1954) had joined the consular service as a student inter-
      preter in 1907 and served in China most of his life. He became Minister to China in 1929
      and served in that position, with the upgraded rank as Ambassador from 1935, until
      1941. Johnson made the cover of Time magazine in 1939. His last appointment was as
      Minister to Australia from 1941 to 1945.
13   三字經. Each line of the poem is made up of couplets of three characters. Chinese chil-
      dren were formerly required to memorise it.

days. He stammered and stumbled and finally admitted that he couldn't recite the lines. "But I can sing them," he added. Nelson T. and some of his fellow students had set the 275 lines of the poem to music and sang it with piano accompaniment. Now, all language students sing it.

In addition to studying the Chinese language, written and spoken, as well as history, law, and customs, each student was assigned to certain routine duties in the legation. The choice job was custodian of passes to the Winter Palace and other forbidden areas in Peking. As these passes were much sought after by tourists, the student in charge was able to get in touch directly and quickly with all the good-looking girls who came through. He kept a supply of passes in his desk but always made a lot of folderol about handing them out, especially if trying to impress a pretty tourist.

Another job was taking passport applications. This was anything but exciting and probably turned up the only instance of graft existing in the diplomatic and consular services. Diplomatically speaking, it was known as "perquisites" rather than graft. Passport applications and other notarial services could not be signed by student interpreters but had to be done by a secretary of legation and, by a quirk in the law, fees for these services were not accounted for. Most of the secretaries were wealthy men who neither wanted nor needed this money. The students, paid the munificent sum of eighty-three dollars a month, always needed more money. They could not take the fees, however, as they were not allowed to receive money in addition to their salaries. This "graft" was usually donated to the students' mess or put to other charitable uses. Subsequently the law was changed and perquisites abolished.

An important job or duty was making calls on all legation officials, our own as well as those of friendly powers. This had been reduced to the simplest terms. We merely borrowed the diplomatic list, dished out the necessary number of cards, and gave them, with corner turned down, to indicate we had called in person, to the "number one boy," who dropped them into the appropriate boxes at the several legations. Thus, in theory at least, having complied with the social and official amenities, we thereafter were permitted social intercourse with our colleagues. In proper time and in similar manner return cards were dropped on us. If you failed in the exchange of cards, your official existence was ignored.

The student interpreter, unless he was an extremely objectionable fellow indeed, soon found himself enmeshed in a chain of social affairs. In my day there were about six British students and ten American. The ministers' wives considered us their personal reserve force to fill in at dinners whenever ministers, secretaries, or the more important fry dropped out. This practice I found a decided bore for, owing to protocol, otherwise known as precedence, the poor student was always ranked last. Invariably I was seated alongside some person who spoke a strange tongue I could not understand.

These dinners were fearsome affairs, consisting of course after course, and the conversation, if one were able to converse, ran to such questions as, " How long have you been in Peking? Do you like it? Isn't the dust dreadful?" When the conversation became really animated the weather was included.

Our number one boy finally solved the problem by answering all telephone calls and lying like a professional diplomat. This did not always save us. Many a time I was picked up on the street and yanked to a dinner willy-nilly by some minister's wife. Our biggest grouse was over formal dances, where the student, being of the lowest rank, could not ask the pretty, slim girl of his choice to dance, but had to make an effort to dance with all the fat and

Temple of Heaven

fortyish ministers' wives, beginning, if possible, with the senior lady present. On the other hand the pot-bellied, bald-headed old ministers danced first with all the lovely young girls.

The American student interpreters endeavored to repay all social obligations by giving a blowout about once a year. Means and facilities were limited, but this problem was solved by the number one boy, who borrowed wine, food, cutlery, and dishes from the legations whose officials were not entertaining at home that night. It was not at all unusual for British legation officials to be served in our mess from their own dinner sets. We took good care, however, that their own wine was not so easily discerned.

For the most part life in Peking was delightful. The classes, or mutual sleeping and study arrangement between students and teachers that I have described, usually started about 9 a.m. and continued for two hours, after which the students went riding on Mongolian ponies and probably took tiffin at the Temple of

Heaven, Temple of Agriculture, Yellow Temple, or some other charming spot. All one had to do was to call in the number one boy and say, "Ten piecee master, missy tiffin Temple of Heaven. Can do?" The reply was always, Can do." And we would find lunch spread for a mixed crowd of ten at the temple when we arrived.

Wang, our number one boy, or major domo, was a fat, jolly Buddha-like Chinese, but it's still a mystery to me how he got fat on the pay he got from student interpreters. He was wise in diplomacy and knew all the tricks of the trade. Perhaps he learned much from the sage diplomatic discussions of green but opinionated students. He received his training in much the same way a boarding-house keeper at the University of Virginia acquired hers. It was said that she was the only person in the world who really understood the *Rule* in *Shelly's Case*.[14] She had learned it by listening to countless freshman law students discuss it. It was Wang who told us when to get up, when to go to bed, when it was time to stop drinking. He told us what to wear and helped us dress and undress. He told us what time to go to parties and what time to leave. He warned us never to leave before the senior diplomat and his lady made the break-away. Although he spoke only Chinese and pidgin English, he was an authority on protocol.

But more important, Wang was adviser on affairs of the heart as well as on things diplomatic. He had a working arrangement with the number one boy of the Wagon-Lits Hotel[15] to notify him of the arrival and specifications of all interesting new female tourists. He remembered all our birthdays and saw to it that we did not forget him at the Chinese New Year.

---

14 1 Co.Rep. 93b (1581). The rule (which is incredibly complex) relates to the inheritance of future interests in land. It has been abolished in most jurisdictions.

15 The Grand Hotel des Wagon-Lits was the only hotel located in the legation quarter in Peking and accommodated many rail passengers to Peking.

PEKING.   Grand Hôtel des Wagons-Lits, Ltd.

The Grand Hotel des Wagon Lits

Naturally we were prone to parade our diplomatic status and immunities, but occasionally we were taken down several notches by the commercial community or by just plain citizens. One day the late Kate Carl[16], American artist famous for her portrait of the Empress Dowager, stopped me on the steps of the Peking Club.

"By the way, young man, send me a carton of cigarettes."

"Most certainly," I replied, "what kind?"

"Oh, you know." And she breezed off.

Her request seemed a little strange, but not yet being thoroughly grounded in diplomatic practice, I sent the cigarettes. Later I learned that Miss Carl thought I worked for a tobacco company.

During our stay in Peking as student interpreters, China, as well as the United States, broke off relations with the Central Powers.

16   Kate Augusta Carl (1854-1938). Through the contacts of her brother, a Commissioner of the Imperial Maritime Customs in China, she painted the portrait for the 1904 Louisiana Purchase Exhibition. She stayed in China until 1930.

Kate Carl's portrait of the Empress Dowager

Both the German and Austrian legations were in the legation quarter, an extraterritorial area administered by the diplomatic body; but when China declared war on them the two countries closed their legations. This was somewhat unfortunate for the students' mess as our number one boy could no longer borrow their excellent Rhine wines.

Because of the rupture of relations and our entry into the war, more legation work than usual was delegated to the students. All of us had to turn to and help with coding and decoding and other tasks, besides keeping up our Chinese studies.

It was a history-making, exciting time. The Russian front had collapsed and, since it was impossible to clear diplomatic dispatches from either Moscow or St. Petersburg to Washington through the usual channels, these were all transmitted through the legation in Peking.

Paul S. Reinsch[17], the American Minister to China at that time, was fond of the students and showed his fondness by keeping us busy. He thoroughly enjoyed his own work and, being a political science expert, his cables were elaborate and detailed studies of the events taking place in Russia as well as in China. Evidently he thought he was writing for history. It was not uncommon for

---

17 Paul Samuel Reinsch (1869-1923) had been appointed US Minister in 1913 and left the post in 1919. He had practiced as a lawyer in Milwaukee and been an assistant professor at the University of Wisconsin-Madison. In 1917 a prosecution was brought against the Publisher of the *Peking Post*, Gilbert Reid, in the United States Court for China for sedition for accusing Reinsch of supporting improper loans to China. See *Gunboat Justice* Vol 2, p203 et seq and Chapter 7.

him to spend all day on a cable, covering pages and pages in his fine script, then assign a student to cipher it while he went to dinner. All too frequently he would come in after midnight and decide to change the cable somewhere in the middle, and the poor devil would have to work several hours longer. Usually I was the poor devil.

I might have chucked the job then and there if it hadn't been for J. V. A. MacMurray[18], counselor of the legation, who always had a warm spot in his heart for the students. We could count on him to come to the chancellery in the early morning hours, with sandwiches stuffed in his pockets and carrying a couple of bottles of beer, to give sustenance as well as a helping hand to the

John MacMurray

Paul Reinsch

18   John van Antwerp MacMurray (1881-1960) joined the US Consular Service in Bangkok in 1907 as Consul-General. In 1924 he served as an assistant Secretary of State and in 1925 was appointed US Minister to China. He resigned in 1929 and joined John Hopkins University as a professor of International Relations. He rejoined the Foreign Service in 1933 and served as Minister in the Baltic States and Turkey. MacMurray took many photos of China (held by Princeton Library) and also shot amateur films of life in China.

sleepy codemaker.

Minister Reinsch was a collector of curios, but, because curio dealers habitually charged him according to his rank, when the canny Minister discovered a valuable piece, he would send me out to try to buy it. I found these dealers a friendly lot and haggling with them over prices and quality was excellent practice in learning Chinese. Occasionally I bought a good piece cheaply. They knew a student interpreter had no money.

After two years' study most of us passed the examinations and were promoted to the rank of interpreter and permitted the privilege of accompanying the Minister or other high legation officers on calls to Chinese officials. My first assignment was to accompany the new American Minister, Charles R. Crane[19], on a visit to the Chinese Minister of War[20]. I boned up in advance on the subject of the interview, but it was soon apparent that Mr. Crane hadn't the slightest intention of sticking to the details of the interview. He was keenly interested in models of junks (Chinese boats), and his conversation about junks was beyond my Chinese vocabulary. I was faced with an embarrassing situation and tried in English to bring the Minister around to the subject. Finally, in desperation, I gave up and solved the difficulty by talking to the American Minister in English about junks and to the Minister of War in Chinese about the purpose of our visit.

Charles Crane was one of Peking's most delightful characters, if a bit eccentric for a minister. When he arrived to take over his

---

19 Charles Richard Crane (1858-1939) was the heir to a large industrial fortune and had contributed heavily to President Woodrow Wilson's election campaigns. He was appointed Minister in March 1920 and served under July 1921. He had been appointed Minister by President Taft in 1909 but was forced to resign by Secretary for State Philander Knox due to his publication of the US Government's objections to recent treaties with China and Japan. Crane, who was a connoisseur of Arab culture, was violently anti-Semitic and admired Adolf Hitler.

20 Either Jin Yun Peng (靳雲鵬) (1877-1951), who was Minister of War and Premier during the period Crane was Minister, or Luo Kaibang, who was Acting Minister of War for a period in 1920 to 1921.

duties he announced to the staff his intention of traveling around the country. He said that, and since he had confidence in us he expected us to do his thinking and his work. He asked the staff to carry on as if he were present but to do no prognosticating as to his future plans. With that advice he left to look, I believe, for junks.

Charles R. Crane

39

III

AN AMERICAN CONSUL'S ODYSSEY

MY APPRENTICESHIP PERIOD ended in 1918 when I was appointed vice-consul and sent to Antung[1] on the Korea-Manchuria border. This was my first official post to run under my own steam. I knew I was merely filling in while the consul went off on a hunting trip, but just the same I was puffed up with importance at the thought of carrying the whole prestige and dignity of the United States on my skinny shoulders.

I remember swaggering into the consulate ready to take over. When hours passed without any duties being assigned me I approached the consul.

"Sir," I ventured, "when do I begin and what affairs do I handle?"

He waved me away. "Oh, don't bother with the files. Your job is to look after my goats."

I was thoroughly deflated but avenged my wounded pride to some extent by ignoring both goats and files. I spent most of my fifty days there visiting with E. T. Hobart, the Standard Oil representative, and his wife, Alice Tisdale Hobart, who was writing her first book, Leaves from a Manchurian Diary[2].

---

1   Later Andong, now Dandong. The city is across the Yalu River from Sinijiu in Korea. In 1951 at the start of the Korean war, General MacArthur ordered bombing of Andong, which brought Chinese volunteers into the war.
2   Published as *Pioneering Where the World is Old: Leaves from Manchurian Diary*. Mrs. Hobart (1882-1967) later published a number of other books on China.

Antung Railway Station

Aside from the Hobarts and the consul there was only one white foreign resident in Antung, but there were many Japanese. The South Manchurian Railway and the Japanese Government Railway in Korea met at this point, and the Japanese infiltration into Manchuria was just beginning. Already there were large Japanese settlements in Antung and the territory north of the Yalu River. A short time after my departure the Japanese provoked fighting with the Chinese in Antung and contrived their trenches so that the United States consulate building was between the Japanese and the Chinese lines. This did not instill any special love between the Japanese and the consular staff.

My first experience with Japanese bureaucracy, which later I came to know so well, was on the train from Mukden[3] to Antung. I was given a form to fill out. To one impertinent question, "What is your business?" I answered, "The pursuit of happiness." This caused great curiosity on the part of the guards. No doubt when translated into Japanese the result was something wonderful.

---

3   Now Shenyang.

Nanking Walled City

No sooner did I arrive back in Peking than I was transferred to Nanking, a thirty-six-hour train ride to the south. Nanking, in the shadow of the Purple Mountains, was a large walled city. At least one-third of it lay sprawled outside the wall and inside there were large wild areas that provided excellent pheasant shooting. A good portion of the city had been destroyed during the Taiping rebellion in the eighteen sixties and the ruins had never been repaired.

Nanking at that time was picturesque but inconvenient. It was not yet the capital, and its American population consisted of a small commercial, and fairly large missionary and educational, groups. There were almost as many cliques in the community as there were persons, and it was difficult to bring two people together who were on speaking terms. I managed to get around without joining any of the cliques, mainly because I was there only three months and went down to Shanghai, an overnight train trip away, as often as I could possibly find an excuse.

My next transfer was north again to the consulate-general in Tientsin, called "Heavenly Ford" by the Chinese. Tientsin, a flat, ugly commercial city on the Peiho (North River), was the center of the Mongolia and China wool trade and was noted for the

Gordon Hall in the Centre of Tientsin

manufacture of Chinese rugs and also for the fact that at one time it boasted thirteen foreign concessions and fourteen different city governments, including the Chinese. Most tourists thought of Tientsin merely as the seaport of Peking. Most foreign residents found it a dreary place. There wasn't much to do. The one lovely spot was a park in what had been the Russian Concession. Here on a lake we skated in winter when the dust permitted. For even with the snows dust blew down from The Gobi.

In Tientsin my chief, Percy Heintzleman[4], was fussy about the form of dispatches and made us write them over and over again. He was diplomatically "correct" and always wanted the principal staff officers to take Saturday tiffin with him.

I was still new when George Sokolsky[5] blew in from St.Petersburg. He bunked with me for a while. I remember that we kept the consul-general in a constant state of alarm by airing

---

4   Percival Stewart Heintzleman (1880-1942) joined the consular service as a student in-
     terpreter and served in various positions in China and for a time in Washington DC in
     the newly-established Far Eastern Division. From 1926 to 1929 he served as a consul in
     Winnipeg, Canada.

5   George Ephraim Sokolsky (1893-1962) had been born in Uttica, New York to a Russian
     émigré rabbi. He went to Russia to observe the revolution but then escaped to China
     where he stayed for 14 years, acting at one point as an adviser to Sun Yat-sen. In later
     life he became a rabid anti-communist, helping movie studios vet actors for communist
     tendencies during the McCarthy era.

George Sokolsky   *Percy Heintzleman*

our liberal political views at his very proper tiffin parties.

George had crossed Siberia a refugee and had lost all but the clothes on his back. I was puzzled one morning when he called downstairs to ask if he could come to breakfast in a kimono. I shouted back, "Yes."

"Well," he yelled, "send up the kimono."

It was in Tientsin that I previewed a Japanese prearranged incident, although I didn't recognize it as such at the time. The United States Fifteenth Infantry Regiment had been stationed in Tientsin since 1901, shortly after the Boxer rebellion. Occasional minor brushes with the Japanese soldiers had worked up a considerable amount of bad feeling. This culminated one night in 1919 in a serious street fight in front of the Empire Theater.

I had an engagement that night to attend the theater with the Japanese vice-consul in charge. When he didn't appear I went on alone. In light of subsequent Japanese policy I don't doubt for a minute but that he knew of "the trouble." The staged fight began just as I and hundreds of other playgoers were leaving, but we were crushed back into the theater lobby and thus escaped injury.

In those days Japanese soldiers wore bayonets as side arms, but when off duty our soldiers went unarmed. Many of our soldiers were injured, but despite lack of arms the Fifteenth gave good account of itself. A number of Japanese went to the hospital with broken heads[6].

By this time I was getting used to the consular routine[7], which included swings around the country. I was just beginning to get comfortably settled in Tientsin when I was hustled off to Tsinan, twelve hours away by train.

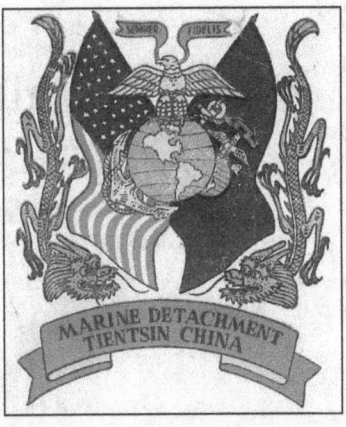

US Marine Detachment Tientsin Badge

Tsinan, the capital of Shantung Province, one of the most densely populated portions of the world, was another picturesque walled city. It was a busy metropolis — the western terminus of the Kiaochi Railway which joined the Tientsin-Pukow Railway and the

A Marine drinking beer in Tientsin

world center of the hair-net industry. (Chinese hair was collected, sent to France for bleaching, and returned to be made into hair-nets for American and European trade.) Tsinan also was an educational

---

6   Allman's account here is rather one-sided. Contemporaneous English reports said there was serious fighting amongst American soldiers which Japanese police (with fixed bayonets) tried to quell. The following day, US Marines seriously beat the Japanese consul. See "Serious Fracas at Tientsin: Fracas Between Americans and Japanese", *North China Herald*, Mar 22 1919, p761.

7   Allman had one additional consular duty in Tientsin, that of Deputy Clerk of the United States Court for China.

The United States Court for China

(Established by Act of Congress of June 30, 1906.)

JUDGE, Charles S. Lobingier of Nebraska.

DISTRICT ATTORNEY, Chauncey P. Holcomb of Delaware.

MARSHAL,
COMMISSIONER, } Nelson E. Lurton of Missouri.
DISBURSING OFFICER,

REPORTER, } William A. Chapman of Ohio.
ACTING CLERK,

DEPUTY MARSHAL, Neville Craig of Montana.

OFFICE HOURS { Judge 9-12.30; 3-5.
{ Staff, 9-12; 2-4.

TIENTSIN:

DEPUTY CLERK, Norwood F. Allman of Virginia.

DEPUTY MARSHAL, William T. Collins of Missouri.

———

All Notices, Announcements, Judgments, Orders and other Proceedings appearing in this department of MILLARD'S REVIEW may be accepted as authentic.

William A. Chapman,

Acting Clerk.

———

Recent Filings :

April 10, 1919; Cause No. 764; United States v. Fred D. Thom ; complaint.

Allman served as Deputy Clerk of the United States Court for China in Tientsin

Cheloo University Gate

center. It was the home of Cheloo University[8], a Union missionary school with both an arts college and a good medical school. The teaching was entirely in Chinese. Only a handful of foreigners resided in Tsinan, although there was a foreign settlement. The substantially constructed German-style houses had one modern convenience — electric lights, usually too dim to read by.

I much preferred the smelly, walled city with its narrow cobblestone streets. In the very center of the city there were tremendous springs, the source of the Hsiao Ching Ho[9]. The springs and a portion of this river within the city walls were lined with temples and tea houses where Chinese gentlemen sat by the hour, sipping tea, conversing interminably, and contemplating this amazing miracle of nature.

I arrived in Tsinan at an interesting time. Several thousand miles away negotiations were leading up to the Versailles Treaty, and the Allied Powers were anxious to obtain information about

8   Cheloo University (济鲁大学). Now part of Jinan University.
9   Xiaoqing River (小清河).

this Germanized section of Shantung[10].

The murder of two German Roman Catholic missionaries in Shantung in November, 1897[11], had given the German government an excellent pretext to seize a part of the Kiaochow peninsula and the village of Tsingtao. In 1898 they obtained a ninety-nine-year lease to Kiaochow Bay with about two hundred square miles of adjacent territory. They demolished the original fishing village and in 1901 built the modern city of Tsingtao overlooking one of the most beautiful harbors of the world. They established the Kiaochi Railway, developed the coal mines along its route, and built up industries in Tsinan. Then in November of 1914, in the triple-threat role of an ally, German foe, and protector of poor China, the Japanese had stepped in and taken over Tsingtao and the German properties.[12]

The newly established American consulate in Tsinan lacked records, and there were daily cabled instructions from Washington to report fully on the Shantung Railway, the Shantung coal mines, or other former German properties. As I was the staff, I was kept hopping and worried until the lucky day I discovered that a German caretaker had been left to guard the German consulate, closed since the Japanese occupation.

I plied the German fellow with glasses of beer at Steins Hotel[13]

---

10 Under the Treaty of Versailles, in 1919, Germany formally gave up all its concessions in China. As Allman notes, most of them had fallen under Japanese influence or control when WWI commenced.

11 In what is called the Juye Incident, on the night of November Richard Henle (1863-1897) and Franz-Xavier Nies (1859-1897), of the Society of the Divine Word, were killed by a mob in Juye County, Shandong Province. It has never been definitely determined who their killers were or why they were killed.

12 See the *Siege of Tsingtao* by Jonathan Fenby for details of the Japanese capture of Tsingtao. This was done with the full support of the British who also provided some troops and naval support.

13 Described by the famous journalist Edgar Snow as "a German inn of long standing reputation ... Besides serving the best beer north of Bavaria, Mr. Schad, the proprietor conducts and establishment such as one dreams of vacationing in, somewhere in a white village south of Berlin." E. Snow and S.Y. Hu, "Through China's Holy Land", *China Weekly Review*, November 9, 1929.

and, without any authority and hence subsequent frowns from the State Department, promised to recommend him for a job in the salt gabelle if he'd open up the files. A job in the salt gabelle, or salt monopoly of the Chinese government, which produced a considerable amount of the government revenue, was not to be sneezed at; so open up the files he did and what's more translated the desired information. Unfortunately for the German, my recommendation didn't carry an ounce of weight.

Ma Liang, Chinese garrison commmander in Tsinan

This was a period of great student foment in all China, but especially in Shantung, where students were agitating to oust the Japanese. They were making trouble for the governor of the province and for the police. The tuchun (military governor) was as anxious as the students to get the Japanese out of his territory but at the same time he was responsible for keeping the peace.

General Ma Liang[14], the garrison commander, was directly responsible for law and order. A devout Mohammedan and a strict soldier, he believed that the best way of handling riots was to shoot the rioters. He arrested a number of students, and they and all Tsinan thought they would be shot.

A few students had escaped arrest. They descended in a body on Sir John Pratt[15], the British consul-general, and me.

---

14 Ma Liang (马良) (1875-1947) was originally from Hebei Province. He had joined the Beiyang Army before the Revolution and moved to Shandong in 1916. His army was supported by the Japanese during World War I. Later, in 1937 he joined Wang Qing-wei's puppet government. He was arrested for treason in 1945 and died of illness in prison in 1947.

15 John Thomas Pratt (1876-1970) served in the China Consular Service from 1898 to 1924 when he transferred to the Foreign Office in London acting as an adviser until 1938 on Far Eastern Affairs. He then served from 1939 to 1941 in the Far Eastern Section of the Ministry of Information. He authored several works including *Great Britain and China*; *Japan and the Modern World*, 1942; *War and Politics in China*, 1943; *Before Pearl Harbour*, 1943; *China and Japan* ; *China and Britain*, 1944; *Expansion of Europe into the Far East*, 1947.

They begged us to intercede to save the others. I was fully aware of State Department disapproval of any such interference in internal Chinese politics. At the same time I knew a number of students were about to be shot for vociferously upholding the very principles we were so sedately advocating at Versailles. As both Sir John and I were on friendly terms with General Ma, we called on him, intimated that we were speaking off the record and without official instructions, and then told him we thought it was a damned-fool idea to shoot students. As a result of our visit he released most of them but had one or two shot as an example.

It was in Tsinan that I met my wife-to-be, Mary Louise Hamilton, who was born in China of American missionary parents.[16] I first saw this hazel-eyed, brown-haired girl playing tennis at the Tsinan Club. She had recently returned from the United States, where she had been graduated from Wellesley and had done some postgraduate work at Columbia University. She was teaching, in the Chinese language, in a mission school. Sir John and Lady Pratt gave a tea and introduced us. They were good friends of both of us, and we've always suspected that the meeting was of their design.

Our courtship was not without complications. Tsinan was frequently under martial law, and I had to cross the city in a rickshaw and pass through two gates to get to Mary Louise's home. When I explained my predicament to the tuchun, he laughed and gave me a military pass. This proved most embarrassing, as each time I presented the pass to go through either gate the guard turned out to give a snappy salute. Sir John and Lady Pratt came to the rescue by inviting Mary Louise to spend weekends at their home. This suited me, as my consulate was close by.

---

16   Mary (1894-1971) was the daughter of Rev. Dr. William Beeson Hamilton and Margaret Woods Hamilton (nee Woods). Her father died in 1912 but her mother remained working in China until 1934. She stayed on after retirement until 1940. Mary Louise at the time she married Allman, was with the American Presbyterian Mission in Tsinan.

Top: Mary Louise on the beach in
Tsingtao, photo courtesy Neal Burnham
Middle: The beach at Tsingtao
Bottom: Tsingtao

A sad note in this romantic interlude was struck by my transfer to Tsingtao, the city of red-tiled roofs. Although it was only an overnight train ride away, it seemed a thousand miles from Tsinan. But despite this I liked Tsingtao. The Germans had done a good job of reforesting all the bare hills, even the fortified areas. The gnarled wind-blown pines, the hills, fine beaches, the rocky coves, and sparkling blue water were reminiscent of the Monterey peninsula of the California coast. After our marriage we built a summer cottage there and spent most of our holidays at this beautiful resort spot, aptly called "Green Island" by the Chinese. It was easily accessible from Shanghai, being a thirty-hour steamer trip and later on only one and a half hours by air.

If memory serves me right, official instructions about my duties there were decidedly odd. I was to proceed to Tsingtao, reopen the consulate, and cultivate social but not official relations with the local Japanese government. My unusual instructions were explained in part by the peculiar situation existing in Tsingtao. The Japs since their occupation had set up both a civil government and a military control over the area. In my consular capacity I was accredited to the Chinese government, but I was functioning in a Japanese-occupied and military-governed area.

The American consulate at Tsingtao had been closed since 1914. Consul Willys R. Peck[17] remained throughout most of the siege, but, when a Japanese shell landed

Willys R. Peck, US Consul in Tsingtao during WWI

---

17   Willys Ruggles Peck (1882-1952) had been born in Tientsin to missionary parents. He was appointed a student interpreter in 1906 and served in the American legation as assistant Chinese secretary (1908-13) and as Chinese secretary (1913-1914) and (1919-1926). He served in consular positions from 1914 to 1919. He was counselor of the embassy from 1935 to 1940 and later in the State Department.

squarely in his office one morning a few minutes before he arrived for work, he and his family were sent out of Tsingtao under a flag of truce.

In the intervening six years, mail addressed to the consulate had continued to arrive in Tsingtao. The Japanese-controlled post office had distributed the consular mail indiscriminately to nearly everybody in the town. I found letters in private houses, offices of Socony, A.P.C. (Asiatic Petroleum Company), Mitsui Bussan Kaisha. Letters had been shoved under all doors of the consulate until there wasn't room for another one.

What appalled me was that I was supposed to answer all of those letters, keep books, and fill out a thousand and one forms, not to mention the maintenance of social but unofficial relations, and I was without even a clerk or typist to help me. I ignored the books and forms and began on the letters, yelling loudly for help. Such lack of respect for red tape brought on more frowns from my superiors.

I was faced with an even graver problem. Soon after my arrival, Admiral Gleaves[18] decided to call at Tsingtao on the USS *Huron*[19], then the flagship of the Asiatic fleet. I was ignorant of the protocol covering such calls, but it was up to me to arrange for exchange of calls between Admiral Gleaves and the Japanese commanding officer, General Yui.[20] It was, as I recalled, the duty of the junior of the two to pay the first call, but I wasn't sure. After frantic cabling to Washington I managed to clear the point. I don't remember now who did call first.

As part of the entertainment for Admiral Gleaves and his

---

18 Albert Gleaves (1858-1937) was in command of the United States Asiatic Fleet at the time.

19 USS Huron (CA-9) had previously been the *USS South Dakota* (ACR-9). She was an armoured cruiser laid down in 1902 and launched in 1904.

20 Mitsue Yui (由比 光衞) (1860-1940) was in command of the Japanese garrison in Tsingtao from 1919 to 1922.

The USS Huron (as the USS South Dakota)

Admiral Gleaves

General Yui

staff, General Yui gave a tiffin party (luncheon) at the top of Laoshan, a mountain some twenty-five miles from Tsingtao. We went to the foot of the mountain in motorcars, but had to walk or take mountain chairs to the top. Someone, probably one of the admiral's younger staff, suggested that we walk. Both General Yui and Admiral Gleaves were getting along in years, but neither

Laoshan Mountain

was going to let the other outdo him. So we all walked up and back, quite an undertaking for even a younger man. The palm should go to the admiral — walking was not his business; General Yui was an infantry officer.

There was also the annoyance of my own immediate calls. This is simplified for the consul, as the Navy sends a boat off with an aid to escort him on board to call on the senior naval officer. One phase of these calls I thoroughly disliked. Believe it or not, a consul draws seven guns! I couldn't get out of my mind the time a colleague, at the conclusion of his call, stood up in the small boat to await his salute. Evidently the naval officer in charge of the saluting party was a practical joker, for he fired over the dinghy. The consul lost not only his dignity but his top hat.

I avoided such a mishap by explaining to Admiral Gleaves that, as we did not wish to accord official recognition to the Japanese occupation of Shantung, it would be just as well to omit this consular courtesy of a salute.

Another incident of the *Huron's* visit occurred one dark morning about three o'clock. I was awakened by loud shouting outside the consulate. Hastily I pulled on a robe and went out. I found something like a platoon of Japanese gendarmes with half a dozen bluejackets in tow. By much gesticulation and sign language I was given to understand that the bluejackets had committed an awful crime. The bluejackets claimed it was nothing more than an argument with a rickshaw coolie. At the end of an hour's argument I persuaded the gendarmerie to turn the sailors over to the Navy shore patrol at the dock. I guaranteed that I would be responsible for any and all crimes committed and went back to bed. Later that day I learned the extent of the crime. The mudguard of a rickshaw had been broken. I settled with the coolie for a few cents and thus avoided an international incident.

I had had previous experience with Jap gendarmerie and government officials. There were constant conflicts between the Americans traveling on the Shantung railway and the railway guards. Nearly all the guards were trying to learn English, and they pestered every white passenger they saw by practicing their words and phrases. There were several British American Tobacco Company youths at Er Shi Li Pu who made frequent trips to Tsingtao and Tientsin. As soon as they caught on to what the guards were doing, they taught them some exceedingly colorful expressions.

A favorite stunt was to teach a guard the proper phrase for greeting ladies, then sit back and howl with laughter when the guard walked up to a missionary lady, bowed politely, and said, "Good-morning, Madame, I am a son-of-a-bitch."

Mary Louise was in Pietaiho[21], the summer capital of Peking's diplomatic set and a seashore resort much favored by Tientsin and Peking residents, more for its accessibility than for its beauty.

---

21 Now transliterated as Beidaihe. The town was established in 1898 as a seaside retreat for senior Chinese officials and foreigners. Even after the Communist Revolution, it was used as a retreat by senior communist officials and was the scene of many a political intrigue.

Peitaiho from the sea

It was a bare, sand-dunish all like "Green Island," but we were to be married there on August 20.

The only way I could get there was by train through Tientsin. But fighting was going on between General Ma Liang's troops and the northern troops at Tehchow. My line of communication was cut. I grew desperate as the wedding date neared.

I made a special trip to Tsinan to see my friend General Ma. He was, he said, quite happy to pass me through his forces but could take no responsibility for me beyond Tehchow. Hoping for the best, I boarded one of the troop trains.

Fortunately my arrival coincided with a lull in the fighting, and I walked unmolested across no-man's land into the area of the northern forces. A couple of days' pleading with the commanding officer got me permission to continue the trip to Tientsin on one of his troop trains.

Soldiers occupied every foot of space. I stood up most of the way but managed to cling to my one small suitcase which contained my white flannel wedding suit. It took four days to make what was normally a ten-hour trip. The food consisted

Mary Louise Hamilton in her wedding dress. Courtesy Richard Allman.

NORWOOD F. ALLMAN

The marriage of Miss Louise Hamilton, daughter
of the late Dr. W. B. and Mrs. Hamilton, of the
American Presbyterian Mission of Tsinanfu and
Norman Francis Allman, American Vice Consul at
Tsingtao, took place on the lawn of the Tewksbury
house on August 10, at Peitaiho, one of the most
popular summer resorts in North China. Rev. John
Murray of the American Presbyterian Mission, Tsinanfu, performed the ceremony, while Dr. J. B. Neal,
of the Shantung Christian College, gave the bride
away. Mr. and Mrs. Allman left on the same evening
for Korea where they will spend their honeymoon.
They will return to Tsingtao after September 2.

Millards Review of the Far East Aug, 21, 1920, reports on Allman's wedding

mostly of watermelon and Chinese tea. But I arrived in Peitaiho
a day before the wedding, much to Mary Louise's relief; for she
had no idea where I was or if I could get there. Looking back on
it, that trip was certainly worth all the trouble and discomfort.
The trip wasn't the only difficulty. We planned to spend our
honeymoon in the Kongo-san (the Diamond Mountains of
Korea), and there was the problem of obtaining Japanese visas.
It was not politic for me to ask the Japanese military authorities
in Tsingtao for a visa, and I knew it would be embarrassing for
my wife to use the passport issued under her maiden name. The
American authorities refused to give her a passport under the
name Allman until after the marriage. This involved too great
a delay. So before leaving Tsingtao I had explained my plight to
the Japanese military governor, suggesting he give me a letter
stating that my wife and I were not spies.

His letter to the Korean authorities baldly stated that Mr. and
Mrs. Allman were spending their honeymoon in Korea. I don't
know what else he said, but I do know that it was the one and
only time in my life I had no trouble with Japanese authorities in
Japanese territory.

Allman and Mary Louise soon after their marriage. Courtesy Richard Allman.

Bad weather almost wrecked the honeymoon, but we survived the Kongo-san floods and returned to Tsingtao, where we made our home until the following spring.

Again we were shunted about the country. This time to Shanghai for three months and then to what in those days was the jumping-off place, Chungking, in the remote western province of Szechwan[22].

The trip to Chungking involved a steamer trip to Hankow, transfer to a smaller steamer in Ichang, and then transfer to a still smaller and specially built steamer to navigate the Yangtze Rapids. The trip may sound easy, but it was fraught with difficulties. Navigation of the rapids was so intricate that each boat carried a Chinese pilot. The ships made about fifteen knots, sometimes bucking a fourteen-knot current. Occasionally it was necessary to send a five hundred to a one thousand foot cable out ahead, tie it to a rock or tree, and warp over the rapid.

Our first child, William, had been born in Tsingtao that

---

22 Chongqing in Sichuan Province. In 1997 it was separated from Sichuan province and became a city directly under the Central Government.

A riverboat takes on the Yangtse Rapids

summer of 1921, and I had to take a wife and a two-months'
old baby up river with me, plus all our personal luggage and
household furniture. It was a great responsibility for, added to
the complications of navigation, a civil war was then raging
in the neighborhood of Ichang between General Wu Pei-fu's
troops and the Yunnanese invaders of Szechwan province. Wu
Pei-fu was on the north side of the Yangtze, the Yunnanese on
the south.[23] Our drawback was that we had to proceed up river
between them.

On arrival at Hankow we found my old friend Percy
Heintzleman, the consul-general there. He was alarmed that my
wife and child were accompanying me. I explained that my wife
had been through the Boxer Rebellion as well as a number of
civil wars and that my son might as well get used to them. The
consul-general did not take kindly to this casualness about war,
but before he could do anything about it we said good-by and

---

23   In 1915 when the President of China, Yuan Shikai (1859-1916), had declared himself em-
      peror, Sichuan supported Yuan, but Yunnan did not, leading to an invasion of Sichuan
      by Yunannese troops supporting the Republic. The war went on even after Yuan died
      in 1916. Wu Peifu (吳佩孚)(1874-1939) had join Yuan's Beiyang Army in the early 1900s
      and supported Yuan as emperor.

sailed up the river.

At Ichang we transferred to one of the new Dollar upper Yangtze boats, temporarily armored with boiler plates stuck up on the outer edges of the deck to protect cabins and bridge. We were fired on several times but with rifles only, and no damage was done.

The very young Acting Consul, in Chungking Howard Bucknell

In Chungking, Howard Bucknell[24], whom I was to relieve, came down to the ship to meet us. I assumed he would go back and turn over the consulate leisurely. Not Bucknell. "Here are the keys," he said. "I'm taking this boat out."

Chungking, another walled city, is built on a steep hillside rising out of the river. In those days the streets were narrow, wet, and dirty, and for the most part merely stairways cut out of the rock. There was not a wheeled vehicle, not even a wheelbarrow, for in the whole city there wasn't a street wide enough to accommodate one.

In my day there were two modes of transportation: walking or going by sedan chair. The consulate owned a very fancy chair with four chair-bearers and two ching ping tis. The function of these two lads was to walk ahead of the consular chair and clear the narrow streets, making room for the chair to pass. This was somewhat disconcerting, as they shoved people aside, roughly jostling them into shop fronts as they yelled out, "Ta jen lai lo"

---

24 (1889-1971) According to Captain Glenn F Howell of the USS Palos, Bucknell was "a very nice youngster ... about twenty-five, a student interpreter who has just finished a marvelous trip through the edge of Tibet with Major Magruder, our Military Attaché in Peking." *Gunboat on the Yangtze*, p138. He was, at the age of 22, temporarily filling in until a regular consul (i.e. Allman) arrived. Bucknell remained in consular service for some years, serving in China and Europe. He later became president of International Telephone and Telegraph Corporation.

which means, "The great man comes." Usually my wife rode in the chair and I, "the great man," walked along behind trying to be as inconspicuous as possible.

Our chair-bearers and coolies went barefooted. Their favorite stunt was to wash their feet in the dishpan, much to my wife's annoyance.

Water was carried in buckets from the river by coolies, and the streets were eternally wet. The climate of Chungking is depressing. It is so foggy and cloudy there that the Chinese have a proverb, "Tu ch'wan Chiao jih,"[25] "The Szechwan dog barks when he sees the sun."

The United States consulate was built squarely on top of the city wall. The execution ground was just below. I could sit on my veranda, and looking down, see men being shot. A semicircle of hills was covered with old graves dug back into the sides. Many

Steps up the steep hill to Chungking

---

25   The normal Chinese expression for this phrase is 蜀犬吠日 or Shǔ quǎn fèi rì. Allman may have mixed up the characters that are used.

of the graves' openings had collapsed. One looked into literally hundreds of yawning catacombs. Few of our associates lived on this side of the river, and it took at least an hour and a half by sedan chair and boat to cross the city and river to the American and British settlement.

I soon understood the reason for Bucknell's hurried exit. At this time the State Department required consuls the world over to submit detailed reports on the physical and living conditions of their posts so that newly assigned officers would know just what to expect. I'll bet a dollar the State Department has never shown my report on Chungking!

Chungking then was not the busy center it is today. There was insufficient work, beyond routine stuff, to relieve the dismal monotony. One of my consular colleagues was so bored he refused to get up before noon. On more than one occasion his nationals came around to see me in the morning to get something done for them. My colleague's sole worry was that his supply of Scotch whisky had been lost in transit from Shanghai.

I claim credit for helping to start modern transportation in Szechwan province. The tuchun, General Liu Hsiang[26], was keenly interested in building a motor road from Chungking to Chengtu. We discussed the possibilities many times as we sat over tea and watermelon seeds. I once mentioned that I could get an engineer up from Shanghai to survey the road. To my surprise General Liu not only agreed to have him come but offered to put up in cash whatever money  *Liu Hsiang*

26   Liu Hsiang (劉湘 Liu Xiang) (1888-1938) was one of the warlords controlling Szechuan and served as civil and military governor of Szechuan on a number of occasions. He invested a lot of effort into modernization. His troops also fought in the second Sino-Japanese war in Shanghai in 1937. The road in question is the Great East Road.

was needed.

I had no engineer in mind but quickly telegraphed Julean Arnold[27], the American commercial attache, to find one. He telegraphed right back that one was on his way. As a matter of fact two came, an American and a Czech to assist him. They went to work immediately and completed the survey in a few months. The road, however, was not built for some years, but it now forms an important part of Free China's transportation system. Incidentally, the first motorcars in western China appeared on this road.

In my time in Chungking, production and transportation of opium was one of Szechwan's major businesses. Every smuggling device known to mankind,

Julean Arnold, American Commercial Attache

plus a few newly invented, were used to get opium down to Shanghai and way ports. The Chinese Maritime Customs[28] and other agencies worked vigorously to suppress traffic in the drug and paid large rewards to informers. This led to a profitable business for informers and development of new and additional techniques by the smugglers. A favorite hiding place was the luggage of foreign officials and diplomatic passengers.

The Chungking commissioner of customs, naturally above suspicion, left on a visit to Shanghai. Luckily, just before the boat docked, he was tipped off that opium was concealed in his

---

27 Julean Herbert Arnold (1875-1946) joined the China consular service in 1902 as a student interpreter. From 1914 to 1917 he acted as US Commercial attaché in China and Japan and from 1917 to 1940 as US commercial attaché in China. He founded the American Chamber of Commerce in Shanghai in 1915 and the China Club of Seattle in 1916.

28 The maritime customs was a Chinese government body, but at the time run by foreigners. For a history, see: Robert Bickers, *Scramble for China*.

luggage. Someone had filled his trunk half full.

Another story goes that an American gunboat went from Chungking to Shanghai for repairs. En route, the captain was "informed" that opium was concealed on board. The captain instituted a search from keel to trucks. Even the bunkers were turned out, but no opium. The disappointed informer, who expected a large reward, was insistent, but everything, including bunks and the crew's duffel bags, had been carefully inspected. Nothing remained unopened except the ship's stores. Finally, a can of peas was opened. There was the opium.

Well aware of these tricks, I feared smugglers would utilize my baggage and effects to get opium past the customs. I had an unusual amount of stuff because I was leaving not only Chungking but China. I was sailing to America on a six months' leave, my first trip home since coming out to China as a student interpreter in 1916. I finished packing the day before sailing. That evening I prepared a notice in Chinese to the effect that I intended to have all baggage searched for opium when it was put on board in Chungking and again at each stop we made down river. I announced that I would seal each piece next morning. I passed the notice around among my house and office staff; even the chair-bearers and coolies who could not read were told about it. That night one trunk mysteriously was repacked, but I landed in Shanghai free of opium and free to sail for a well-earned holiday back home.

IV

The International Mixed Court

In 1922 I returned from my first home leave a full-fledged consul and was assigned to duty at the consulate-general in Shanghai.

Edwin Cunningham, US consul-general in Shanghai

Edwin S. Cunningham[1], the consul-general, was the first officer I served under, except for that brief period under Mr. Heintzleman in Tientsin, and I gathered that in the beginning he was dubious about our getting along together. Cunningham, I suppose, had been tipped off that while Allman had been in charge of various posts and had gained some experience, he was not overfond of red tape and had a dangerous contempt for protocol. As soon as he realized that I did not intend to start a revolution, we got along famously. But Cunningham was taking no chances. He kept me away from more delicate diplomacy by putting me to work on the International Mixed Court, and all unwittingly set me on the path that led to my practicing law.

---

1   Edwin Sheddan Cunningham (1868-1953) joined the United States consular service in 1898 and served in a number of positions before being appointed consul in Hankow in 1914. He served there until 1919 when he transferred to Shanghai where he served until his retirement in 1935.

The International Mixed court pre 1911

The Mixed Court goes back to April 20, 1869[2], when, through the efforts of Sir Harry Parkes[3], the Chinese government appointed a Chinese resident official with the rank of subprefect to hear cases involving Chinese of the International Settlement. If a foreigner were concerned in a case his consul or the consul's deputy was entitled to sit with the subprefect at the trial. In the cases where only Chinese were concerned, the subprefect could adjudicate the case independently and the consuls might not interfere.

The Chinese revolution in 1911 brought about the collapse of Manchu authority in the Shanghai area. The Manchu magistrate made a hurried departure and the Shanghai consular body authorized the Shanghai Municipal Council to take over the courts in the Settlement. The Chinese judges were continued in office, but the British and American consuls deputed consular officers to sit with them.

2   In fact, the Mixed Court was established in 1863.
3   Sir Harry Smith Parkes (1828-1885) GCMG, KCB, the British Consul in Shanghai in 1863. He subsequently became British Minister in Japan and then British Minister in China. Parkes had been held prisoner by the Chinese during the second Opium War in 1860.

Chinese Mixed Court Magistrates in 1911. Magistrates Kwan, Neoh and Wong with Secretary Yang.

During this period of political transition in China, the tenure of the Chinese judges was insecure, and by custom and usage the consular officers came to be a deciding factor in the court's judgments. At first only the British and American consulates deputed judges, known locally as assessors. Later, other nationals, Germans, Italians, Japanese, asserted the right to depute assessors whenever interests of their own nationals were involved. The Chinese courts in the French Concession were organized separately from those in International Settlement, and only French assessors sat in those courts.

The Mixed Court was interesting but the work exacting. The court had jurisdiction over all Chinese citizens or persons subject to Chinese jurisdiction including, later on, Russians, Germans, Austrians[4], and all other non-extraterritorial aliens. The court had unlimited jurisdiction in both civil and criminal matters. Its great weakness was a lack of a court of appeal. In lieu of appeals,

---

4   Soviet Russia gave up extraterritorial rights in 1922. Germans and Austrians lost extraterritorial rights when China declared war on Germany and the Austro-Hungarian Empire in 1917.

applications were made for rehearings, invariably granted.

Criminal cases, prepared and brought by the Shanghai municipal police, were conducted by the municipal advocate. The official court language was Chinese. Cases involved every known violation from over-parking to armed robbery and murder.

As many as fifty or sixty cases were heard in one day. My day as an assessor often began at 9 a.m. and continued until 6 or 7 p.m., sometimes later. All traffic violations were heard on Thursday afternoons, and a week's collection was rarely under seventy-five cases. Procedure in traffic cases was simple. Those who had informed the police of their intention to plead guilty were heard first and fined a minimum penalty. The police encouraged this. It certainly simplified things for the court. Usually about half the accused lined up to plead guilty. It was merely a matter of calling a man's name and writing down the amount of the fine. More complicated or technical cases came last and the too involved were adjourned for special hearings.

The Mixed Court was anything but elegant. It was held in an unpretentious red brick building on Chekiang Road, a one-time mansion which was not unlike the old county courthouses

The Mixed Court on North Chekiang Road

I've seen in many a small American town. The building was enclosed in a typically Chinese walled compound, but its rusty tin roof could have topped any down-at-the-heels tenement. It was uncomfortable at all times. In summer the sun beat down unmercifully through the roof to bake out our brains. There was always an almost over- powering stench, especially bad in the garlic season when the odor oozed out of the coolies, who ate the herb in quantities to keep up their strength.

The Mixed Court was far from dressy. Unlike other Chinese courts the judges did not wear caps and gowns but heard cases in their ordinary business suits.[5] In winter we added overcoats, for the building was inadequately heated by coal stoves and we were always cold. I recall seeing witnesses and parties coming to court fortified with charcoal braziers for their feet and hot-water bottles to warm their hands.

In appearance the Mixed Court rooms were similar to American court rooms of the police court or municipal court variety with judge's bench, witness stand, and prisoner's rail. The women's prison and house of detention was right next door.

Very often the minor cases were amusing. It was necessary for the assessor and magistrate to listen with all ears, for these petty lawbreakers were ingratiating fellows with entertaining if not authentic alibis.

There was Li Ah-tsung, a smiling, toothless old coolie, who came before the court so many times we greeted each other like old friends. One time he was charged with breaking into the godown of an American firm with intent to carry away a quantity of flour sacks. The night watchman had seen Li enter and had trapped him hiding in a corner. To this, Li, bland as always, demurred. He was not hiding, he said, but had caught his foot

---

5   Until the Republic Revolution in 1911 when the Municipal Council had taken over the court, the Chinese Magistrates had worn traditional robes and caps.

A Mixed Court Court Room

Entrance to the Mixed Court showing detention cells

on some obstacle in the dark and had fallen into the corner. His excuse wasn't good enough and so he stumbled into a cell at the municipal jail for a month's stay.

Often magistrates and assessors were taken in by these smiling pilferers. One of my colleagues heard a minor case which involved the theft of several chickens. The evidence was a bit sketchy, magistrate and assessor agreed on acquittal, the accused was released, and the judge hurried home to tiffin.

He noticed that throughout the meal his Chinese boy seemed unusually interested in details of the case and the assessor, delighted to have such an enthusiastic audience, expounded fully. He finished and looked up, expecting the boy's admiring smile. But the boy was a picture of woe. It was soon clear why.

"Oh, master," he wailed, "chickens belong you!"

I, too, was caught. If consistency be a virtue, as the philosophers say, then one Wong, delightful old rascal, is wearing a halo now. Wong was accused of passing counterfeit *yuan* (dollars) on various shopkeepers, and one brought in a heavy load of evidence to lay against him. But Wong contended that he had no suspicion that the coins were bad. Indeed, he had obtained them at a presumably reliable money exchange shop, and if his confidence had proved misplaced surely he was a candidate for commiseration rather than prosecution.

Despite his plea for sympathy we found him guilty and fined him two dollars. He paid and left. In the midst of the next case I was swept by a horrible thought. As soon as possible I consulted the custodian of the cash. My hunch was right. Wong had paid his fine with two counterfeit *yuan*.

I learned early that a judge, or a lawyer for that matter, must not let himself be swayed by sad stories. He must carefully close his heart and open his mind only to the cold facts of evidence and reason. I had opportunity to listen to many heart-rending stories in the Mixed Court. I remember the particularly pathetic one told by a blind man who had spent ten years in search of a missing wife. As I recall it:[6]

Sometime in the year 1913, Zee Kung-soong and Zee Zee-sz were married in their native village of Yangchow and there they lived happily for three months. Then the bride disappeared. Rumor was that Liu Ching-san, an unsuccessful suitor, had abducted and imprisoned her in Shanghai.

Zee, following this thin thread, started out on his search. For five weary years he toiled in Shanghai by day and combed the city by night. He gave up finally and returned to his own village. There his family and his wife's were engaged in a bitter quarrel. The father-in-law accused Zee of selling his wife into slavery. To prove this charge false Zee once again journeyed to Shanghai.

Poor Zee, hard luck dogged his heels. As he left the steamer, Liu (who for some reason could keep track of the husband) dashed up, threw lime in his eyes, and pushed him off the dock. A boatman rescued him, but the lime had blinded him for life. This incident, however, convinced the father-in-law that Zee's story was true, and he joined in the search. They worked together and in 1923 their efforts were rewarded. They found the wife in bondage and notified the police, who arrested Liu, prosperous manager of a Chapei theater.

Zee's troubles were not yet over. As he left court after the first hearing, several men jumped him and stabbed him seven times. After hospital treatment he returned to court, insisting that the men were gangsters Liu had employed to assault him.

So much for Zee's story. Had that been all there was to it, the court might have been moved to tears. Unfortunately for

---

6   Allman did not sit as an assessor in this case. Otherwise the story is accurate. It was heard by Magistrate Yui and Assessor Blackburn. The complainant was represented by American Chinese lawyer Hua Chuen Mei and the Defendant by H.D. Rodger. "A Ten Years' Search for Missing Wife" *NCH*, Sept 23, 1922, p910

Zee, irrefutable evidence produced against him, although far less dramatic, was based on the cold facts and proved that Zee's pathetic story was pure fiction. To bring the story of a long, involved case to a close, Zee and his wife were nothing more than a couple of extortionists who had seen rich pickings in Liu. Previous records showed that the Zee couple had been imprisoned numerous times on other extortion charges, and this was but one of the many money-making schemes they had dreamed up over their opium pipes. The Zees were members of a notorious guild of extortionists which at one time was so large that a hotel in Shanghai was maintained for their exclusive use.

One of my earliest and more serious cases was a murder. A man had beaten his wife to death and afterward for good measure had chopped her up with a hatchet. There was no doubt as to his guilt. He admitted the crime. The difficulty was that the magistrate and I could not agree on the sentence. I took the view that because of the revolting nature of the crime and because of his admitted guilt the man should be executed. The magistrate,

Allman on the Mixed Court with Magistrate Li. H. Bucknell is assisting Allman.

an old-style gentleman and to my mind out of date in his ideas, thought that ten years was enough. After all, wasn't the woman the man's own wife!

As neither of us would budge from his opinion we agreed to transfer the case to another assessor and another magistrate. They sentenced the culprit to life imprisonment.

Another time the magistrate and I came to a unanimous decision which we were convinced must have approximated exact justice, as both plaintiff and defendant were dissatisfied with the judgment.

An American citizen had filed a claim for breach of contract against a prominent Chinese, and this case was fought out bitterly on both sides. When the judgment was handed down, the plaintiff went so far as to complain to the American legation of the lack of justice he had received at the hands of the American assessor. He was informed that the legation was in no position to interfere. The Chinese party to the case also complained through several sources about the Chinese magistrate.

Naturally, there were many other such complaints, but as far as I can remember there were no actual threats against my life, although one irate Chinese murderer upon whom the magistrate and I were forced to pass the death sentence cursed us thus: "May my ghost come back and haunt you all the days of your life!" Possibly because I'm not a believer in ghosts that's one spirit I've never met.

The Mixed Court had unlimited jurisdiction in all civil matters, including admiralty cases. An admiralty case with complicated questions of jurisdiction was that of *Patstone and Patstone versus R.J. Ellerder*, agent for the Soviet owners of the Russian Volunteer Fleet. This case was pending before I went on the Mixed Court, came up for hearing a number of times while I was sitting as assessor, and continued for several months after I had left both

IN THE MIXED COURT
AT SHANGHAI

No. 108.

ding at _____, Shanghai.

Between _____ **Plaintiff,**

_____ **Defendant.**

You are hereby required to attend at the _____

_rt on_____, the_____day of_____192 , at

_hour of_____in the_____noon to give evidence in the_

_ve action on behalf of the_____

In default of your attendance you will be liable to fine or

risonment.

Registrar.

nghai,

正會審官

十年七月十四日

形照兹抗法庭懲罰毋慎切切

易所質證如屆時無故不到應酌量情

下午二時半至本公廨以備為日爰交

此傳知該王鳴正於十年七月廿四日

案內應需居住閘北之王鳴正作證爲

傳知事茲有由爰交易所訴張伯勳一

上海會審公廨

爲

Mixed Court Witness Summons

court and consular service.

The plaintiffs in the case, two American citizens, had been
employed in Shanghai by the Russian merchant marine in

77

prerevolution Czarist days when the Russian Volunteer Fleet was a privately owned concern. After the birth of the Soviet Republic, when the fleet became state owned, a dispute arose between the Americans and their employers over monies advanced by the Americans for wages to crew, medical attention, supplies, and so forth, while acting as agents for the fleet.

I remember that during the trial the plaintiffs attempted to attach the steamers *Erivan* and *Astrakan* and this brought up an interesting point: Did the Shanghai harbor fronting the Settlement come under the jurisdiction of the Mixed Court? After much discussion the opinion was that a portion of the harbor came under the Mixed Court's jurisdiction, and we could proceed with the main issue.

What with questions of admiralty, Chinese law, American law, Russian law, private and public international law, it's no wonder that the case dragged on for nearly three years. And then after all the litigation the case finally ended, I believe, in a compromise.[7]

The White Russian residents of Shanghai themselves presented untold legal problems. The complicated Russian law was based on church as well as state law. Whenever two Russians were involved in civil disputes, particularly in those cases where questions of domestic relations and wills came up, it seemed better to put the whole thing in the hands of a Russian deputy of the consular body. Russian law was applied and the case was treated as though it were heard in a Russian consular court. Chinese law applied in all criminal cases, as Russians were non-extraterritorial aliens. Where the plaintiff was a non-Russian and the defendant Russian, Chinese law was generally

---

7   Allman, sitting with Messrs Ivanov and Kuan, in fact, gave judgment for Patstone and Patsone and ordered the sale of the ships. "Russian Volunteer Fleet: Fifteen Months' Case in Mixed Court Concluded by Order to Sell Vessels", *North China Herald*, Jan 13, 1923, p122. It was announced later that negotiations were pending to settle the judgment. "Transfer of Soviet Ships", *North China Herald*, Jan 27, 1923, p245.

Some Mixed Court Celebrities

Some of the many foreign lawyers who appeared before the Mixed Court

applicable and that's how I happened to hear the case brought by an American garage owner against his Russian mechanic, Michael Beilin.

Beilin sold his employers on the idea of sending him to Vladivostok to buy up used cars. But once in Vladivostok Beilin used his employers' funds to purchase cars and accessories for the garage he planned to open on his return to Shanghai. His only purchase for his employer was a fourth-hand car which looked as though it had gone through the revolution.

There was no doubt of Beilin's guilt, but the magistrate and I decided to refund his bail and let him out. Beilin, we thought, had received just punishment. He had been out-swindled by the

Vladivostok dealers, who, it turned out, had sent him cases of scrap iron and steel, not so valuable then as now, instead of the accessories he had purchased.[8]

One of my early and difficult civil cases involved the American publishers, G. & C. Merriam Company, and the *Commercial Press* of Shanghai.[9]

The *Commercial Press* had translated Webster's *Collegiate Dictionary* and then had published it bilingually, retaining the English version to interlard the translation. The Merriam company sued the *Commercial Press* for alleged piracy of copyright and infringement of trade mark. This case was a bitter fight and involved the interpretation of treaties between the United States and China, as well as Chinese law.

In producing the bilingual edition the Commercial Press inadvertently had reproduced the title page of the dictionary including the trade-mark owned by Merriam and recorded at the American consulate-general and the Chinese Maritime Customs at Shanghai. This trade-mark, as most dictionary users have never noticed, consists of "Webster and Webster's Collegiate

THE NORTH-CHINA HERALD.

MOTOR CARS FROM
VLADIVOSTOK

Proceedings in the Mixed Court
Respecting a Supply of Cars
for Shanghai

At the Mixed Court on Tuesday morning, before Mr. Li (Magistrate) and Mr. Allman (American Assessor), Mitchell Beilin, of Russian nationality, residing at Tungheng Road, Chapei, was charged on the complaint of the Hongkew Motor Co. (through its manager, Mr. G. F. Grout) that on or about September 20, 1922, he did at Shanghai, deceitfully, unlawfully and fraudulently obtain from the complainants the sum of Y. 4,000, contrary to Aricles 382 and 383 of the Chinese Provisional Criminal Code.
Mr. L. K. Kentwell represented the complainants and Mr. A. N. Roushkovsky appeared for the defence.

A report of the Beilin case

---

8   Allman tried the case with Magistrate Li. The Defendant's name was Mitchell Beilin. Hongkew Motor Co had provided Beilin with money to buy cars in Vladivostok. Mr. Lawrence Kentwell prosecuted and Mr. A.N. Roushkovsky defended. Beilin's bail was returned and Allman and Li acquitted Beilin on the basis there was no criminal intent. "Motor Cars from Vladivostok", *North China Herald*, Mar 10, 1923, p692 and "A Motor Car Deal" *North China Herald*, Apr 28, 1923, p269.

9   Judgments: *G. & C. Merriam Company v Commercial Press, Ltd, China Weekly Review*, Oct 6, 1923, p232. *North China Herald*, Sept 29, 1923, p940. Trial: *North China Herald*, Aug 25. 1923, p563. Krisel & Krisel and Davies & Brian for the Plaintiff and William S. Fleming and Alexander Ting for the Defendant.

"below the colophon, a representation of a wreath in which is enclosed the letter "W" in fanciful form.

The decision, in which both the magistrate and I concurred, was that under the Sino-American treaties, and the then state of the Chinese law, there had been no copyright infringements, as the Merriam company had no Chinese copyright on the book. But we did agree that there had been a trade-mark infringement, and the G. & C. Merriam Company was awarded damages to the amount of two thousand dollars (Chinese currency).

Shortly after Chinese copyright laws were enacted some years ago, I registered copyrights on a number of textbooks for several American publishers. But in later years the Chinese government stopped granting these copyrights and held that its copyright law was intended to apply to Chinese authors and publications only or, in the language of the treaty, to those works "especially prepared for the use and education of the Chinese people."

The Chinese view this copyright question as an economic rather than a legal or moral one. Chinese students, they say, need our text and technical books but cannot afford to pay our prices, which when translated into Chinese dollars are prohibitive. Some efforts have been made to induce American publishers to bring out cheaper editions, especially in textbooks, but nothing has come of these efforts.

Piracy of all types of British and American books has been a flourishing business in Shanghai. An American best seller could be reproduced and sold for two or three Chinese dollars. The leading British and American bookstores, Kelly and Walsh, and the Chinese American Publishing Company had difficulty in disposing of legitimately printed books. Most foreign residents in China waited for the pirated edi- tion, which they bought for thirty cents instead of three dollars.

New treaties may change all this, but at the present time unless

Sapajou on the rendition of the Mixed Court

a book, map, print or engraving, or any other literary material can be interpreted as "for the use and education of the Chinese people" it can not be copyrighted. Trade-marks are something else again — another headache which I'll leave for a later chapter.

On the whole the Chinese were never too satisfied with the International Mixed Court. If I remember rightly it was in 1922 that members of the Peking judiciary headed by Chang Yao-tsen[10], a former Minister of Justice, paid a visit to the International Mixed Court as a part of the movement for return of the Court to Chinese control.

There had always been controversy between the Chinese

---

10   Chang Yao-tsen (張耀曾 Zhang Yaozeng) (1885-1938) served a number of times as Minister of Justice between 1916 and 1924. From 1924 he practiced as a lawyer in Shanghai.

JUDGE CHIU.

THE PROSECUTING SOLICITOR.

MICHAEL PARSHEKOFF, THE ACCUSED.

COUNSEL FOR DEFENSE.

DR. ANNING OF PUBLIC HEALTH DEPT.

A scene from the Provisional Court before Judge Chiu. Mr Maitland prosecutes on behalf of the Municipal Council, Dr Fischer defends

government and the foreign governments over the court. Boiled down, this controversy meant that the Chinese government claimed that the operation of the court was contrary to the treaty provisions, while the foreign governments contended that during the period of China's political transition, its operation was essential for administration of justice at Shanghai.[11]

On October 31, 1926, just fifteen years after the revolution, an agreement signed by the consular body at Shanghai and the

11 One of the main drivers for the agreement had been reached was the May 30 Movement of 1925 when the Shanghai Municipal Police had shot and killed a number of protestors in Shanghai. Chinese public anger pushed foreign governments to agree to the rendition of the court.

Kiangsu provincial government provided for the establishment of the Shanghai Provisional Court to succeed the Mixed Court.[12] This agreement went into effect on January 1, 1927, and thereafter assessors no longer sat with judges in Chinese civil cases. The senior consul, however, could appoint a deputy to sit jointly with the judge in criminal cases which "directly affected the peace and order of the International Settlement" and in cases involving contraventions of the Land Regulations, Municipal By-laws, and Sino-foreign treaties.

Dr. Showin Wetzen Hsu, American educated head of the Provisional Court and later head of the newly established Special High Court.

But the Provisional Court also proved unsatisfactory, and a new agreement concerning the court was signed by the Chinese government and interested foreign powers on February 17, 1930, and came into effect on April 1, 1930. This new agreement abolished the practice of consular assessors appearing to watch the proceeding and to sit jointly with the Chinese judges. Under the new agreement the Chinese government established a Chinese district court and a high court in the International Settlement. But by that time I had long since said my farewells to the Mixed Court and to the American consular service.

---

12   Allman signed the agreement on behalf of Mexico in his capacity as Consul for Mexico.

V

PROTOCOL AND OTHER PROBLEMS

FOR A YEAR OR MORE the highfalutin title of "Judge" — really a nickname given me by the Shanghai Rotary Club[1] — was mine by day, but from 7 p.m. on, with time out for a hurried dinner, I was just another overworked consular officer. The American consulate-general was such a busy place that both Joseph E. Jacobs[2], my colleague on the court, and I were required to do considerable routine consular work in addition.

One of my most interesting consular jobs during this period was handling the incoming and outgoing cables concerning the Shanghai-Peking Blue Express kidnapping, otherwise known as the "Lincheng Outrage." The kidnappers made quite a haul and got several prominent Americans.

That early spring of 1923, a large gang of bandits under the leadership of Sun Mei-yao operated along the borders of Kiangsu, Anhui, and Shantung provinces adjacent to the tracks of the Tientsin-Pukow Railway. The de luxe Blue Express was proceeding through the southern part of Shantung when, at two-fifty in the morning of May 6, about six hundred bandits held it up and overpowered the guard of some thirty soldiers. The foreign and Chinese passengers were left at the bandits' mercy.

---

1   Allman continued to use the title "Judge" after the WWII, even after he had returned to the United States.
2   Jacobs had been a student interpreter with Allman. See Chapter 2 for biography.

Derailed Blue Express

Bandit Chief Sun Mei Yao (in long robe). J.B. Powell is on the left side of the photo.

The passengers included J. B. Powell[3], Shanghai newspaperman, Max Friedman[4], Shanghai automobile dealer, a Shanghai attorney, and a number of world tourists. In this group the bandits bagged

---

3   John Benjamin Powell (1886-1947) was first came to China in 1917 to co-found *Millard's Review of the Far East*. In 1922 he took over the paper and later renamed it the *China Weekly Review*. Powell published a series of articles on the Lincheng Outrage in the *China Weekly Review* in April and May 1939. See Chapter 17 for more details.

4   It was, in fact, Leon Friedman (died 1961), Max's brother, who was captured. Max Friedman (died 1942) and Leon promoted aviation and organized airshows in Shanghai from 1910 to 1918. They then worked as automobile dealers at the China Motors and Star Garage from 1919 to 1940.

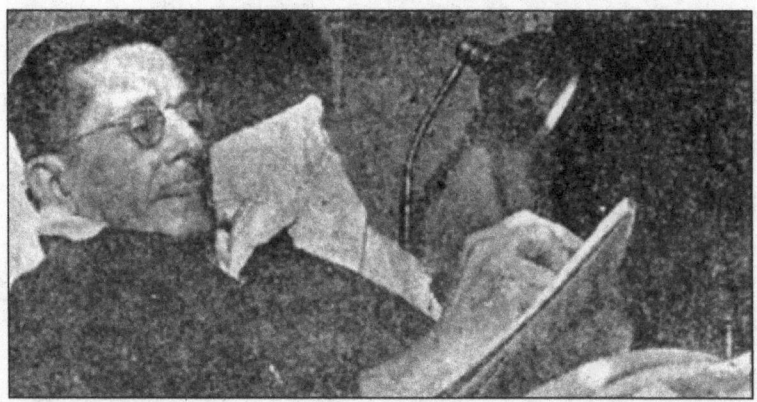

J.B. Powell

two United States army majors on vacation from their posts in the Philippines, and one well-known American woman, Miss Lucy Aldrich[5], daughter of the late Rhode Island Senator and sister-in-law of John D. Rockefeller, Jr.

Before Miss Aldrich left New York she visited her brother-in-law and asked his advice about traveling in China. He told her jokingly that in case of any trouble to call on the nearest Socony agent. The story went that when the bandits invaded her compartment Miss Aldrich called out, " Socony! Socony!" But there wasn't a Standard Oil man within hearing distance.

About thirty foreign passengers were on the train and possibly one hundred Chinese, all of whom were taken into the mountains. After a few hours the bandits released the women, who didn't move fast enough over the rough, mountainous country. Among the prisoners were a Mexican merchant and his wife, Mr. and Mrs.Verea[6], who were on their wedding journey, and Mrs. Verea flatly refused to leave her husband in spite of anything the bandits could do.

---

5   Lucy Truman Aldrich (1869-1955) was the eldest daughter of US Senator Nelson W. Aldrich. Her sister Abigail Aldrich married John Davidson Rockefeller.
6   Manuel Ancira Verea and his wife Teresa Campos Verea nee Kunhardt. Mrs Verea was released by the bandits despite her protests.

Manuel Ancira Verea , Mexican kidnapped by bandits

Released by Bandits

MISS LUCY C. ALDRICH.
Daughter of late Senator Aldrich of
Maine, and sister-in-law of John D.
Rockefeller, jun., who was captured by
Chinese bandits, with a score of other
foreigners.

Lucy Aldrich

As for Miss Aldrich, she was simply abandoned in the mountains on the second day, which the bandits certainly would not have done had they known her identity. She finally made her way back to civilization, none the worse for the adventure, but with a story that outclassed all experiences of world travelers for many a year. I helped to send cable after cable for her and about her to distraught State Department officials and her anxious family at home.

At first the prisoners were taken to the top of a mountain which had been previously fortified for the purposes of defense. Here they, as well as the bandits, were besieged all day by Chinese troops, whose efforts proved futile. The bandits notified the troops that all foreigners would be shot unless the troops withdrew immediately. One of the foreign captives was forced to write a letter to the commander of the besieging force, warning him against attempting a rescue since it might result in their slaughter.

Late one night the prisoners were marched to another mountain, Paotushan or "The Calf Carrying Hill." This hill was considered impregnable because there was only one mountain path, so steep no grown oxen were able to climb it and farmers

Mt Paotushan – the bandits' lair

"The Sap Club" – a dugout where some of the captives were held

bought baby calves, carrying them to the flat, cultivated summit where they grew up and died.

Here, where further pursuit was impossible, the bandits and their prisoners settled down while negotiations proceeded for their release. The bandits, who now numbered two thousand, demanded five million Chinese dollars in ransom, and in addition demanded that they be taken into the Chinese army and stationed on the Tientsin-Pukow Railway where they could levy further tribute on the traveling public and loot the railway as well.

Altogether the prisoners spent about six weeks as guests of the bandits, who won out in their demand for incorporation into the army, but compromised on the money end. Instead of the five million dollars, they finally accepted the equivalent of five hundred thousand United States dollars paid over in hard Chinese silver dollars. Some six months later, by a ruse, the

Chinese governor of Shantung succeeded in getting the bandits away from their rifles and executed practically the whole gang. To prove his action, the Chinese general in command sent each of the ex-captives a photograph showing several hundred bodies of the late bandits all piled up against the stone wall which had served as their background when they faced the firing squad.

An ex-captive told me, after his release, that for a man possessing a sense of humor the experience of being a bandit's captive was not too painful. To be sure, for the first two weeks there was little food and the captives had to make forced night marches over stony ground wearing very little clothing except pajamas. Eventually, however, most of the prisoners secured clothing by begging or bartering with the bandits who had stolen their things from the train. No one was able to get his own; hence some interesting trading took place among the captives, usually in the night after the guards had gone to sleep.

Among the group was Leon Friedman, a man of considerable avoirdupois. He fell heir to the clothing of a Mexican who weighed one hundred and twenty-five pounds. Chevalier Musso,

Chevalier Musso, Italian lawyer from Shanghai, and his bandit captors

a prosperous Shanghai attorney, even larger than Mr. Friedman, never did succeed in finding his clothing and was forced to continue in the attire which he wore when captured, a night shirt reaching barely to his knees. The others called him the Roman senator, as he strode about camp in his "toga."

The captives subsisted on an enforced diet of one raw egg daily

Leon Friedman and a bandit

and some tasteless cakes, the consistency of leather (made from kaoliang or millet seeds, crushed and mixed with water), until an American missionary in the adjoining valley succeeded in smuggling some food into the camp. This food consisted of a Chinese ham, the nether portion of a Chinese pig, which is of commercial use chiefly as a supplier of bristles. The reading matter sent by the missionary consisted of several copies of the New Testament. But after all, ham is food and the New Testament is reading matter.

After partaking of the ham and settling down to discover the New Testament, Captive Friedman was heard to say, "What is a good Jew boy going to do in the circumstances? We starve and they send us ham! We have nothing to read and they send us the New Testament!"

After his release one of Friedman's first acts was to send a handsome contribution to the missionary, Dr. Yerkes.[7]

Once the victims were freed, the Chinese government dispatched the party in style in a palatial private car to Shanghai, where we all turned out to give them a royal welcome. The Chinese government on recommendations of the American

---

7   Rev Carroll Harvey Yerkes D.D. (1876-1971) of Yihsien Station, an American Presbyterian Mission at Yishien (Yixian), Shantung.

Rev Yerkes who smuggled food to the camp with a bandit

Minister, Dr. Jacob Gould Schurman[8], finally paid for property stolen by the bandits, and in addition gave each captive a sort of "compassionate grant" figured out on a per diem basis for the time held captive.

I was in the midst of cables about this affair — I had to do most of this work at night, since the Mixed Court kept me busy all day — when the phone rang one morning about one o'clock. It was Dr. Anne Walter Fearn[9], then famous as a Shanghai hostess, who was giving a tiffin party next day to all the diplomatic, judicial, and consular ladies in town. She asked me to make out a seating list according to protocol. I surmised from the cables then at hand that the kidnapped party had no chance of immediate

---

8   Jacob Gould Schurman (1854 to 1982) was born in Canada but moved to the United States in 1886 and became the third president of Cornell University in 1892. He served as the US Minister to Greece from 1912 to 1913 and as US Minister to China from 1921 to 1925. He was appointed ambassador to Germany from 1925 to 1929. He retired in 1930. He opened the American Club in Shanghai in 1924. See Chapter 10 for a photo of the cornerstone.

9   Born Anne Walter (1865-1939). Fearn moved to Suzhou in 1893 after graduating from the Women's Medical College of Pennsylvania. She stayed in Suzhou until 1907 and after briefly returning to the United States with her husband John Fearn, returned to Shanghai in 1908 where she established the Fearn Sanatorium. She retired to Berkeley, California in 1938.

J.B. Powell and Lloyd Lehrbas arrive at Shanghai station

release and that taking a couple of hours to spend on this seating arrangement would not prejudice their safety seriously.

I drew up a seating plan and placed every lady according to her official precedence. Even the Quai d'Orsay or Number 10 Downing Street would have approved my plan as a work of art. It had, however, one serious drawback from Dr. Fearn's point of view. The ladies to her right and left she thoroughly disliked. I sent this plan to Dr. Fearn about 3 a.m. and she phoned at once to know if it couldn't be changed. I told her, " No. It's according to protocol."

At the tiffin she took matters in her own hands, mixed up the ladies and placed them according to her own ideas. She threw protocol out the window, she thought, but in her rearranged seating she trod on numerous official toes. She had placed too many people "with but after" instead of "with but before." Dr. Fearn, no mean diplomat herself, claimed, "That damned fool

93

Dr Anne Walter Fearn

Allman made the mistake in seating." She knew that I'd take it as a good joke.

Both consular and court work were interesting and thoroughly enjoyable, but conditions under which we worked in the consular service were discouraging. I had completed all of the student interpreter work, and promotion therefore had been rapid. I could not complain on this score. Nevertheless, the pay was low; we had neither entertainment nor retirement allowances and had to pay all our own expenses on home leave. Most consuls did not earn enough money to go home more than once in ten years and consequently were out of touch with the American scene.

My daughter, Nancy English, was born in Shanghai in 1926, and I did not see how I could stay in the consular service with two children to support and educate. I regretted leaving such pleasant and agreeable surroundings and colleagues, but I came to the conclusion I'd better resign and go into private practice of law in Shanghai, especially as the State Department frowned upon any idea I might have had of telling my congressman from Virginia how badly we were treated. Later Congress did better by the consular service.

I also came to the conclusion that I had better resign before I was asked to do so. It was my belief that the major duty of a consul was to go to bat for his nationals; that he should first make sure that the claims of his nationals were reasonable, then work like hell to get quick results. At the same time I realized that sooner or later this method would get me into trouble and fired. Whenever I found an American in trouble I tried to get him out, regardless of red tape. And I was just as fond of protocol as a bull is of a red rag.

I have referred to protocol so often that perhaps an explanation of this monkey business is in order. Protocol, in the sense I've used it, is the oil that keeps the diplomatic social and ceremonial machinery from creaking too loudly. A sure-fire way to put a diplomat in high dudgeon is to seat him a few ranks lower than he is entitled to be. This sometimes is done by design but more often it is accidental, especially if a number of army, navy, Judicial, and other officials are in the same large party. The offended official is almost certain to get up and walk out on the party. I have seen this childish stunt pulled time and time again. Once or twice I have been assigned the wrong seat, but, certain that it was accidental, I did not feel that the dignity and prestige of the United States were thereby irretrievably damaged. To me it seemed more than adequate to drop a hint that at the next party the seating should be put in order. It never seemed worth the bother to carry on angry correspondence over such a small matter.

But aside from my dislike of protocol I was never able to dress the part of a diplomat. As soon as our little student interpreter group arrived in Peking, our colleagues broke the sad news to us that we had to buy and, worse luck, wear top hats, morning coats, and striped pants plus spats. This rig makes any man look like a crow, and all the bowing one has to do in diplomatic life merely emphasizes the resemblance. But I could not resist the pressure and was compelled to buy one of these costumes, thereby postponing the purchase of a Mongolian polo pony for two months.

Shortly after I resigned from the consular service, my wife announced that she had given my morning coat and striped pants to the church rummage sale. I was a little surprised at my luck, as she usually gave away my favorite old suit. The top hat came in handy now and then. I used it for paper hunting (the Chinese version of fox hunting). Incidentally, in spite of my wife's best efforts, I've consistently held the title of being the worst dressed man in China and was reputed to have had my tailoring done by the Whampoa Engineering and Dock Works. This was downright slander of such an efficient company. Later when I was elected to the Shanghai Municipal Council I shocked my colleagues by refusing to buy or wear morning dress. They were no little offended when I intimated that they looked like crows. In any case, I thought councilors were elected to work, not just look pretty.

To our Western way of thinking many things were done backward in China. It wasn't at all unusual for a judge to resign to practice law; Chinese lawyers frequently get their start as judges.[10] This is also true of some of the European systems. But under American and British legal systems the lawyer usually graduates from attorney at law into "his honor the judge."

No one was much surprised when I announced that I was ready to join the group of fifteen or so practicing American lawyers. I had started my study of law at the University of Virginia

---

10   This remains true today. Many Chinese lawyers start their careers as judges.

and had continued it as a part of my student-interpreter course. While in the consular service I had read law under the expert guidance of the late E. P. Allen[11], one of the ablest of the American lawyers in China, who had offices in Tientsin and Peking. Too, I had access to the extensive Chinese-American law library of the Pei Yang University in Tientsin. And during my consular days I had translated into English

Edgar Pierce Allen, Allman's mentor

the Chinese trade-mark, patent, and copyright laws. Later I translated the Chinese company and labor laws.

While still a member of the consular service I had taken and passed the bar examination of the United States Court for China[12]. I was a member of the American Far Eastern Bar Association[13], and now I was ready to practice.

I received offers from almost every American law firm in Shanghai and Tientsin, and in those days there were a good many law firms.

American lawyers in China practiced in the United States Court

11 Edgar Pierce Allen (1866-1921), was born in Shanghai to Rev Young John Allen and Mary Allen (nee Houston). He practiced principally in Tientsin. He died in Peking in 1921.
12 Allman was admitted to the bar on 29 June 1918.
13 The Far Eastern Bar Association was established in 1916 by Judge Charles Lobingier of the United States Court for China. Its objects as set out in its Constitution were: "The better to maintain the dignity, honor and interest of the American legal profession in the Far East, to promote and improve the morale, efficiency and solidarity of its members, to enable them to keep in touch with the progress of judicial science and its promoters throughout the world and especially in America, to assist in the due administration of justice the courts in which they practice and to secure the general observance of the American Bar Association's Canons of Legal Ethics which are hereby declared part of the rules of this Association." Active membership was open to "any American citizen residing in the Far East who has been regularly admitted to practice in the Federal Supreme Court, the United States Court for China, or the highest court of any American state, territory or possession."

for China, which corresponds to a Federal district court, and in all the American consular courts, similar to our minor municipal courts. By courtesy they also practiced in the Chinese courts and in the courts of other extraterritorial powers, such as the British, French, and others. The lawyers of those nationalities, likewise by courtesy, practiced in the United States Court for China.

William S. Fleming, Allman's first law partner

As every American lawyer in China had tried cases before me in the International Mixed Court, I had had good opportunity to study them all. I decided to throw in my lot with William S. Fleming[14], whom I admired and respected both as a man and a lawyer. He was one of the first six members of the American bar in China and had been practicing in the United States Court since 1907. He was a former deputy attorney general of the Hawaiian Islands.

To my mind a lawyer needs three things — courage, loyalty, and integrity — and Fleming, scholarly in appearance and fiery in temperament, had all three in a greater measure than any other man I've ever known. He also had one of the largest law practices in China.

Living in Shanghai where there are few if any secrets and everyone knows all about the other fellow's business, I knew that Fleming was highly regarded by most people, especially his colleagues of all nationalities and by the British and Chinese in particular. I also knew that Fleming had been held in contempt of court and sentenced to six months in jail by Judge Charles S.

---

14 William S. Fleming (1877-1932) was born in Napa, California and died suddenly in Shanghai in 1932.

Lobingier[15] of the United States Court for China.[16] But I understood, too, that this was due to a conflict of temperament and that it did not reflect on Fleming's moral integrity. On the contrary, it proved to me that he was a fighter. In fact, I'd had many a conflict of opinion with him myself in the Mixed

> Mr. Norwood F. Allman, Junior American Assessor, has resigned from the American Consular Service. He will be associated with Mr. W. S. Fleming in the practice of law in Shanghai. Mr. Howard Bucknell, jr., Consul, lately at Canton, will succeed Mr. Allman on the Mixed Court bench. Mr. Bucknell was appointed student interpreter in 1919 and has served at Chungking, Changsha, and Canton. He was recently promoted to Consul's rank.

Allman to join Fleming

Court. Just because we didn't agree on occasions I saw no reason why I should have any less respect for him.

As assessor on the Mixed Court I went on the assumption that there were three sides to every case: the plaintiffs, the defendant's, and the right side. To Fleming there was only one side, his client's, even if this meant an argument with the judge.

The Fleming contempt trial, which set the whole town agog and divided Shanghai society into two camps, had occurred in 1921 while I was acting consul in far-off Chungking, where little if any news reached us. I didn't hear about the case then, or if I did I was not sufficiently interested to be impressed. But naturally when I returned to Shanghai it was still a major topic of conversation. I doubt if even now it has been entirely forgotten by some of the old-timers.

---

15 For more on Lobingier and the US Court, see Chapter 7.
16 In 1921, Fleming had published a pamphlet "The United States Court as an Institution" that was highly critical of the United States Court for China and the huge power the single judge wielded. He had challenged this power by trying to force Judge Lobingier to recuse himself by accusing Lobingier and others of corruption and bias. Instead, Fleming was found in contempt of court by Lobingier, a sentence up held by the Ninth Circuit on appeal. See Gunboat Justice, Vol 2, Chapter 42.

What actually happened was this:

In the opening stages of a hearing before Judge Lobingier, Fleming asked for a change of venue, charging the judge with malfeasance in office.

Contempt proceedings abruptly followed and Fleming was adjudged guilty. He had been confined in the American prison for eleven days of his six months' sentence when he was released under a thousand American dollar bond, pending outcome of his appeal to the Ninth District Court of Appeals in California. Some months later this court passed upon the case and affirmed Judge Lobingier's judgment. Fleming then took the case to the United States Supreme Court, which a year later also affirmed the judgment.

> **LOBINGIER, ENTIRELY VINDICATED, BACK TO SHANGHAI COURT**
>
> Judge of United States Tribunal for China Upheld by President Harding Against Accusations Made.
>
> **FLEMING'S CONTEMPT SENTENCE AFFIRMED**
>
> Appeal Court Rules for Penalty of Six Months' Imprisonment — Fleming Charges Held Baseless.
>
> Judge Charles S. Lobingier, judge of the United States for China, reached Yokohama yesterday morning on the President Grant, returning to Shanghai from the United States, where he has been for the last ten months in connection with the President's investigation of his court. The result of that investigation has been the complete refutation of the charges against the American Court for China placed with the Washington authorities early last year by William S. Fleming, a Shanghai attorney.

Judge Lobingier vindicated

While the case was wending its way through the various courts, all American court procedure in Shanghai was disrupted. Fleming had also filed a list of charges against Judge Lobingier with the Department of State at Washington, D. C, and both men had to spend some time there during the investigation. As there was no provision in the court code for the judge's absence from the country during his term of office, all court cases went unheard for more than a year.

To bring a long story to a close, the day after Christmas in 1922, the judge, exuding the season's good will to men, remitted Fleming's unexpired sentence. Fleming, in turn, apologized, and once more all was peace and harmony in the United States

Court.[17]

When the news got around that I was set on joining Fleming, I remember that one conservative old codger called on me with the warning, "If you join Fleming, you are finished before you begin."

I already had made up my mind that it was to be Fleming, but I hadn't formally accepted his offer. That settled it. I lost no time in getting over to Fleming's office. "Well," I asked, "when do I begin?" Then and there we drew up papers and from that

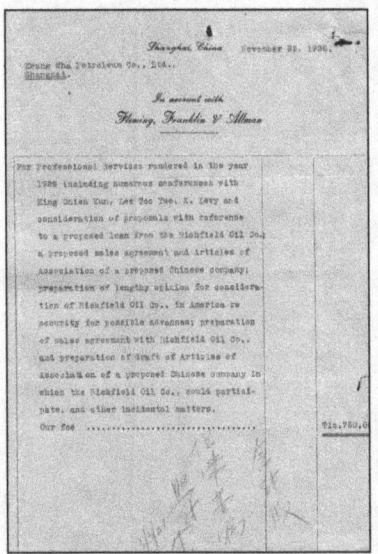

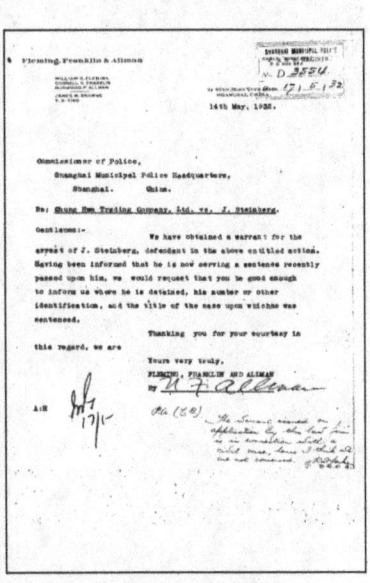

A fee note Fleming, Franklin and Allman in 1930. The other partner was Cornell Franklin

A letter from Allman on Fleming, Franklin and Allman letterhead

17   It appears that the remission of the sentence was a deal that Lobingier had done with US President Harding to retain his position. Lobingier was a very erudite judge who wrote long judgments citing English and American cases. In the case of his judgment releasing Fleming, he cited no cases but merely cited Victor Hugo's Les Miserables and the story of Jean Valjean who had been caught stealing candlesticks but been forgiven by the archbishop. Lobingier made a point of saying that while candlesticks could be restored, a good name could not. *United States v Fleming*, *North China Herald*, December 30, 1922, p881

moment on, we were partners until his death in 1932, when I established my own office.

Now I was a practicing American lawyer in Shanghai. At first I missed the official life that had been mine for seven years, but I soon acquired a sense of freedom I hadn't known in ages. I could do anything I wanted to do, within reason of course, without having someone ten thousand miles away enter a mark on my efficiency record.

VI

AMERICA IN CHINA

FOREIGN LAWYERS, AS WELL as the
merchants and missionaries,
philanthropists, and promoters
who made their homes in
Shanghai and other treaty
ports during the past century,
owe a debt of gratitude to the
brilliant Massachusetts lawyer,
Caleb Cushing[1]. For it was he
who negotiated the first treaty,
clearly defining the rights of
the foreigner in China, and

Caleb Cushing

interpreted the most important and controversial of all the
rights — that of extraterritoriality.

It's impossible to discuss a law practice or any other subject
concerning the foreigner in China without dragging in that
confusing and unwieldy word extraterritoriality, commonly
contracted to extrality. Without extraterritoriality, or to give
it still another term, consular jurisdiction, there would have

---

1   Caleb Cushing (1800-1879) served as a US Congressman and as Attorney General under
     President Franklin Pierce. He was appointed by President Tyler as Ambassador to China
     to negotiate a treaty after the British had signed the Treaty of Nanking. Cushing also
     served on the Massachusetts Supreme Court and was nominated by President Grant to
     be Chief Justice of the United States. The Senate did not approve the nomination.

been few American and other foreign lawyers in China, and I, for one, would have missed the fun and experience of trying cases of every description in the courts of half a dozen different nationalities.

Shorn of its weighty legal phraseology, extrality meant that a foreigner was amenable only to the laws of his own country. He was subject to detention and trial only by his own officials and could be sued in civil action only in his own country's court. This was one of the most important and most controversial of the rights secured by foreigners through treaties negotiated with the Chinese government. I speak of extrality in the past tense because the British and American governments relinquished their rights (gained by nineteenth-century treaties) in treaties signed simultaneously on January 11, 1943. All other governments, including the Axis nations, followed suit.

But why such a privilege in the first place?

China's huge total population was always fascinating to foreigners, and in the early sailing days traders were lured across the treacherous seas by the Chinese market of four hundred million or more potential customers. But until 1842 Canton was the only port in all China opened to foreign trade, and at that time trading with the Chinese was done under most unsatisfactory conditions. Chinese restrictions varied from day to day and there were constant quarrels over application of strange Chinese laws and "unchristian" punishment of foreigners.

Manchu law peremptorily required "life for a life" whereever foreigners were concerned. In 1821 an American sailor who had killed a Chinese was strangled without trial at the public execution grounds at Canton.[2]

---

2   Francis Terranova, an Italian serving on an American ship, the *Emily*, was accused of murder in Canton in 1821. All American trade was stopped until he was handed over. There does appear to have been a trial, however, no foreigner was allowed to attend. He was then strangled and his body returned to the Americans. Trade was resumed.

104

British traders and sailors had suffered similar treatment. Eventually this led to hostilities. When the smoke of battle cleared away the first British treaty with China was negotiated. This treaty, signed on board a British warship off Nanking on August 29, 1842, opened five ports to trade and granted special privileges, including extrality, to British merchants.

News of the Treaty of Nanking caused quite a stir in European and American commercial circles. The various

Kiying who negotiated with Cushing

governments hastily dispatched emissaries to open trade and take advantage of the British wedge. At President John Tyler's request, Congress authorized funds to "send a mission to treat with the people of the Middle Kingdom," and late in 1843 Mr. Cushing and his little party of merchants and secretaries sailed for China with Commodore Parker in the frigate *Brandywine*.

They anchored off Macao, the Portuguese colony, in February of 1844, but it was not until June that Cushing communicated the project of a treaty to Kiying, the emperor's special commissioner. Provisions of the treaty were discussed day after day until it assumed the form in which it was finally signed on July 3, 1844, in the little village of Wanghia on Macao Island.

This treaty of Wanghia secured for the American trader the right to carry on trade and reside in the five ports opened by the British treaty—Canton, Amoy, Foochow, Ningpo, and Shanghai—plus the right of extraterritoriality. Actually it contained few provisions not already included in the British treaty, but Cushing rewrote the British document in such exact legal phraseology that for ninety-nine years it was generally accepted as the standard treaty and served as the basis for Sino-foreign relations.[3]

At the time the treaty was signed the Manchu rulers of China barely tolerated the white foreign devils, and looking down from their lofty peak of superiority they let it be known that if the foreign barbarians wanted to punish their own wrongdoers it was all right with them.

But it wasn't all right with the Chinese residents of Canton, who disliked the strange white barbarians as much as they did the Manchu interlopers.

While the dignified diplomatic representatives of the two governments were deliberating in polite terms over the treaty and Cushing was assuring Kiying that "the United States desired to treat on the basis of cordial friendship and did not desire any portion whatsoever of Chinese territory and wanted only a free and secure commerce," Chinese mobsters attacked Americans in the Canton factories where foreigners were permitted to reside and trade.

One gang broke into a company garden and hurled stones at some Americans who were walking there, forcing the foreigners to flee by boat. Three Americans, escorting a fellow countryman to his house, were set upon by Chinese hoodlums who threw stones and other debris. One American, firing low to drive the attackers back, unhappily killed a native. The case was

---

3   The terms of the treaty establishing extraterritoriality were: ARTICLE XXI. Subjects of China who may be guilty of any criminal act towards citizens of the United States shall be arrested and punished by the Chinese authorities according to the laws of China, and citizens of the United States who may commit any crime in China shall be subject to be tried and punished only by the Consul or other public functionary of the United States thereto authorised according to the laws of the United States; and in order to the prevention of all controversy and disaffection, justice shall be equitable and impartially administered on both sides. ARTICLE XXV. All questions in regard to rights, whether of property or person, arising between citizens of the United States in China shall be subject to the jurisdiction of and regulated by the authorities of their own Government; and all controversies occurring in China between the citizens of the United States and the subjects of any other Government shall be regulated by the Treaties existing between the United States and such Governments respectively, without interference on the part of China.

investigated by the district magistrate, who reported it to the Governor of Canton, who, in turn, asked the American consul-general to deliver up the murderer. The consul-general, knowing what that would mean, refused.

Then Kiying brought the case to Mr. Cushing, and there was more diplomatic palaver. But finally the arguments of Cushing, coupled with the stipulations in the British treaty and the landing of marines from the corvette St. Louis, convinced the Emperor's commissioner that the foreign powers weren't fooling about holding on to their treaty right of judging their own countrymen.

Kiying solved his problem by deferring to the irate Chinese petitioners who demanded "life for a life" until they cooled down. Then he appeased relatives of the slain man with a small donation.

Twentieth-century China, quite naturally, has resented consular jurisdiction, contending that it was in derogation of her foreign rights. And in all fairness it must be said that the United States was ready to relinquish extrality years ago. We said so in the treaty of 1903[4].

But there was always some good reason why it was not the right time for the foreign powers to give up the privilege. Until 1911 the Chinese did not have a modern code of laws but followed the ancient code laid down during the Tang Dynasty (619-905 B.C.). Rightly, I think the Western nations resisted giving up extrality until Chinese laws were modernized.

After the overthrow of the Manchu monarchy in 1911 the Chinese government attempted to improve China's legal system, but without much success because of the country's

---

4 Allman is stretching the truth a little here. By Article XV of Treaty Between the United States and China for the Extension of the Commercial Relations Between Them, the United States would "be prepared to relinquish extra-territorial rights when satisfied that the state of the Chinese laws, the arrangements for their administration, and other considerations warrant it in so doing."

social and political instability. It was not until the establishment of the Legislative Yuan in 1928 under the National government in Nanking that a real effort was made to re-write the laws of the land. Eventually a series of codes, based on the French and continental codes, were enacted; the civil code in 1931 and the criminal code as late at 1935.

The hundred years of extraterritoriality in China was a period of civil war, unrest, and readjustment, and in my opinion extrality was a help rather than a hindrance to the Chinese during these unsettled years. Undoubtedly it spurred on the Chinese to reform their legal and judicial systems, and the contact of Chinese lawyers with their Western colleagues greatly influenced the formation of their modern codes.

Aside from the fact that extraterritoriality gave lawyers a chance to live and practice in China, it did not solve all problems. In some ways it complicated administration of the law. When a foreigner having extrality rights was arrested by the Chinese authorities he was handed over to the nearest consulate of his own country and tried by his own country's laws. Often this was inconvenient to all concerned, especially when the scene of the crime was a thousand or so miles away from the nearest consulate and it was necessary to transport witnesses.

During my consular days in Chungking I ran across a story which perhaps illustrates this difficulty. According to the records, an American landed at Wan Hsien[5] and started overland on foot for India, literally working his way. He carried a sign which proclaimed in Chinese characters that he was a doctor and could cure all ills. He stopped overnight in small wayside inns, hung out his sign, and treated those brave enough to take a chance.

---

5   Wanxian in Sichuan Province.

The patients paid him in food and in a few coppers.[6]

Ultimately the doctor arrived at the Tibetan border, taboo to foreigners. The Chinese magistrate tried his best to persuade the doctor to turn back. Failing, he insisted on supplying an armed guard. The doctor was barely able to feed himself, much less provide food for a squad of soldiers, and after a week of worry he decided to get rid of

Henry De Menil, American doctor who killed a Tibetan lama

them. Arising early one morning he hid all the rifles except one, which he kept for himself. When the soldiers awoke and found themselves disarmed, there was a great hullabaloo. Thoroughly frightened, the doctor grabbed the rifle he had saved out for himself and, to paraphrase, "He shot his rifle into the air, the bullet landed he knew not where."

That is, he didn't know for a day or two. Then he learned that to his misfortune his unaimed shot had struck and killed a Lama priest who had been walking in the hills a quarter of a mile away. Thereupon the magistrate detained the doctor and notified the nearest American consulate at Chungking.

The consul ordered the doctor brought back to Chungking under guard, but the doctor refused to backtrack. He intended to keep right on his way to India. Finally, after much telegraphing back and forth between consul and magistrate the doctor was

---

6   Allman is recounting here the story of Dr. Henry De Menil who shot and killed a lama in Tibet. De Menil was, in fact, prosecuted and tried by Judge Wilfley of the United States Court for China, but acquitted. At least one witness was brought from Tibet. Wilfley expressed doubts about De Menil story but acquitted him. The acquittal led to a fierce protest from the Chinese authorities. William S. Fleming, who became Allman's partner represented De Menil. See *Gunboat Justice*, Vol 2 pp88-95.

sent to Chungking and from there to Shanghai for trial in the United States Court for China. The doctor was charged with manslaughter and later released because the district attorney could not (1) produce the body, nor (2) bring witnesses down from the Tibetan border to appear in court, some forty days' travel away.

I believe that had the case been tried in a Chinese court the doctor would still have been released. There was conclusive proof that the shooting had been purely accidental, and the more modern Chinese laws of this time no longer demanded "life for a life" where a foreign devil was concerned.

Few Americans, even those who resided in China for years, understood the real meaning of extraterritoriality. There were many who were under the delusion that by living in China they were immune to all law. This was not so.

C. C. Julian, the notorious American oil promoter who had been charged with fraudulent sales of oil stock, held this belief. Indicted in Oklahoma, he skipped bail and came out to China. He soon found out that the long arm of American law might reach across three thousand miles of ocean, pick him up, and return him to the scene of his alleged crime. But before Oklahoma authorities had a chance to institute extradition proceedings, Julian committed suicide in his Metropole Hotel room.

I was never his lawyer, but Julian's hotel was just across the street from my office and he dropped in frequently to talk. He always said he wanted to retain me, but I'm sure that what he really wanted was a little companionship, for like all hunted men he was lonely.

Too, American citizens in China were often surprised to find that although they were under American law some of their fundamental rights were not available to them under extraterritorial privileges. For instance, the democratic right of

*Courtney Charles Julian,
fraudster free in Shanghai*

Courtney Charles Julian, was a Canadian businessman who jumped bail in Oklahoma charged with oil stock fraud. As a Canadian he was a British subject and not subject to American law in China. America had no extradition treaty with China or Britain so he could stay in Shanghai freely. On arrival in Shanghai he stayed in the Metropole Hotel opposite Allman's office in Hamilton House under the alias of T.R. King. He later moved to the Astor House hotel where, having run out of money after 10 months living in Shanghai, he and his "pretty secretary and intimate", 29 year-old Miss Leonora Levy, tried to kill themselves by poisoning. Julian succeeded and died at the Country (now Huadong) Hospital. A coronial inquest was conducted by Mr. Idwal Morris in the British Police Court. A verdict of suicide was returned.

C. C. JULIAN RECEIVES HUNDRED PER-
CENT EXTRALITY PROTECTION

C. C. JULIAN Canadian born stock salesman and promoter of oil-wells which allegedly had no existence outside the well-printed pages of his high-power publicity, has arrived in Shanghai and apparently intends to reside here permanently. Mr. Julian departed from Oklahoma City exactly one day before his trial was scheduled to be held in U. S. Federal Court in that city. In leaving the United States so suddenly he defaulted on a G.$25,000 bail-bond which had been put up to guarantee his appearance for trial on a charge of using the U. S. mails to defraud. Mr. Julian arrived in Shanghai about a month ago and first resided at the Metropole hotel under the name of T. R. King. Later, when he had employed attorneys and apparently had satisfied himself that he could not be arrested or extradited back to the United States, he discarded his pseudonym and removed to the Cathay hotel where he is residing in more or less comfort and issues interviews to the local reporters and correspondents for American papers. Julian is a picturesque character; he started in life as a well-driller, but shortly discovered there was move profit in selling stock than in wearing greasy overalls with an oil-gang. His first well in the Los Angeles field turned out happily and he floated a twelve million dollar company. But the company failed, so he went to the Oklahoma field and floated another, also for twelve millions. According to his story, he was double-crossed by his lawyers and this company also failed. Then the Oklahoma state and federal authorities stepped in and started prosecution against Julian on charges of using the mails to defraud. He forfeited his G.$25,000 bail and came to Shanghai, allegedly because he feared he would not receive a fair trial in the United States.

The way it works out in Julian's case is somewhat as follows: Julian was born in Canada, hence is a Canadian or British subject. His stock-selling activities which caused his legal complications were conducted in the United States. Julian cannot be extradited to Canada because he allegedly committed no crime in Canada. He cannot be arrested by the American authorities in Shanghai and extradited to the United States because he is not an American citizen. He is a Canadian. And since there is no clause in any Anglo-American treaty providing for extradition of their respective citizens while residing under exterritorial jurisdictions in China, Mr. Julian apparently is entirely free to reside in Shanghai and tell the American authorities to "go to hell" as he is alleged to have done. If there was no exterritoriality, or if the exterritorial system could be modernized, Julian would be subject to Chinese jurisdiction, in which case he could be arrested by the Chinese and handed over to the American authorities. But this cannot be done under the present circumstances—which indicate quite clearly that exterritoriality has its handicaps as well as its alleged benefits. The Chinese authorities obviously will not overlook the Julian case in pressing their claims for a modification of this obsolete system. In the meantime, Mr. Julian is one man among the considerable number of foreigners in Shanghai who really receives 100-percent benefits from exterritoriality. We recommend him for the presidency of the newly organized Shanghai Foreign Residents Association, one of the objects of which, we understand, is to oppose revision of the extrality treaties!

C.C. Julian Receives Hundred Percent Extrality Protection

trial by jury was denied them — and denied them by no less an authority than the United States Supreme Court.

In 1880, when we still had extrality privileges in Japan, John M. Ross, a seaman, was tried and convicted for the murder of the mate of the American ship *Bullion*. Thomas B. Van Buren[7], consul-general at Kanagawa, Japan, sentenced Ross to be hanged. But President Rutherford B. Hayes commuted the sentence to life imprisonment.

Thomas Van Buren, US Consul General in Yokohama

Ross appealed his conviction all the way to the Supreme Court. One of the grounds for appeal was that he had not been indicted by a grand jury. But the Supreme Court held that " by the constitution of the United States a government is ordained and established 'for the United States of America' and not for the countries outside of their limits; and that the constitution can have no operation in another country." The decision also made it clear that extraterritorial Americans were not entitled to trial by jury.[8]

Americans in China, however, lost nothing by this decision. Even the modern Chinese legal code does not provide for trial by jury.

Sometimes it was difficult to determine just what the extraterritorial nations could and could not do under their

---

7   Thomas Brodhead Van Buren (1924-1889), was a nephew of President Martin Van Buren. He fought on the Union side as a Colonel. He was brevetted as a Brigadier-General in 1865. In 1874 he was appointed US Consul-General in Yokohama and served in that position until 1885.

8   *Ross v McIntyre* 140 US 453. This was a *habeas corpus* application where Ross alleged he was illegally detained because (1) he was Canadian and should have been tried by a British court in Japan and (2) he had been denied a jury trial. The case led to a major diplomatic incident between the US and the United Kingdom. See *Gunboat Justice*, Vol 1, Chapter 14.

Japan Punch on the Ross case. American and British officials argue over who can try him while British Judge for Japan Richard Rennie looks on.

extraterritorial privileges and to what lengths they could go in disciplining wayward citizens. During the First World War the United States went so far as to deport an American citizen from China.

Dr. Gilbert Reid[9] was arrested in Peking in April, 1917, and charged with printing German propaganda and slandering President Wilson in the Peking Post. Major C. P. Holcomb, the United States district attorney at Shanghai, filed charges of sedition against him. But when Dr. Reid expressed regret and promised not to do it again, the charges were withdrawn. Dr. Reid, however, continued to be a thorn in the side of the British

9   (1857-1927) Reid was a missionary and ran the Mission among the Higher Classes in Shanghai. When WWI broke out he took over the *Peking Post* and published articles highly critical of loans being made to China. After he was deported, he returned to China in 1921. Reid also founded the International Institute in Shanghai whose aim was to foster better relations between religions. A bust was placed in its building on the corner of 318 Avenue Joffre (Huaihai Road) and 831 Avenue Edouard VII (Yanan Road). For more on Reid's trial see Gunboat Justice, Vol II, p203-208.

THE NORTH-CHINA HERALD.

DR. GILBERT REID
DEPORTED.

According to information received here on Saturday Dr. Gilbert Reid was deported from China by the Chinese Government, after it had obtained the acquiescence of the American officials. He was placed on board the U. S. transport Warren at Chinwangtao and is now *en route* to manila.

The information states that last Monday the Chinese Government sent notice to the American Minister that Dr. Reid's presence in China was not wanted, and that he be ordered to be deported outside the territorial limits of China.

Dr Gilbert Reid, accused of sedition

government, the American government, and the Chinese government. The British minister went so far as to lodge a protest against him at Peking.

Then, in December of 1917, legal steps again were taken against Dr. Reid, this time at the request of the Chinese government. As Dr. Reid was an American, the Chinese government could not try him; under extraterritoriality this was the duty of the American government.

It was about the middle of December that the Chinese government sent word to Dr. Paul S. Reinsch, the American Minister, that Dr. Reid's presence in China and his transactions with the enemy were distasteful and dangerous to the Republic and they requested his deportation from Chinese territory. Dr. Reinsch turned this communication over to Major Holcomb, who had brought and dismissed the sedition charges, and who now filed a petition in the American consular court in Tientsin requesting that a writ of deportation be issued and an order be made for Dr. Reid's removal outside the territorial limits of China by the marshal of the consular court. The writ and the order were issued, and Dr. Reid was put on board the United States transport

Warren bound for Manila.

In a way this case put American authorities on the spot. It was a moot point whether the United States Court or the American consular courts had authority to extradite or to deport persons from China. It also exemplified some of the practical difficulties of the extraterritorial courts. The offense was committed in Peking, the district attorney had his headquarters in Shanghai with the United States Court for China, and the deportation proceedings were tried in the consular court in Tientsin, ten days away from Shanghai by boat, or three days by train. In those days, because of civil wars, the trains seldom ran.

I took no part in these proceedings, but I did play a very small part in one nation's decision to relinquish extrality privileges.

About the time I resigned from the American consular service to practice law, considerable trade was developing between China and Mexico in rugs, lingerie, and antiques, and most of all in the one item, pig lard. For some years several hundred thousand dollars' worth of pig lard annually was exported to Mexico, and Mexican consular invoices were required for all shipments. A consular representative was needed to handle the documents. As I had studied Spanish in my youth and at one time considered myself quite proficient in this language, I was pleased to take on the job.

I was appointed honorary consul for Mexico in China in 1925 and continued as such, with an occasional interruption, until shortly before Pearl Harbor. I soon discovered that along with my honorary title I had become a "judge" again, and, too, I had inherited quite a gambling problem.

Gambling flourished in the International Settlement through the protection of extraterritorial laws. The establishments were run by citizens of the countries whose laws did not prohibit gambling. Raids and arrests were futile, because according to the statutes of

Shanghai Municipal Police and the problems of the Wheel

his own country the proprietor of the gambling house was a law-abiding citizen. The Mexican law was comparatively mild. No matter who the real owner was, it was advantageous to have a Mexican as a front. Under Mexican law the maximum penalty was a five hundred pesos fine or thirty days imprisonment whereas under the British, American, or Chinese laws the penalty for the same offense averaged from six months to two years in prison with or without a fine.

Gambling, however, was not confined to the Mexicans. It was a

Dr Oscar Fischer, lawyer and patron of the Wheel　　*Garcia prosecuted in the Mexican court before Allman*

favorite Shanghai pastime. All ages and sexes and nationalities gambled at the dog races, the races, at jai alai (pelota Basque), and the numerous lotteries. As a matter of record Shanghai has always tolerated gambling and some of it was quasi-legal, or at least the Shanghai Race Club, a number of savings bond companies, and lotteries thought so. Too, one of China's sources of income was derived from its government-controlled state lottery.

One of the most spectacular "wheels" was operated by a Mexican, Carlos Garcia. He catered to the carriage trade, and his establishment was so luxuriously equipped that his wheel gained greater notoriety and patronage than those of his several competitors. Periodically he was raided by the Shanghai municipal police and prosecuted. Cheerfully he paid his fine and went his way. He could afford an almost daily fine without taking any serious business losses. As soon as one place was closed he opened up a new one in the neighborhood.

It was when I was sitting as judge on the Mexican consular court that three of Garcia's wheel operators were brought before me. They had been rounded up by the municipal police in a routine

Sapajou on the SMP barricading the Wheel

gambling raid of the Settlement. They were charged with conducting gambling places and having in their possession paraphernalia contrary to the Mexican code which applied to gambling. I fined each one the maximum of five hundred pesos, plus costs, and to their horror ordered confiscation of all equipment.

Then, to my amazement, their lawyer, Dr. Oscar Fischer, a fiery little Austrian noted for his flowing black beard, which was almost as long as he was tall, rose up wrathfully. He threatened to appeal the case to the higher courts. He would take it all the way to Mexico City if necessary. I couldn't understand why he was making such a fuss over such a piddling case. But he made good his threat and appealed. It was then I learned that in ordering confiscation of the equipment I had stepped on his toes. Dr. Fischer was the wheel's number one patron.

Dr. Fischer's case never reached Mexico City. And Shanghai's gambling problem, insofar as the Mexican element was concerned, was suddenly and unexpectedly solved.

Some time earlier I had suggested to the Mexican consul-general in Hong Kong that the extraterritorial clauses in the Sino-Mexican treaty could be dropped as they were of no particular advantage to Mexico, and only a dozen or so Mexicans actually received practical benefits of consular jurisdiction. It was foolish, I thought, to cling to extraterritoriality for the few who like Garcia abused the privilege for gambling purposes. The Mexican government, of the same opinion for some time, concurred that it

Victory for the prosecutor, R.T. Bryan, in the case against Carlos Garcia in the Provisional Court

was a good idea to let the treaty lapse and did so in 1929.[10]

The police now prosecuted Garcia under Chinese law, and he found himself face to face with a year's prison sentence. That, however, did not put an end to gambling in Shanghai.

Mexicans were not the only ones who tried to hide behind extrality's skirts. One American judge in imposing a prison sentence and a fine on an American who had assaulted a rickshaw coolie, said in passing sentence:

"The court will not tolerate such acts by American citizens. This court functions as much to protect Chinese as Americans appearing before it. The American court will not protect Americans who act in this country as they would not dare to act in their own."

Later on the sentence was suspended on plea of the defense attorney that it was a "common offense."

Then, take traffic cases. In the Chinese courts conviction on a drunken driving charge meant at most a fine of ten dollars, while in the United States Court for China on several occasions fines of fifty American dollars and six months in jail were imposed.

Chinese, on the other hand, always claimed that the consular officials who supposedly were meting out justice knew nothing about law, especially the Chinese law. This may have been true in the early days of consular jurisdiction. The story was often told of one consular judge who said of himself, "I may be short on law, but I'm hell on equity."

Those days of hit-or-miss jurisdiction ended with the establishment of the United States Court for China.

---

10 The prosecution against Garcia started in the Mexican court before Allman. It was transferred to the Provisional Court when Mexican extraterritoriality came to an end. Garcia did seek to argue in the Chinese courts that the Mexico-China treaty had not expired. He was after a long trial convicted and sentence to 1 year in prison. See: *China Weekly Review*, September 7, 1929, p68 for a report on a rejection of their appeal.

VII
CROOKS AND THE UNITED STATES COURT

MUCH HAS BEEN WRITTEN about the white crooks, confidence men, adventuresses, gun runners, and opium smugglers who have plied the China Coast since clipper-ship days, and there were many. But since the establishment of the United States Court for China in 1906 the American criminal element in Shanghai, the city with the greatest number of United States citizens in China, has been no larger than in any American city of comparable population. Americans always had the reputation of being the biggest crooks in China, but this was more apparent than real. We were simply more diligent in prosecuting the criminals than were other foreigners, and in giving their crimes and trials I wide publicity. In fact the United States Court was an unfailing source of front-page newspaper material in the days when the local scene was barren of sensational copy.

In an international community like Shanghai even an ordinary breach-of-contract suit was written up fully in the local newspapers and followed avidly by some of our international competitors who could say to their Chinese customers, "See, all those Americans are crooks."

There were numerous defalcations by foreign but non-American bankers and employees of other foreign firms, but

McNeil Island Penitentiary where US prisoners were sent from the mid-1920s

none ever reached the headlines, and the defalcators quietly left the Shanghai scene for home. This was not so with us. Every time we caught one of our community, banker or clerk, in a misdeed, we aired his crime in public, then retired him home to McNeil's Island in the state of Washington, or some other prison to which the United States Court for China was authorized to commit Americans convicted of crime.

Despite the feeling in some quarters that such cases were derogatory to American prestige, we nevertheless prosecuted these cases to a conviction and never made the slightest attempt to soft-pedal or conceal them. The same was not true of other nationals, as they sometimes put prestige and face first and repeatedly failed to prosecute offenders for fear of the attendant publicity.

About the time that the trial of a minor United States official was headlined in every Far East newspaper, a paymaster in a European navy was caught embezzling funds. Instead of prosecuting him his commanding officer discreetly shipped him home.

The United States Court for China has had a somewhat stormy career, but on the whole its record compares favorably with any other court in China, regardless of nationality. None has been without scandal, but the American court probably has had the best record for bringing its erring members speedily to justice.

Until 1906 the only courts for the trial of Americans in China were the consular courts. They served their purpose while the American communities were small. For a long time the only Americans who came under the court's jurisdiction were American sailors who imbibed too freely of cheap whisky in Canton dives and then worked off excessive exuberance in waterfront brawls. But with the shifting of foreign trade to Shanghai, that city's growth, and the great increase of American interests in China, these consular courts soon were inadequate.

By an act of Congress dated June 30, 1906, the United States Court for China came into being, with headquarters in Shanghai. The establishment of the court created consternation among those Americans whose activities were of such nature as to be open to serious interference by a stricter enforcement of the laws of the United States. Since the Boxer Rebellion in 1900 and the Russo-Japanese War of 1904-1905, Shanghai had been the scene of operations for numerous undesirable foreigners of all nationalities, including a great many Americans. Ladies of easy virtue and adventurers of every description, ranging from the shady operator who stayed just inside the law to the garden variety of beachcomber, had found Shanghai easy pickings.

But with the opening of the Court, Shanghai was no longer a paradise for American adventurers. There have been five American judges on the bench since 1906, and all of I them have been men of strong character. From the very first they did their best to see that their nationals obeyed the law. If ever there was any bias on the part of the judges it must be said that they leaned toward severity rather than leniency.

Both American and British judges were inclined to inflict

Lebbeus Wilfley First judge of the US Court for China

heavier punishment for an offense than was inflicted by Chinese judges for the same offense. Some of them went so far as to say, rightly or wrongly, that heavier penalties ought to be inflicted, on the ground that it was the duty of the alien in China to behave himself.

Lebbeus Redman Wilfley[1] of St. Louis, Missouri, who had been serving as attorney-general in the Philippines, was the first judge appointed for the prescribed ten-year term. He has gone down in Shanghai history as "the reform judge."

There's no doubt that he was anxious to establish the court on the highest possible plane and that his main idea was to compel respect for the court. His first act burst a bomb in legal circles. He issued a blanket challenge to the whole bar when he announced that only Americans who could pass an examination in law, and who, moreover, could furnish proof of good moral character, would be permitted to practice in the American court. This edict infuriated the legal profession. Most of its members protested, but to no avail.

True, there were some shysters among the lot, and perhaps their moral characters were not all that they should have been, but there were a number of good lawyers whose only fault lay in the fact that they were some years out of law school, and, while they retained the practical principles of law, they long ago had

---

1   Lebbeus Redman Wilfley (1867-1926) was born in Mexico, Missouri and graduated from Central College, Fayette Missouri and Yale University Law School. He was admitted to the bar in 1893 and practiced law in Missouri until 1901. He was appointed a judge of the Court of First Instance in the Philippines but then quickly appointed Attorney-General. After leaving China, he practiced in St Louis and New York.

The US Court for China in 1906. Left to right: Arthur Bassett, District Attorney, Hubert O'Brian, US Marshal, Judge Lebbeus Wilfley, Frank Hinckley, Clerk of the Court

Wilfley administers exam to US Lawyers. Thomas Jernigan and Stirling Fessenden stand at the back

forgotten school textbook rules and theories. When suddenly confronted with a bar examination they were flabbergasted. Only two passed and were admitted to the Court. Aside from Arthur Bassett, the United States district attorney who arrived with the court, the only two who could practice for the first month or two were the scholarly T. R. Jernigan, a former American consul-general in Shanghai and a consular judge, and Stirling Fessenden[2], subsequently secretary-general of the Shanghai Municipal Council, and always an erudite student of the law.

Most of the lawyers were of the opinion that Judge Wilfley would have been fairer had he brought disbarment proceedings individually against any unqualified member of the bar instead of issuing his blanket challenge. Presumably his motive was good but his method unfair. I say presumably because this was long before my time, and I knew none of the lawyers involved except the two who passed. Those who failed had no other choice than to leave and hang out their shingles elsewhere. Many went back to their old home states where they had first been admitted to the bar.

From that early date there have been few disbarment proceedings brought in the United States Court. In the early 1920's one lawyer was disbarred after he was caught appropriating for his own use securities that clients had left with him for safekeeping.[3]

Earl B. Rose, disbarred

---

2   Fessenden: See Chapter 15, footnote 15. Thomas Roberts Jernigan (1847-1920). He served as US Consul in Kobe and then in Shanghai from 1893 to 1897. Jernigan Road in Shanghai (now Xianxia Road) was named after him.

3   Earl Brown Rose (1882- 1954) a former clerk of the court. He had been a name partner of the firm Jernigan, Fessenden and Rose. Rose had at times also acted as Commissioner of the Court and as Acting District Attorney. Rose fled Shanghai hours ahead of a warrant being issued for his arrest. He arrived in Seattle on April 8, 1921. An unsuccessful application was made to extradite him from Seattle in 1923. He appears to have resolved the matter by paying back the money he embezzled. "Lawyer disbarred", *Shanghai Times*, Mar 12, 1921.

A year or so earlier another lawyer, a former American vice-consul[4], was suspended from practice for one year because of misconduct. The judge said he showed a lack of adherence to the ethical standards which should govern a member of the bar. To my mind this lawyer did no more than many another wide-awake attorney might have done for a client under similar circumstances. Unfortunately he met with bad luck.

Alexander Krisel, suspended from practice for a year

To enable his client to catch a debtor who was attempting to escape jurisdiction of the court the lawyer advised his client to hire a launch which would take him to the trans-Pacific steamer anchored off the mouth of the Whangpoo, twenty-five miles distant. So far so good; but the only available launch was one owned by the Standard Oil Company. The lawyer and his client, being in something of a hurry, neglected to ask permission of the company manager to use the launch and merely bribed the Chinese *laodah* (head boatman) with two hundred dollars to let them borrow it. The lawyer knew that the *laodah* had no right to make such a deal, and when the boat was wrecked on the return trip the company sued. The suspension came soon afterward.

By the time I was ready to make my debut, Shanghai's legal profession had outgrown its rowdy beginnings and had become respectable, with such eminent organizations as the American

---

4   Alexander Krisel (1890-1983) Krisel's offence was much more serious than that de-
     scribed by Allman. The court found that Krisel had given false evidence in the British
     Supreme Court for China when his client Ellis Ezra was prosecuted for corruption.
     Krisel was later able to redeem himself and became a commissioner of the court. Re A.
     Krisel, *NCH*, December 28, 1918 and February 22, 1919 and Lobingier, Extraterritorial
     Cases, Vol, 1 846.

Far Eastern Bar Association[5], the Chinese Bar Association, and the British Bar Association, to keep its members in line.

Judge Wilfley's next great reform effort, after he had purged the legal profession, was directed toward the oldest profession in the world. He was not so successful in his second clean-up campaign.

For some unknown reason it was the fashion for all the ladies who resided in the popular Kiangse and Soochow Road districts to claim American citizenship. Their luxurious business residences were known as "American houses" and they persisted in calling themselves "American girls," though in fact most of them were anything but girls and were of other nationalities. This caused considerable annoyance among the more strait-laced members of the American community.[6]

Judge Wilfley had subpoenas served on them charging vagrancy. They were warned to leave town before charges were pressed; otherwise they would all be jailed. The general opinion was that the judge could not drive these ladies out by any arbitrary action and by no means were all the residents of Shanghai in favor of any such drastic step. The judge's campaign blew up when he discovered that the majority of the women were not Americans. The few who were Americans jumped his jurisdiction by hurried marriages with men of other nationalities,

---

5 Established by Judge Charles Lobingier in 1916. See Chapter 5, footnote 12.
6 One of the reasons for establishing the US Court for China given by Secretary of State Elihu Root was: "As a result of this peculiar arrangement the vice which seems to thrive in the atmosphere of the Orient has long tended to seek shelter under the flag of the country whose administration is the most lax and ineffective. American administration in Shanghai had long been notoriously lax and ineffective, and the gamblers and prostitutes of Shanghai generally flourished under the claim of American citizenship and the protection of American indifference. To such an extent had this gone that prostitutes generally in Shanghai, and, to a considerable extent in the other cities, whether American or not, were called American girls and the two expressions were practically synonymous." *Charges against Lebbeus R Wilfley Judge of the United States Court for China and petition for his removal from office*, Letter to the President from Mr. Root dated February 29, 1908.

mostly sailors who conveniently sailed away after the ceremony, the "bride" having paid over a marriage fee which ranged anywhere from one hundred to one thousand Chinese dollars.

The judge did succeed in exposing the canard of an American monopoly, and the women lost their profitable trade name. He did not escape criticism, however, and his attempted house cleaning did not go unchallenged. The pickings had been too good for the lawless not to put up a fight. They brought impeachment proceedings against him in 1908. Nothing came of that President Theodore Roosevelt not only exonerated him but commended the work of his court. But Judge Wilfley resigned and left Shanghai, serving only two years of his ten-year term.[7]

He was succeeded by Judge Rufus H. Thayer[8] of the District of Columbia. Thayer was a man of much calmer temperament than his predecessor, and, being a likable and kindly soul, he soon established himself in the confidence of the better element of the American community without all the pyrotechnics that had characterized the Wilfley regime. Too, he was extremely popular with the British, probably because he wore a Vandyke and bore a striking resemblance to King Edward VII.

Rufus Thayer Second Judge of the US Court for China

---

7   See *Gunboat Justice*, Vol 2 Chapters 32 and 33 for the full story of the rise and fall of Lebbeus Wilfley.
8   Rufus Hildreth Thayer (1850-1917) was born in Plymouth Michigan. He graduated from the University of Michigan in 1871 and was appointed assistant to the Librarian of Congress. He studied law and graduated in 1874 and then was appointed a law clerk to the Treasury Department. He resigned after 10 years to establish Thayer & Rankin. He was the brother-in-law of the head of the New York Republican Party who recommended his appointment.

But he was not without enemies. In 1913 charges against him were laid before the House Committee on State Department Expenditures. He was charged with leaving his court in Shanghai and spending much time in Canton while prisoners awaited trial before him. It was also charged that the court's expense accounts were irregular.

The irony of this action was that charges were brought after Judge Thayer, because of ill health, had resigned of his own accord and was already on his way back to America. The charges were dropped, but he served only four of his ten years.

Perhaps more was accomplished by the court during the term of Judge Charles S. Lobingier[9] than at any other time. Lobingier was the third judge of the United States Court for China and the first to serve a full term. He rendered brilliant service. A thorough student of the law, Lobingier insisted on writing up all judgments in full. He viewed all parties and facts before him with cold logic. This may have been because he had to stand alone in his decisions. Judges in the United States Court for China were deprived of the assistance of a jury upon whom so much responsibility

Charles Lobingier Third Judge of the US Court for China

9   Charles Sumner Lobingier (1866-1956) was born in Lanark, Illinois. He practiced as a lawyer in Omaha for 10 years from 1892 to 1902 and also was a professor of law at the University of Nebraska from 1900 to 1903. He was appointed a judge of the Philippines Court of First Instance in 1903. While in the Philippines, he was on the Commission to codify Philippines law and a member of the law faculty of the university of the Philippines. He had written nine legal books including books on stocks and stockholders, Constitutional Law, Equity, Foreclosure, Insurance and Evidence.

could be shifted. The judge alone bore the burden of unraveling intricate questions, not only of law but of fact.

The bill creating the court had laid down no specific code of laws to apply to it, merely stating that the court was to be governed by the laws of the United States, which included the laws of Alaska and the District of Columbia[10]. Where such laws were deficient or unsuitable the common law and the law of equity were to apply. Lobingier made a useful contribution to the court and to the law by compiling and publishing in two volumes of Extraterritorial Cases, the most important decisions handed down from the court's beginning until the end of his term in 1924. This gave lawyers a ready reference to the law of the land as administered by the United States Court for China.

It was during Lobingier's term that a rule was made that each applicant for admission to the bar had to present a diploma from a recognized law school. Until then office study and the ability to pass the examinations were acceptable for admission.

Judge Lobingier, however, was not without his troubles, as I have mentioned in an earlier chapter.

Judge Milton D. Purdy[11], the fourth of the five judges in the United States Court for China, was the first judge who did not have charges of some sort brought against him. He completed

---

10   The act did not state that the laws of Alaska and District of Columbia would apply but only that the law of the United States would apply. This created problems because federal law did not deal with many crimes nor regulate commercial transactions. In *Biddle v United States*, the Ninth Circuit, the appellate court for the US Court for China held that the law of Alaska and the District of Columbia were the law of the United States.

11   Milton Dwight Purdy (1866-1937) was born in Mogadore, Ohio. He graduated from the University of Michigan in 1891 with a BA and 1892 with an LLB. He started his career as a city attorney in Michigan. He served briefly as a federal judge in Minnesota from July 1908 to May 1909 having been given a recess appointment, but had failed to obtain confirmation in the Senate. Before that, Purdy had been a special assistant Attorney-General in the Roosevelt administration handling anti-trust actions. He had become well-known as "the chief trust buster." After his nomination for a federal judgeship failed, he re-entered private practice and between 1912 and 1916 he was a national committee member of the Progressive Party. In 1916, he returned to the Attorney General's office in the Harding administration.

his ten-year term gracefully and left the bench with the friendship and respect of all the members of the bar.

Not that the lawyers weren't often annoyed by the judge's habit of taking the examination of witnesses out of their hands and examining them himself. As he never followed the lawyer's plan of organization, this was bound to slow up procedure. And they were often bored by the judge's favorite story which went something like this:

Milton Purdy Fourth Judge of the United States Court for China

A judge in trying a Negro asked him who his lawyer was.

"Ah ain't got one," replied the Negro.

"In that case," said the judge, " I'll appoint one."

Purdy on the bench of the US Court for China on his retirement with members the American Bar Association. Standing, left to right: Ferno Schul, Cornell Franklin, unknown, Thomas Sellett, H.D. Rodger, Sterling Fessenden, Chauncy Holcomb, Robert Bryan, Edwin Cunningham, US Consul General, Hua-chuen Mei, Viola Smith, Jim Davies, Norwood Allman, Paul Kops, Roy Allman

The Negro shook his head. "No suh, jedge, ah doan want to be hindered by no lawyer."

Milton J. Helmick[12], the last judge to sit in the United States Court (from 1934 until the Japs took over on December 8, 1941), was without a doubt the most popular of all with Americans as well as with other nationals, especially the Chinese. Because Judge Helmick always viewed cases from the human angles and flavored common sense with a sense of humor, I, like all the other lawyers, enjoyed trying cases before him.

Milton Helmick Fifth and Final Judge of the US Court for China

The judge gave judgments both in my favor and against me. In fact Judge Helmick, unknowingly, was the cause of my most embarrassing moment.

This was the one and only time I ever failed to appear in court for a client. My client, Carl Crow, then a Shanghai advertising man and later internationally famous for his *Four Hundred Million Customers* and other books about China and the Chinese, was being sued for a small amount in the American court by an Italian plaintiff.

I did not appear because the United States Court for China sat on a day observed as a holiday by other courts. Previously our court also had observed it. I still don't know why Judge Helmick chose to change the custom, unless he was anxious to clear the calendar of small cases before leaving to hear an important one in Tientsin. Anyway, I neglected to check up and was not on

---

12   Milton J. Helmick (1886-1954) was a native of Colorado and graduated in law from Denver University. He served as attorney-general and as a judge in New Mexico.

hand to present the documentary evidence, which we thought would have defeated the claim, and to argue the matter, nor did my client put in an appearance. The plaintiff was awarded all he asked, and as this was just about the amount of my fee, I did not present a bill.[13]

Judge Helmick did much to discourage shady promotion deals. Prior to his arrival the right to summon a judgment debtor for examination into his property and other assets was somewhat vague. Several slick promoters in particular had failed to pay judgments against them in the belief that they could not be brought into court to explain what and where their property was. Judge Helmick took advantage of a rule-making power, formerly exercised by American Ministers and inherited by the United

Italian Gets $750 In Suit Against Carl Crow

Judgment for $750, one month's salary, was granted Mr. Bruno Perme, an Italian citizen, against Messrs. Carl Crow, Inc., advertising consultants, by Judge Milton D. Purdy in the United States Court for China yesterday morning.

Mr. J. B. Davies of Messrs. Schnhl, Davies and N E. Lurton who appeared on behalf of Mr. Perme moved that the court give judgment for six months' salary amounting to $3,750, claiming that the contract had been cancelled by Carl Crow, Inc., six months before expiration.

Judgment was only given for salary for the month of May amounting to $750. Mr. Norwood F. Allman, appearing on behalf of Messrs. Carl Crow, moved to file an answer, but the plea was denied by the judge and judgment for $750 was accordingly passed.

Chinese Infant Killed By Omnibus During Rain

Little Yeh Biao-zu, three years old, is dead and his father is in a critical condition in the Red Cross Hospital, the result of being run over by a Shanghai Omnibus Co. motor bus at the corner of Bubbling Well and Yates Roads yesterday afternoon during the shower. The bus was driven by A. Yamalidinoff, a Russian.

The father of the infant youngster, who is at the Red Cross hospital suffering from serious internal injuries, is Mr. Yuen Chinchen. He is a native of Pootung. The body of the little boy was taken to a French mortuary after the child had been pronounced dead at the hospital.

Carl Crow loses suit

13 According to the *China Press* report, Allman did appear in court and made a motion to be able to file an answer, but Helmick refused this. He entered judgment for $750 out of the $3,750 claimed. "Italian gets $750 in Suit against Carl Crow" *China Press*, July 11, 1933.

Inside the Grand Theatre

States judge on establishment of the court, and promulgated a rule that judgment debtors could be brought into court and examined as to property and other assets.

The first case to test this rule became famous in Shanghai as the Grand Theater[14] case.

Max George[15], although that is not his true name was the arch type of promoter and at one

The Grand Theatre on Park Road

time had done well in Shanghai. He had started a number of companies on a modest scale but decided to be a big shot and began promoting on expansive lines. He promoted luxurious

---

14 The Grand Theatre on Park Road (now Nanjing West Road) opposite the racecourse was built between 1928 and 1933. It is still extant.

15 Real name: Grant Mark, President of the China Finance Corporation. In addition to the Grand Theatre he was also a promoter of the Cathay Theatre. The story Allman recounts here is essentially accurate. The case went on for some time and produced numerous case reports. Some key reports are: "New Rule of Court for Creditors" *NCH*, August 1, 1934; "Grant Mark Grilled Before American Court", *NCH*, Oct 10, 1934; "Judgement for L.E. Hudec," *NCH* June 26 1935, p535; and, "Attorneys Sue Mark for Fees" *NCH*, Aug 9, 1936.

cinema palaces and soon was deep in financial difficulties. He went on the theory that the law was made for other people.

One of my clients was an architect[16] whom Max had engaged to start one of his theater projects. Max made the mistake of signing the contract personally before he organized his high-sounding syndicate. This was a curious oversight on his part, as

Ladislav Hudec Famous Shanghai architect, represented by Allman

he could have formed a corporation within twenty-four hours. When the project flopped he told the architect to "Go whistle for your fees." The architect came whistling into my office.

The claim was for twenty-five thousand dollars. In order to avoid the trouble and expense of a lawsuit my client was willing to compromise for fifteen thousand dollars. When I suggested this to Max and his attorney they laughed loudly and intimated that we were fools if we thought we could collect anything. Max boasted that he was judgment-execution proof. We finally got judgment against Max for the full amount and hailed him into court for examination into his assets as per Judge Helmick's ruling, but again he laughed.

Max appeared to be legitimately execution proof, as he had transferred all his property and money to his mother, who in the meantime had left Shanghai[17]. She had left a bank account in

---

16 Allman's client was Ladislav Hudec (1893-1958), a Slovak who arrived in Shanghai as a WWI refugee. He designed many of Shanghai's most famous buildings including the True Light Building on Yuanmingyuan Road and the Park Hotel.

17 Mark's mother Myra Louise Mark had not left Shanghai. She was, however, Canadian and not subject to the jurisdiction of the US Court for China, but the British Supreme Court for China — a fact Judge Helmick lamented in one judgement. See "Another Glaring Abuse of the Extraterritorial Principle" *China Weekly Review*, Oct 20, 1934 Myra Mark was later sued by the China Realty Trust in the British Supreme Court for China. *NCH*, July 27, 1938, p163.

NORWOOD F. ALLMAN

Marks' mother, Myra, was later sued in the
British Supreme Court

Shanghai in her own name, which Max could dip into through power of attorney. Max claimed in court that he was practically destitute, but at the same time he lived luxuriously in one of the most expensive suites in the Cathay Hotel. He blandly explained this anomaly away by saying that his mother wanted him to live comfortably, even though penniless.[18]

Max was quite annoyed when the marshal searched his suite for property upon which to levy execution. Everything was marked with his mother's name, except the beautiful blonde stenographer whom the marshal found there. We couldn't very well levy on her.

After weeks of tedious search we found leads to property, but all of it led to the mother's name. About this time directors of one of the companies in which he had an interest decided that in view of so much publicity they could struggle along without Max's valuable services, and he was discharged.

Discovering that he had a claim against the company for two and a half years' salary for this breach of contract, I warned the directors that if they paid this money to Max or any of his blinds

18   Judge Helmick commented sarcastically: "The Defendant testified he is virtually a pauper, possessing nothing of his own subject to execution, but lives and does business in Shanghai on money in his mother's name under a sweeping power of attorney from her. In this melancholy state, he is restricted to membership in three clubs, and reduced to living in a hotel at a monthly expense of $2,000." By way of comparison Helmick's annual salary as a judge at the time was US$10,000. See: "Melancholy State" and "Simply Haven't the Money", *China Weekly Review*, June 29, 1935, p141

137

I would hold the directors personally responsible for obstructing justice. This at least made the directors cautious. They forced Max to deposit with them a cash guarantee in the amount of our judgment. They then paid Max his claim but made the check payable to his mother to forestall us from executing on it. His claim had been for about fifty thousand dollars, but the company had whittled it down to twenty-five thousand.

We heard of the guarantee deposit and started after that. But we found it had not been made directly by Max. He had arranged for a Belgian friend[19] to make the deposit for him. This, of course, greatly complicated our procedure as we had to sue the Belgian in the Belgian consular court. I warned the Belgian that he would be held responsible for obstructing justice, and this is a serious offense under Belgian law.

By this time all the parties were frightened. The money was paid over. The net result was that this smart promoter who might have settled the claim for fifteen thousand dollars, ultimately paid nearly fifty thousand including costs.

In the entire thirty-five years of the court's history only three court officials have been charged and convicted of wrongdoing. One was a district attorney who was sentenced to two years' imprisonment at McNeil's Island and fined three thousand American dollars after he had been tried and convicted of accepting a bribe and embezzling property of the United States.[20] A clerk was convicted on an embezzlement charge[21] and a marshal for dealing in arms.

---

19   Mr A. Loonis of the China Realty Company.
20   Leonard Goodwin Husar (1889-1974) who served as District Attorney from 1922 to 1926. His case was extraordinary. He had taken bribes from opium smugglers to not prosecute them. His defence was that he had made the money smuggling guns – three years earlier he had launched a campaign to prosecute gun runners and successfully prosecuted a number of them. See Gunboat Justice, Vol 2, Chapter 49.
21   William Alden Chapman (1881-1952), the clerk of the court was convicted of embezzling US$15,000 and sentenced to 3 years and five months imprisonment.

HON. JUDGE MILTON PURDY.

DR. GEORGE
SELLETT,
U.S. DISTRICT
ATTORNEY.

LEONARD G. HUSAR,
THE ACCUSED.

MRS. PORTER,
COURT STENOGRAPHER

DA Husar on trial before Judge Purdy. George Sellett prosecuting.

This last case occurred just before Pearl Harbor. Usually the marshal was sent out to China from some town in the United States as a small reward for his political party work, but because of wartime conditions and difficulties of trans-Pacific transportation in 1941, he was chosen locally on the recommendation of several leading citizens who, however, were unaware of the man's past, which included a prison sentence.

The man[22], anxious for the job and knowing his prison record would automatically bar him from it, cleverly substituted a set of fingerprints for his own and all went well until, hard up for cash, he sold a pair of pistols confiscated by the court. Unfortunately for his own good he wasn't careful about the purchaser and sold the pistols to a Chinese policeman of the Shanghai municipality. The Chinese, unaware that he had come upon his purchase illegally, checked the pistols with the Shanghai municipal police. The latter discovered their history.

William Chapman, convicted of embezzlement.

This brought the United States district attorney into the case. His investigations turned up not only the marshal's past but the false set of fingerprints. The marshal was tried, convicted, and sent to McNeil's Island, where to the best of my knowledge he still resides.

Various charges were brought against other court officials. One district attorney was charged with accepting monthly retainers from two keepers of the town's brothels under threat to drive them out if they didn't pay[23]. But there was no evidence and the charge was dismissed.

This brings me to one of the China Coast's prize stories

22 The man was identified as Sam Titlebaum. However, this may not have been his real name. Titlebaum made news in Shanghai when he arrested Jack Riley, the "Slot Machine King" in 1941. Riley had escaped from prison in America 15 years before. See *Gunboat Justice* Chapter 59.

23 Allman is probably referring to Leonard Husar. The allegation was put to Husar by the new DA Thomas Sellet in his corruption trial that he had been receiving money from two prostitutes Virginia Nelson and Blanche Bennet. Husar responded: "The only business I ever had with these unfortunate women was when some of your people — missionaries — came to me with an affidavit that they had gone into some of the houses and spent money and asked me to help get them out of town."

Sam Titlebaum, US Marshall (left) arresting Jack
Riley, the slot machine king

Riley with his face uncovered

concerning both a wayward court official and a crook, told so
often it has become a legend. It is about a man who escaped the
long arm of the law. There are several versions, but I'll tell mine
because it shows that the jurisdiction of the United States Court
for China was far-reaching, and that extraterritoriality, insofar as
Americans were concerned, was no bar to justice.

Peter Grimes, alias John Rogers, came out to Shanghai shortly
before the First World War. He had just finished a year's term in
San Quentin for forgery, but that, of course, was not known until
later. He had been in Shanghai only a few weeks when he began
signing the names of locally prominent and highly respectable
men to chits at bars and houses of ill fame. He ran up prodigious
bills before he was caught, tried, convicted of forgery, and
sentenced to serve three years in his former abode, San Quentin.

Following the customary procedure Grimes was taken by the
prison keeper from the American jail in Shanghai to Nagasaki.
Here they were to meet the United States Army transport
Sheridan, which was to convey the prisoner to his new place of
incarceration. Unfortunately for the prison keeper, a twenty-two-

year-old youth, there was a three-day wait in the dreary Japanese port.[24]

Pals by this time, the prisoner and his keeper whiled away the time by visiting all the water-front saloons together. We have only the word of the two men as to what actually happened. According to Grimes, after a night of drinking beer and somewhat stronger spirits, the jailer remarked, "It's a damned shame a good guy like you has to go across to San Quentin."

The crafty Grimes, believing himself out of jurisdiction of the United States Court, thought so too. Then the idea was hatched of substituting another in the prisoner's place. The plan was followed and on the next evening the jailer, Grimes, and a drink-befuddled bar fly who had agreed to act as substitute took a sampan (small boat) from the wharf to the transport. Leaving the other two on a lower deck, the jailer presented his commitment papers to the commanding officer, who summoned the deck officer and directed him to take charge of the prisoner. The jailer identified the substitute as Grimes and received a receipt.

Thereupon, leaving the substitute in the officer's company, Grimes and his companion left the ship and started out that same evening for Yokohama. And for a few weeks they had a high time on funds Grimes obtained by means of fraud and forgery. But the ever-suspicious Japanese soon caught him. He was convicted and sentenced by them.

The jailer, his binge with the convict over, decided to return to Shanghai, and realizing that the game was up wrote a five-page self-disparaging letter asking the court's leniency in his crime of aiding Grimes to escape. Because of his extreme youth and his plea of guilty the jailer was sentenced to serve five months in his

---

24   See *U.S. v P.A. Grimes*, NCH, Jan 30, 1914, p358; *Shanghai Times*, Feb 1, 1915, p3. His hapless jailer was Willis B. Kilgore. The substitute was, apparently, a Swede. See: *US v Kilgore*, *The Shanghai Times*, Oct 26, 1914, p2.

own jail and fined five hundred American dollars.

Grimes, after serving time in Japan, was returned to Shanghai by the Japanese, who were not required to do this, since the United States had no extrality privileges in Japan. Grimes was sentenced to serve one year in the Shanghai American jail after completion of his three-year forgery sentence in San Quentin, where he was sent under somewhat more reliable guard.

VIII
ALL IN THE DAY'S WORK

IN HIS EVERYDAY WORK the American lawyer in China came up against problems that the average "homeside" lawyer in Kansas or Vermont in all likelihood wouldn't meet in a lifetime of practice.

For one thing, law practice in China was unique in that the ordinary lawyer had cases in half a dozen different national courts. He might be in the Chinese court one day, the British the next, the French or American court another. The one court he didn't bother much about was the Japanese. A favorite story among Shanghai lawyers was that you'd file a petition with the Jap court, wait two years, and then the case would be dismissed in favor of the Japanese party. You could be sure of one thing — you'd always lose the case.

All law offices in Shanghai were bilingual. It was absolutely necessary for an American firm to have associates who knew both the Chinese and the English language. If an American lawyer intended to practice in the French or continental courts a fluency in French, plus a good working knowledge of the Code Napoleon and of Chinese and English law, was highly desirable. It also came in handy to have a staff assistant who had at least a nodding acquaintance with other continental codes.

It was taken for granted that the American lawyer in Shanghai knew something about international law, maritime law, the laws of the District of Columbia, the decisions of the federal courts, equity, and the laws of most of the forty-eight of these United States. Cases in the American court frequently turned upon the law of any one of the states, not to mention the laws of the Philippine Islands.

It wasn't any too easy to assemble an A-1 law staff. Those dime-a-dozen, fresh-faced juniors just out of law school and willing to work for almost nothing as they learned, who once flooded the United States law offices, were never plentiful in the Far East. Few United States lawyers were even aware of the existence of a United States Court for China. Occasionally, when some reference to it was made in newspapers, we'd get a flock of applications for jobs. Once in a great while a law school graduate who wanted a year or two of exciting adventure in the Orient before settling down to humdrum work in the Middle West would write asking particulars. But usually such applicants were discouraged when told of the necessary requirements, which included, among other things, horsemanship.

Most of the American lawyers in China played polo. A new lawyer who neither rode nor tried to learn the game was not likely to last long. One young lawyer in a rival firm was heard to remark somewhat ruefully, as he nursed a broken shoulder bone after a tough spill in a paper hunt, "Why the hell couldn't I have joined a firm of chess players!"

Hamilton House (right), home of Allman's law office. On the left is the Metropole Hotel

The first partner I took into my office in the modern skyscraper, Hamilton House, was Paul Kops. He joined me shortly after Fleming's death[1], when I branched out into practice for myself. Kops was a former trade commissioner in China with the United States Department of Commerce. I was satisfied as to his legal qualifications and knew he could ride, but I made him promise to learn polo before we joined forces. He proved satisfactory in all departments.

Allman advertises his new office alongside some other service providers

[1]　Allman's partner, William S. Fleming, died at the age of 57 on September 2, 1932. The firm of Fleming, Franklin and Allman was dissolved automatically with Cornell Franklin choosing to continue to practice as Fleming and Franklin. Allman went his own way. *NCH* Sept 14, 1932, p418.

Allman's Partners

	**Paul Franklin de Bruyn Kops** (1906-1984) studied law at the University of North Dakota and George Washington University and was admitted to the DC bar in 1928. He was commercial agent of the Department of Commerce in DC and New York from 1927 to 1930. He came to Shanghai in 1930 to be Trade Commissioner and served in that position until 1932. He was laid by the US Government off as part of a series of general cost savings introduced during the Great Depression.
	**James Benjamin Davies** (1880-1958) graduated from Detroit College of Law with an LLB in 1904. He came to China in 1911 as clerk of the US Court and served in that position until 1913. That year he entered private practice with Fleming, Davies and Bryan until that firm was dissolved in 1921. He stayed in partnership with Mr Bryan. In 1928 he served as acting DA in Shanghai for a number of months.
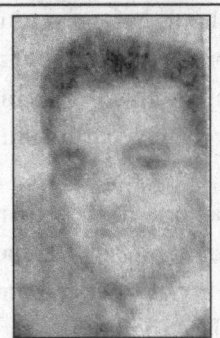	**Roy Glynn Allman** (1904-1977) arrived in Shanghai in 1933 and was admitted to practice by Judge Purdy on the motion of Cornell Franklin. He had practiced law in Charlottesville, Virginia for 2 years before moving to Shanghai. He left Allman, Davies and Kops in 1936 to set up in partnership with J.L. Winkleman a Dutch lawyer. He had been hoping at the time to be appointed US District Attorney for China. Roy returned to the US in 1940 and practiced in DC and Virginia.
	**James M. Lee** (李澤民 Li Zemin) (1907-1970) became a partner in the firm after WWII and it was re-named Allman, Kops & Lee. After the Communist Revolution Lee moved to Taiwan and re-established the firm as Allman, Kops & Lee there. In 1970, the firm was renamed Lee & Li. It is now the largest law firm in Taiwan and continues to have a strong intellectual property practice.

Jim Davies, the other American partner, had practiced law in Shanghai for many years and was the doyen of the American lawyers. But he wasted his spare time playing golf and couldn't be induced to get nearer a pony than the race track bookmakers. He always claimed that the office polo players discriminated against him by giving him all the tough cases so we'd have more time for practice.

For a time my brother, Roy, was a member of the firm, but when two Allmans in the same office proved one too many he resigned and in 1939 returned to the United States to resume practice.[2]

Our firm was unusual in that the three of us started our Far Eastern careers in government service: Kops in the Department of Commerce, Davies as secretary to a United States Ambassador to Japan, and I as a student interpreter in the consular service. Kops and Davies had graduated from law schools before coming out to China. Davies and I had a common bond in the fact that at one time he also had been a partner of Fleming. This was many years before my time, and they had dissolved that partnership by mutual and friendly agreement.

James M. Lee, our Chinese associate, was one of those rare treasures all Shanghai law offices dreamed about but seldom met in reality. He had a thorough knowledge of both American and Chinese law and, most unusual, was equally at home in either the English or Chinese language, although he had never been out of his own country.

---

2   After leaving Allman, Kops and Davies, Roy entered into a partnership with J.L. Win-
     kelman a Dutch lawyer (and son of the famous Dutch general) In 1937, Winkleman
     sued to dissolve the partnership on the basis that establishment of a law partnership
     with a foreigner was illegal. (Winkleman had been convicted that year by the Dutch
     consular court of being drunk and disorderly.) Judge Helmick agreed with Winkleman
     but was overturned by the Ninth Circuit. Former judge of the US Court, Charles Lob-
     ingier was one of the lawyers representing Roy before the Ninth Circuit. *Allman v Win-
     kleman NCH*, Dec 27, 1939, p542.

Lee, a graduate of St. John's University in Shanghai, had been one of my most promising students at the Comparative Law School, where I taught from 1924 to 1929. His chief fault was that he was not robust enough to ride as a jockey or play polo.

Lee appeared mostly in the Chinese court. For that matter

Davies, N. Allman, Kops and R. Allman

we all did. Kops and Davies used an interpreter, but I tried cases in Chinese unless the judge spoke a different dialect from the ones I knew. I was one of only three American lawyers in all China who could practice in Chinese without an interpreter. Once I acted as an interpreter for the judge. I had a witness who spoke only Cantonese and English. The judge spoke only Mandarin. The witness told his story in English and I translated it into Mandarin for the judge.

As a large percentage of our work was in the Chinese language and law, we employed numerous Chinese whose sole duty it was to copy letters and documents into Chinese. The firm of Allman, Davies and Kops was the only law office in Shanghai which used dictaphones. Lee usually kept two going at once, one in English and the other in Chinese.

My first secretary, Vera Hahn, left me to get married. Lillian Rice, an American girl born in Japan and a former secretary to Dr. H. H. Kung[3], also walked out on me for the same reason. Marriage was the main drawback in having women in the office. My next was Mrs. Hannah Lee (no relation to James), who

---

3   Kung, Hsiang-hsi (孔祥熙 Kong Xiangxi) was a Chinese banker of the 20th Century. He married Soong Ai-Ling, the elder sister of Soong Ching-ling and Soong Mei-lin, who had married Sun Yat-sen and Chiang Kai-shek. He served as Premier of China from 1938 to 1939 and was also Minster of Finance for a time.

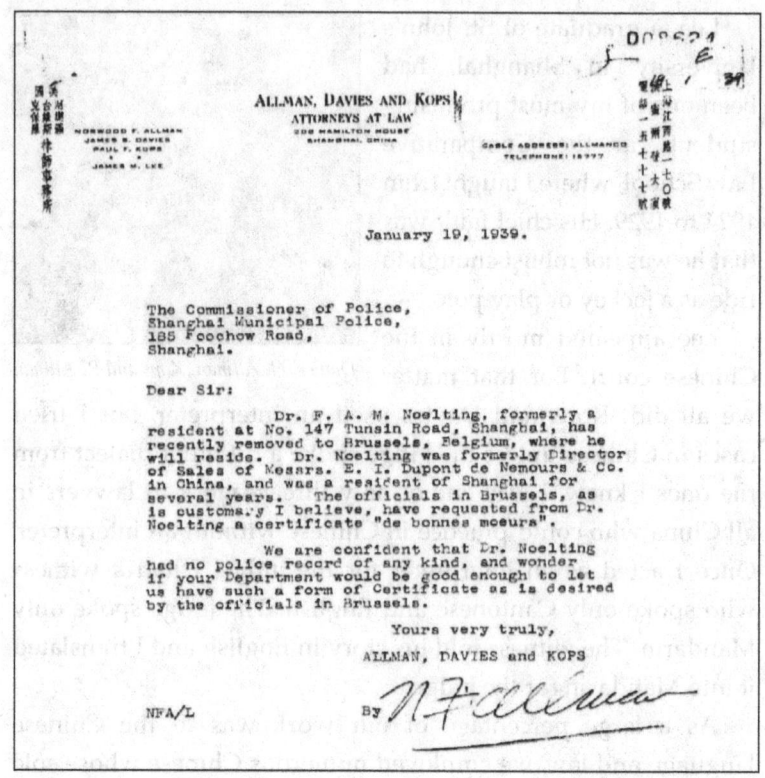

Allman, Davies and Kops letterhead

already had a husband and needed the job.

Kops with his Department of Commerce background was our tax expert, although actually we did not divide up on the work. Usually we all had a finger in the same case, especially if it was an important or troublesome one. As a rule it took two of the firm to handle an out-of-town case. The one trying the case, in Tientsin or Canton, say, often was without access to legal reference books and would have to ask the court for a recess to give him time to telegraph back to Shanghai, where another partner was kept busy looking up law points in our Shanghai office. Incidentally, ours was probably the best and most extensive American law library outside the United States.

Our firm always had at least one or two Chinese employees whose sole duty it was to track down the counterfeiters of our clients' products. It was often necessary to augment our private detective force with additions from an outside agency.

In the Sino-American Commercial Treaty of 1903 China agreed to establish copyright, patent, and trade-mark laws. The copyright law I mentioned earlier. A tentative patent law is available only to Chinese, but China has enacted an effective trade-mark law for protection of all trademarks, regardless of nationality.

This does not mean there were no trade-mark infringements. Quite the contrary. Every nationally or internationally advertised product has been imitated and counterfeited extensively. But the law has made it possible to prosecute an infringer criminally and also sue him for damages in a civil action. The civil suits seldom amount to anything because most infringers are petty pirates without property or money. A favorite article with counterfeiters was the EVEREADY battery, distributed in China by our client, The National Carbon Company. The batteries were counterfeited by small factories scattered all over China and sold for about one-fifth of the cost of the real article. Once brought to light there was no difficulty in getting convictions. The trouble was in unearthing the counterfeiters, so numerous and so well hidden were their small factories.

Chu, an office boy who had been promoted to number one detective, was a whiz at this. He combined infinite patience and perseverance with ingenuity. He kept his tricks secret, but I do know that his first step in tracking down a counterfeiter was to go or send a friend to a suspected shop to purchase an article or obtain a receipt. Unless he dealt in counterfeits exclusively, the shopkeeper tried to sell the counterfeit for the same price as the genuine. In that case Chu bargained and bought the counterfeit at a reduced price. The receipt was used in evidence and the shopkeeper usually found it difficult to explain the reduction.

As soon as Chu made his purchase we applied for warrants to arrest the manager and search his shop. The search often disclosed the manufacturer's address and sometimes, with good luck, we found the names of wholesalers and chains of dealers. At other times it was not so easy. The wary dealers kept false records or none at all. In one case we arrested a manufacturer in Hankow, searched his premises, seized his records and followed a trail of distributors from there to Canton to Swatow to Shanghai to Tientsin. Altogether a distance of 2,500 miles. It also led to the arrest and conviction of the printer of the counterfeit labels. The printer was doing a large-scale business in Shanghai and maintained a big printing and lithographing concern for counterfeit purposes only.

Often it was difficult to tell the counterfeit from the real article and usually it was the label that gave it away. Labels invariably were on thinner and cheaper paper, and because the counterfeiters copied without knowing English, there would be a blurred or upside-down letter that led to detection.

A few years ago another client, the General Electric Company in China, was bothered when Japanese-made counterfeit GE light bulbs flooded the market. We knew the Japs were manufacturing them. But where was the factory?

Chu got on the trail, posing as a dealer in cheap bulbs. He discovered the identity of one of the Jap brokers and arranged a meeting with him in a Chinese hotel to conclude the contract for distribution rights. When the contract was ready for Chu's signature the police walked in.

The Jap, in an attempt to phone a warning to his factory, gave away the telephone number. The police jotted it down, clamped

NORWOOD F. ALLMAN

Local Attorney Unfolds Plot Of Counterfeiters And Imitators At Canton

Mr. N. F. Allman, Recently Returned From Canton, Tells Of Criminal Infringements Of American Utility Goods

What has turned out to be a veritable nest of counterfeiters and fraudulent imitators of well-known and largely advertised utility articles in constant use throughout China, has just been unearthed by Mr. N.F. Allman, of the local legal firm of Fleming, Franklin and Allman, who has just returned to Shanghai from a business trip to Canton undertaken on behalf of the firm's clients, two large and important American manufacturers of electric batteries and flash-lights. The "Ever-ready" Electric Company, and The Winchester Repeating Arms Company.

PROLONGED SEARCH

It was known by Mr. Allman that there were certain headquarters who were distributing the spurious imitations throughout China, and Hongkong and Shanghai particularly were singled out as especially suitable to unload same. Criminal prosecutions have from time to time been undertaken by the legitimate owners of the registered trademark covering both flash lights and batteries, against shopkeepers who sold or displayed the imitations in their establishments, and while fines and imprisonment were imposed, it was found to be extremely difficult to uncover the real source from which these base articles were being obtained.

Large sums of money were expended by the real manufacturers, and an immense amount of time was involved in trying to unravel the vexing problem, and it was not quite recently that definite and reliable information was secured, which led to the trip of Mr. Allman to the South.

GLARING IMITATIONS

On the 8th of this month, however, following what were believed to be veritable clues, Mr. Allman left suddenly for Canton, and with

(Continued on Page 4, Col. 1)

One of Allman's counterfeiting cases makes front page news

the receiver back on the hook, and placed the Jap under arrest before he had a chance to give the alarm. While he was being taken to the police station for questioning, other police traced the call to a house in Hongkew. The Jap blustered that we had kidnapped him, but even the Japanese consular authorities with all their sibilant smiles couldn't list counterfeiting under the heading of legitimate business. To save face they seized and destroyed all the counterfeit bulbs in the factory. The only conviction we could get against the counterfeiter was his promise not to do it again.

There were certain things expected of every American lawyer in China. Sooner or later, for instance, he was always called on to defend a soldier, sailor, or a marine. I disliked these cases as too many of them involved breaches of discipline and I, as an officer in the Shanghai Volunteer Corps, was inclined to sympathize with the disciplinarian's side of the case rather than with the defendant's angle. Once, how- ever, my sympathy was wholly with the defendant.

153

A marine's sweetheart came to me in tears. Her fiance, a noncommissioned marine, had been court-martialed and sentenced to serve two years for robbery. She was convinced that he was innocent. Because the girl painted such a sincere picture of a clean-cut, honorable American youth my curiosity was aroused and I consented to see the boy. His straightforward story and wholesome appearance convinced me too.

I obtained a copy of the court-martial record and found that this lad and several other marines had spent an evening at the jai alai games, where one of the number had won a considerable sum of money.

The accused, who was not as inveterate a gambler as his pals, returned to camp ahead of the others and supposedly retired. Later on when the winner came into the barracks he was hit over the head and robbed. Circumstances showed that several marines, other than the accused, might have committed the robbery and at least two possible offenders had bad records and needed money, whereas the accused's record, up to that time, had been excellent and he was not suspiciously short of funds.

Furthermore, an identification parade had been ordered immediately after the robbery. The accused was present at the parade but the victim had been struck from behind and could not identify anyone.

I studied the record thoroughly and interrogated everyone who had the slightest connection with the marine or the jai alai party. My efforts were rewarded when I discovered that one of the possible offenders had failed to turn up at the identification parade, and through some oversight his absence had not been noticed.

When this was pointed out on a review of the case, the sentence was canceled and the accused restored to his former rank and pay. As to my fee? I was satisfactorily repaid by the gratitude of the boy and girl.

In addition to those where the lawyer conveniently forgot to present a bill, there were the out-and-out charity cases.

Almost all the American lawyers in Shanghai were members of the American Association, and a good many of us took turns in donating legal services to the association's Civilian Relief Committee. Our work for the Committee consisted mostly of details dealing with repatriation of Americans stranded high and dry on the China Coast. Fortunately, there weren't many, just enough to keep us busy. I remember spending countless hours trying to unravel nationality mix-ups and institute legal proceedings to provide food, shelter, and some form of education for children of destitute parents, at least temporarily until they could be shipped home.

One nationality mix-up concerned Edith, an American child who had been legally adopted by a Japanese professor and his English wife before Judge Ben Lindsay, during a brief residence in Denver, Colorado.

Soon after their arrival in Shanghai, Professor Motono deserted his family and returned to Japan. Mrs. Motono sought help from the American Civilian Relief Committee. The good ladies of the American Women's Club rallied round, provided food and clothing for the girl and placed her in St. Joseph's School.

Meanwhile as the committee's legal adviser I sought legal methods of taking the girl away from the mother and repatriating her. The mother was a queer character, but, although we feared the worst, there was no proof that she was mentally or morally unfit. She refused to give up the child, and as adoption papers were in good order, there was nothing we could do. By being strong willed we did manage to keep Edith in school for a few years, but in 1937 our suspicions were realized. We were forced to yield to Mrs. Motono's importunings to have the daughter at home, and forthwith she placed Edith in a brothel in Shanghai's Hongkew section.

The American community's perennial problem was the Jones family. Jones, a free-lance writer, punctuated short term newspaper jobs with lengthy drunken periods during which time his wife and ever-increasing brood were dumped on the Civilian Relief Committee. Jones claimed American citizenship, but the American consulate was not convinced.

It was plain to see that Jones would never support his children, and the relief Committee was stuck with them. After some years of this we decided to solve the Jones family's nationality mystery once and for all. If he were an American, the best thing would be to send the children to an institution in the United States; if he were not American, it was time an agency of his real nationality shouldered our burden. It was my job as the committee's legal adviser to take him into the United States Court for China. Under examination and cross-examination he stuck to his story – Jones was his name and he was an American.

I tried every device to break his story. Then by sheer good luck one day when I was calling on his wife I found an old photograph stuck in a pile of papers. It was a picture of Jones and his buddies taken during the First World War. I wasn't at all sure that the man in the picture really was Jones, but it bore a strong enough resemblance for me to take a chance. I put Jones on the witness stand and flashed the picture before him. I intimated that I knew all.

The photograph in my hands so startled him that he broke down and told the truth. He confessed that his name wasn't Jones at all. He was an American, but the reason he'd never been able to prove it to the American consulate's satisfaction was because his real name was Bronski, a name he disliked. He had been born in Pennsylvania of Lithuanian parents.

I suppose the decision might be called a draw and both sides won. Jones, or rather Bronski, celebrated his acknowledged status as an American citizen by going off on a bender. As far as I know he is still in Shanghai and still known as Mr. Jones.

But the Civilian Relief Committee at last was rid of the Bronski children. Just before the outbreak of the Sino-Japanese war in 1937, we sent the boys to a school in the United States. Mrs. Bronski, a mixture of Chinese, Portuguese, and Irish, and her daughters were shipped across the Pacific to friends in San Francisco.

During the most frightful part of the bombing of Shanghai a cablegram came through to us from the San Francisco Y.W.C.A. advising us that Mrs. Bronski and daughters wanted to return to Shanghai and would we cable funds. We cabled back the one word, "No."

At least once in his career every American lawyer in Shanghai was called upon to defend Willie Fondell, or "Little Willie" as he was better known. This strapping big Negro had come to the China Coast as a piano player in a Jazz band, but drink and a battling fist had put him on the rocks. American lawyers took turns in trying to get him out of jams and into jobs. We also did our best to get him out of town, but he liked Shanghai and as Negroes were rarely seen in Shanghai there was always someone to buy him drinks. He wouldn't leave.[4]

It was during one of his many clashes with the law that Little Willie sent Judge Purdy the letter that became a Shanghai classic. He wrote:

To Whom It May Concern:

I Willie Fondell demands a new trial on the following conditions:

---

4   Fondell, who claimed to be of Japanese descent, was in and out of the American courts in Shanghai. Fondell was eventually forced to leave when he was sentenced to 15 months imprisonment at McNeil Island in Washington State. "Negro Fondel is Given 15-Months Sentence in Spite of His Appeal", *The China Press*, Oct 23 1926, p1. The letter he is alleged to have written is set out in this article as well.

SHANGHAI LAWYER

THE NORTH CHINA HERALD.

AMERICAN PROBLEM IN SHANGHAI

Negro in Court Convicted of Assault After Drinking Sunnybrook

William Fondell, an American negro whose activities have been given considerable publicity through his frequent appearances in the United States Court for China and the American Consular Court since he became stranded in Shanghai several months ago, appeared again on Tuesday morning before Judge Purdy in the U.S. Court for China. He was charged with assault and battery while drunk in Seward Road on the night of June 24, and later in the Hongkew Police Station, where he is alleged to have struck a Russian constable.

Mr. Leonard G. Husar, U.S. District Attorney, appeared to prosecute, and Fondell was represented by Mr. N. F. Allman, who was appointed by the Court to defend.

The District Attorney, after the defence had been closed, told the Court that Fondell's case had become a real problem to the Court and to the American community. Though the charges were assault and battery, he wished to take the occasion to say that the defendant had been before the Court three times and each time he was gaoled for a short time, after which he was only turned loose on the community.

Mr. Allman said that he had been to the Shipping Office of the Consulate and they refused to do anything in the case. Neither would the American Association do anything in the matter.

Allman represents Fondell

SAM JOHNSON'S LIFE IN U. S. COURT

Eccentricity Not Insanity: Will Fondell Declared Sane

At the conclusion of the hearings into the alleged insanity of Will Fondell, an American negro, a jury sitting in the United States Consular Court on Wednesday deliberated 20 minutes and declared the man sane.

The proceedings were brought to a close by an exceedingly interesting argument on behalf of Fondell, by Mr. C. S. Franklin of Messrs. Chalaire & Franklin, in the course of which he pointed out that eccentricity is not incompatible with soundness and clearness of mind, and illustrated the point by a reference to the life of Dr. Samuel Johnson. That most able writer and vigorous thinker, Mr. Franklin recalled, hoarded up orange peel for some mysterious purpose he would never divulge, believed in ghosts hunting in Cock Lane, in walking was constantly gesticulating, and would not go in or out of a door unless he could effect his entry or exit in a certain preconceived number of steps, at times would sit in company and drink a dozen cups of tea, engaging in no conversation, but continually muttering to himself, and was generally so inconsistent in his habits that sometimes he practiced great abstemiousness and at other times devoured large quantities of food and wine with great voracity—yet who would say that Sam Johnson, with his remarkable and clear mind, was insane?

Mr. Franklin, pointed out that to one who understood the negro, Fondell was typical of those found in the Southern sections of the United States, and that his qualities and eccentricities were ordinary and in no manner unusual. Should men of Fondell's type be adjudged insane, concluded the attorney, the cotton plantations of the South would be denuded of labour, the famous American fried chicken would have to be born fried, and the insane asylums would be incapable of accommodating the hordes consigned to them.

An extraordinary case regarding Fondell's sanity

1st That I be tried by a colored gentleman

2nd That I have a chance to choose my own witness

3rd That the district attorney remain silent during the trial

4th That the jailer who messed things up so during the trial be barred

5th That all charges against me be dropped to a small liquor charge

6th That my segar and chow allowance be raised forthwith.

(Signed)   LITTLE WILLIE.

But we escaped many of the messy cases most lawyers dislike. Few breach-of-promise cases came up in the American court. Perhaps there were others, but in over a quarter of a century I can recall only one. This one occurred back in my consular days and no doubt the stiff judgment the judge gave the defendant made a lasting impression on me. The defendant, a young American vice-consul stationed in Shanghai, had to pay the girl five thousand American dollars in monthly payments of fifty dollars. And that out of a yearly salary of twenty-four hundred dollars! How well I knew the struggle to exist on consular pay! This heavy judgment probably served as a severe warning to all the gay blades who came under jurisdiction of the United States Court and may have been the reason why so many Shanghai bachelors shied away from proposing marriage.[5]

In all my twenty years of practice I was asked only once to

---

5   Miss Henrietta Weil sued Mr J.T. Wright for breach of promise and seduction. They were engaged in 1917. Ms Weil had discovered they were no longer affianced when Wright married Miss Dora Emens in 1921. Weil was a stenographer who was living with her widowed mother. Wright was a US Navy yeoman. Weil had become pregnant and had to have an abortion which damaged her health. She was awarded US$5,500 in damages. All was not lost for Miss Weil. She married Henry Alwin Quade in 1923. "Breach of Promise Action", NCH, August 13 1921, p502; E. Scully, Bargaining with the State from Afar, p 174.

take a breach-of-promise suit. It smelled so high of blackmail that I turned it down. I don't believe the girl, a Russian dance-hall hostess from Tientsin, found anyone who would handle the case.

Bankruptcy cases seldom came up. In China no odium is attached to being in debt, but the foreigner who escaped his creditors by going bankrupt had a hard time living it down. The Chinese themselves lost face if they went bankrupt. For the sake of white prestige, the better foreign clubs had rules which automatically expelled a bankrupt member.

All in all the foreign lawyer's day was filled with any number of scheduled and unexpected occurrences, and if he was smart he usually began it early. My day started at daylight, when I left home for the Race Club. There I exercised a couple of horses, bathed, shaved, and breakfasted. At that I was in the office before most Shanghai lawyers were up. Sometimes I had done a day's work by the time my partners and staff appeared. But they stayed long after I had closed my desk and left for the polo field to end the daylight hours with a stiff workout.

IX
CHIH FAN CASES

A LAWYER'S CHIEF AIM is to keep his client out of court. Usually when a client's case comes to court the lawyer feels that he has failed in some way. I know I always did. I'll admit that to the layman court work is more exciting than office routine, which at times even to the lawyer is dull, exacting stuff. But in Shanghai as elsewhere contracts, conveyances, and opinions on legal phases of the clients' business were what the Chinese would call chih fan, or "eating" cases.

Most of the law firms were small, and there was no tendency toward specialization. The Shanghai lawyer, like the country doctor, was more or less a general practitioner. Personally I preferred corporation law and whenever possible I devoted myself to this branch. It has been a matter of pride with, me that our firm had a hand in organizing the majority of the American companies formed to do business in China. As it was customary for the company to retain the law firm assisting in its organization, I did not lack for corporate law experience. My firm had as clients banks, schools, colleges, mission boards, manufacturers, construction companies, importers and exporters, insurance companies, transportation companies, and public utilities.

Since the days of the first clipper ships, Americans have played an important part in China trade. Very often our efforts were amateurish, and especially was this true in our foreign trade expansion during and immediately following the First World War. Some of our business firms, notably banks, employed an undue proportion of non-Americans. Their excuse was, "Not enough Americans trained in foreign trade and international banking." No doubt the Scottish started this story because an amazing number of Scotsmen were employed in the foreign branches of American banks.

My consular job in Shanghai had given me firsthand knowledge of the ins and outs of American trade in the Far East. It seemed to me, as it did to a good many others, that our laws were throttling American trade and enterprise. An American-operated company organized under one of the state laws paid a federal income tax and in many cases a state income tax. This meant that the tax was added to the cost of the goods sold in China, and it was just that much more difficult for us to compete with government-subsidized businesses and British firms organized under the Hong Kong Ordinances, a law which permitted them to do business in China without paying taxes to the British government, or any taxes for that matter except a nominal registration fee to the Hong Kong government.

In 1921, during my first stint at the American consulate-general in Shanghai, Congressman Dyer of Missouri[1] came out to China. A practical statesman, Dyer was

Congressman Dyer, a strong support of China causes

---

1   Leonadis Carstarphen Dyer (1871-1957) served in Congress from 1911 to 1933. He was a noted reformer, including seeking to have anti-lynching laws passed. One of his daughters, Mrs. D.J. Collins, lived in Shanghai and he visited the city regularly.

sincerely interested in improving Chinese-American trade. After a series of talks with me and several others, including older, more experienced business men and officials, he returned to Washington and introduced a bill in Congress. When passed this became the law known as The China Trade Act. Companies organized under this law were exempt from income tax.

At last American business had an even break with British, French, and other foreign firms. The act's main purpose was to assist in distribution of goods produced in the United States. It didn't say so in so many words, but an implied purpose was encouragement of Chinese and American money mergers in such distribution. A company could be formed under this law without any American money; the only provision was that the company's president, treasurer, and a majority of the directors be American citizens. Neither did the Hong Kong Ordinances require British capital, only that the principal officers of the company be British.

But like most laws, the China Trade Act had its drawbacks. It was almost choked to death by red tape. Usually it took from two to three months to organize a company under this act. Under the laws of Delaware, or under the Hong Kong Ordinances, a company could be formed in twenty-four hours.

Well do I remember the time two clients, one British, the other American, rushed into my office. One waved a cable advising them of their exclusive distribution rights for an American aircraft company. It was generally known that the Chinese government was on the verge of placing a large order for planes and my clients had a chance to make a big sale, if they could organize a company immediately. The Chinese government, naturally, preferred to deal with a duly authorized company rather than an individual. To avoid the China Trade Act delay, we formed a company under the Hong Kong Ordinances. At the same time under the China Trade Act we organized a company to distribute airplane accessories. Three months later, after the boys had sold and delivered the planes, this charter came through.

The act itself excluded some businesses. It did not provide for organization of either American insurance or banking companies to do business in China. Connecticut is one of the few states that permits organization of companies to do banking outside the state, and thus it was that the American-Oriental Banking Corporation was organized in that state. This bank filled a long-felt need in Shanghai's American community by immediately identifying itself with local interests and accepting small personal as well as big business accounts. This was something new, as the American banks in China were tied to the apron strings of the New York offices and had not gone "all out" in identifying themselves with local interests. British banks, on the other hand, devoted themselves to local trade. Their officials made their own decisions and did not depend on someone halfway across the world to pass judgment on a loan.

The failure of the American-Oriental Banking Corporation in 1935 shocked the China Coast speechless[2]. When people had recovered their voices, some shouted loudly that it was the law's fault that the bank had failed. I can't agree with this. To my mind the blame rests wholly with the men who ran the bank and not with the law under which it was organized. Perhaps it would have been better all around had the China Trade Act or some other national law authorized organization of banks, and the proper authority kept a wary eye on them. True, the main purpose of the China Trade Act was encouragement of trade. But we might as well wake up to the fact that we can't do business

2   The AOCB was owned by Frank Raven a church-going pillar of the community, who it turned out was a fraudster. His group of companies collapsed in 1935 causing many to lose their life savings. The ultimate payout in liquidation was only 7 cents in the dollar. Raven was convicted of fraud and sentenced to 5 years in prison. See further: *Gunboat Justice*, Vol 3, pp90-99

Sapajou on the collapse of the AOCB

in foreign countries without proper American banking facilities.

The day the American-Oriental Banking Corporation closed its doors I was trying a case before Judge Helmick in the United States Court for China then sitting in Peking. The judge and I

Crowds mill in front of the now closed American-Oriental Banking Corporation

flew back to Shanghai immediately[3], but for different reasons. The bank's failure had affected practically every American in China, most of whom had accounts either in the bank itself or in one of its affiliates.

The notice read that the American-Oriental Finance Corporation had been closed by order of the Board of Directors.

The judge was anxious to appoint a liquidator. At first he wanted an American lawyer, principally because of the numerous legal entanglements; but it was impossible to find a lawyer who was free to take the job. Obviously the bank's own lawyers were out of the picture, and the moment the failure was known every other lawyer in town had dozens of claims to file against the bank. Finally Frank Hough[4], a prominent and reputable businessman, agreed to shoulder the responsibility. He did a fine piece of work, but it broke his health and he died on the job.

---

3   In fact, Helmick remained in Peking trying the Peking Union Medical College case (see Chapter 16). Allman flew back to Shanghai for one day to meet with clients and then flew back to Peking.

4   Frank L. Hough (1866-1936) was the Managing Director of the R.C.A. Victor Radio Co. in Shanghai. He had come to Shanghai in 1933. Before that, he had run a number of companies in America, Argentina and Indonesia.

My office had telegraphed me in Peking to obtain various restraining orders against the bank officers and get claims started. This I had done, sitting right in the lap of the court, as it were. In Shanghai there was plenty to do. In addition to local clients several New York banks and insurance companies had cabled us to protect their interests.

Our first job was to stop delivery of our clients' mail to the bank and its affiliates. Under Chinese postal laws a

Frank Hough, liquidator of the AOBC

sender can stop mail in transit. Immediately we asked for and received an order from the postal commissioner authorizing delivery to us of all our clients' mail addressed to the bank. We obtained this order several days prior to appointment of the liquidator. In. all the excitement it completely slipped my mind, and the minds of my partners as well, to notify Mr. Hough.

When he found out what was happening he was furious. He phoned the office, accused us of trickery, and demanded the mail. Kops, who took the call, nonchalantly read him the postal laws on the subject, but he was not convinced. Indeed, it took many phone and several personal calls before he would believe that we were well within our rights. When he cooled down we arrived at a speedy settlement, for some of the mail contained drafts, bills, and contracts in which the liquidator had a just beneficial interest.

By taking advantage of the Chinese postal law we saved time and money for many clients. We could force immediate settlement of a number of drafts, remittances, and other contracts on the ground that they had not come into the bank's possession before its failure. The bank has not yet been completely liquidated, and if we had not rerouted the mail, many of our clients' claims would be outstanding today.

Banks in China required more legal advice in a week than did ordinary business firms in a year. We had several banks among our clients. Their transactions were so varied and involved so many different nationalities that there was seldom a day when we weren't called upon for some advice. Too, the banks made constant use of their legal advisers on the "ounce of prevention is worth a pound of cure" theory. No system is foolproof, however. One of the strongest and most cautious British banks in Shanghai was the victim of a million dollar fraud.

In order to import an expensive line of leather goods, Harrendorf, a Shanghai importer, established a million-dollar letter of credit with the British bank. The bank advanced the money, paying it over to Harrendorf's partner in Hamburg.[5] Invoices, insurance papers, and other documents were forwarded to Shanghai in good order. Shortly thereafter the merchandise arrived, a thousand cases in the bank's name which were stored in the importer's godown.

Following the Shanghai custom, Harrendorf was to sell off the goods from within four to six months and repay the bank as the merchandise was sold. When four months went by and the bank had received suspiciously little in the way of repayment, it examined its thousand cases of leather goods. Most of them were

---

5   Holder Harrendorff was a German merchant in Shanghai. He obtained credit from a number of banks including the Hongkong & Shanghai Banking Corporation, Chartered Bank of India, Australia and China Ltd, Deutsch-Asiatic Bank and the National Commercial Bank against shipments of worthless products that shipping documents stated were of value. HSBC obtained search warrants to search Harrendorff's office, whereupon Harrendorff left Shanghai for Japan. HSBC used its influence to have Harrendorf arrested and returned to Shanghai. As a German he did not have extraterritorial rights. He was tried in the Provisional Court (which had taken over from the Mixed Court) before Judge-Hsu-Moh with Allman defending. He was convicted of fraud and sentenced to six and half years imprisonment. Allman made numerous applications on his behalf to be released early due to ill health. This was ultimately granted over strong objections from the banks. "Harrendorf is Released from Jail Yesterday", *The China Press*, August 16, 1929, p1.

filled with cheap glass trinkets.

The others held baled newspapers. Harrendorf was arrested, but the partner and the million dollars had vanished into thin air. Harrendorf asked me to take his case. He insisted that he was innocent; that he had been swindled. It is possible he was telling the truth, for neither the bank's hawk-eyed investigators nor I could find a cent in Harrendorf's name. He was convicted and sentenced to two years' imprisonment. He came to see me after his release. He was penniless, he said, and I felt so sorry for him that I returned half the hundred American dollars he had paid me. With the money he purchased passage on a freighter and went to South America, where he may have joined his millionaire partner. It is just possible that I, too, was swindled.

Insurance is another business that required much of a lawyer's time. Most insurance branches in China did not maintain their own legal departments. Insurance cases provided the soy sauce for much of a law firm's rice. Not a day passed that we weren't consulted on at least one legal question. Enough international problems popped up to occupy all the lawyers in China.

An insurance case with international complications concerned *The Republic of China versus the Merchant Fire Insurance Company*. We represented the insurance company. A sum of $66,238.12 (the insurance covering the premises of the Wuchang Telephone Administration Building destroyed by fire in February, 1926) was due the Chinese government. Our client was perfectly willing to pay. There was no question about that.[6] The sole problem was, pay whom? The policy had been taken out and paid for by the Peking government. In the meantime the National government

---

6 Allman is being, at the politest, "economical with the truth" here. His client was not
   willing to pay at all. They fought the case as hard as possible, including entering into
   a consent judgment with the former Chinese government in 1928. Judge Purdy found
   this had been done by collusion between the parties. See *Gunboat Justice*, Vol. 3 pp17-21;
   and, *NCH*, June 15, 1929, p448 and Aug 17, 1929, p257.

had been established in Nanking, but at the time the case came to court the United States had not as yet recognized the Nanking government. The case was argued on the basis of whether or not the new national government had the capacity to sue in our court. The case dragged on for more than two years and was settled shortly after July 25, 1928, when the United States, by recognizing the National government at Nanking, automatically wiped out our problem.

It was in connection with another internationally complicated case that my firm brought suit against Chang Hsueh Liang, "the Young Marshal," who achieved fame as abductor of Generalissimo Chiang Kai-shek in 1936.[7]

Just prior to 1931, McDonnell and Gorman, American engineers and contractors, built a residence and some other buildings in Mukden for the Young Marshal. The contract price had not been paid when the Japanese seized Manchuria and Chang fled to Shanghai. He ignored all requests for payment. Acting for the builders we filed suit against him in the Chinese court in the French Concession where he was residing at the time.

Chang's lawyers claimed that he was not a resident of Shanghai but of Mukden and that anyway the buildings were for the account of the Manchurian government. The first defense was silly, as Chang was an actual resident of Shanghai. Even if we'd wanted to bring suit against him in Mukden the Japanese would not have permitted his return. As for the second defense,

---

7   Chang Hsueh Liang (張學良 Zhang Xueliang) (1901-2001). His father had ruled Man-
    churia. In 1928 his father was assassinated by the Japanese and Zhang took over. He
    formed an alliance with the Kuomintang, but his power was weakened when the Japa-
    nese invaded Manchuria in 1931. In 1936, he kidnapped Chiang Kai-shek in Xian to
    force him to negotiate with the Communist Party. Zhang was placed under house arrest
    by Chiang until 1975. Allman sued Chang in the 2nd Special District Court, in 1933 on
    behalf of R.T. McDonnell for $158,000 and J.M. Hermann, architect, for $28,000. "Young
    Marshal Sued", NCH, Sept 13, 1933, p431. McDonnell at one point had been rumoured
    to become the American Minister to China. He later served on the Shanghai Municipal
    Council with Allman.

the lower court held that although the contracts had been signed in the personal name of Chang Hsueh Liang, the buildings were for the account of the Manchurian government and he was not personally liable. In the meanwhile the Young Marshal had sailed for Europe. Our clients

Chang Hsueh Liang , the "Young Marshal" with Chiang Kai Shek. Allman sued Chang in a Chinese court in Shanghai

decided against appeal. Even if they were awarded judgment it would have meant trailing Chang all over Europe to collect[8]. And since he personally had signed the contracts, suit against the Japanese-sponsored government in Mukden appeared futile.

The net result was: our clients were out time, labor, and materials, the Japs were in possession of several good buildings at no expense to them, and the Young Marshal had the experience of being sued for the first and perhaps the only time in his life.

But a large part of a Shanghai lawyer's business concerned the important but routine work of real estate. Registering a land title in a foreign settlement in China was far more complicated than tracing a deed or drawing up a mortgage in the United States.

In the years between 1844 and 1853 the plan of marking off separate plots of land for the residence of foreigners at each of the five treaty ports was adopted. From these grew the concessions or settlements governed by the various extraterritorial nations.

At the time the Chinese gave away nothing that was of any particular value to them. When the British took Hong Kong in 1840 it was a barren rock, inhabited only by a band of pirates.

---

8   Chang returned to China after 9 months in Europe in January 1934.

In 1842 Shanghai was an unimportant fishing village. The areas ceded to the British, French, and Americans consisted of mud flats which were submerged at high tide, and the only water supply came from the muddy Whangpoo. Both Shanghai and Hong Kong became places of great wealth and importance, but largely through the efforts of the foreigners who went there to live and carry on their businesses. Incidentally, Americans have never had a concession or settlement in China.[9]

In our first treaty with the Chinese Caleb Cushing[10] made it plain that the United States did not desire any portion of China. However, when the British obtained their mud flats at Shanghai, John A. Griswold[11], the American consul and a partner in the influential firm of Russell and Company, refused to be outdone. On his own initiative he made a deal with the Tao-tai and selected the mud-flat section north of Soochow Creek now known as Hongkew. Communications being somewhat slow in those days, the State Department did not learn of the consul's action until several months later. When they did they immediately repudiated it. Nevertheless many Chinese, even in recent years, continued to call Hongkew "mei kuo tsu chieh," which literally translated means "American Concession."

Theoretically, the concessions and settlements were set aside for the exclusive use of the foreigners, but in the early transitory and revolutionary period these areas served as oases of safety for all persons and property, including the Chinese themselves. As a matter of fact, there being more of them, the Chinese received the

---

9   This is not entirely correct. The Americans did have a concession in Shanghai that was merged with the British Concession in 1863 to form the International Settlement. America also had a very small concession in Tientsin from 1860 to 1880. This became part of the British Concession in 1902.

10 See Chapter 6

11 John N.A. Griswold (1821-1909). At the time, the United States would often appoint local merchants as consuls. Griswold was a strong supporter of the union during the Civil War and later became President of the Illinois Central Railway and Chairman of the Chicago, Burlington and Quincy Railroad.

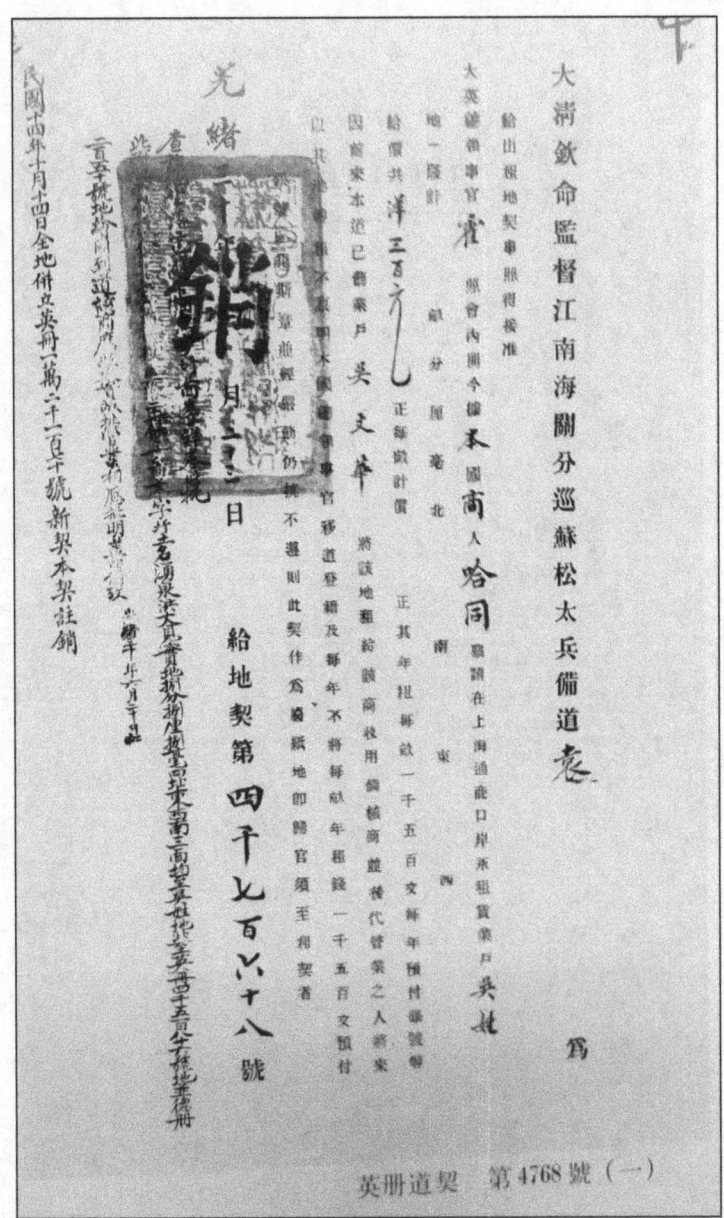

A title deed leasing land to Silas Hardoon

SHANGHAI

[TRANSLATION.]

Tāo lai's copy

TITLE DEED.

Yuan Superintendent of Maritime Customs for the Province of Kiang-nan Intendant of the Su-sung-tai Circuit, &c., &c., hereby gives this Deed for the Renting of Land.

I have received a communication from His Britannic Majesty's Consul-General, stating that

Silas Aaron Hardoon

[herein described and called the Renter] has applied to Rent in perpetuity from the Proprietor

Wu Wan-hua

a Lot of Land, situated at the Port of Shanghai, measuring in area

_____ mow, _____ fun, _____ li, _____ hao, bounded

North by _____

South by _____

East by _____

West by _____

That the said Renter has paid to the said Proprietor a sum of *Dollars Three hundred*

($300.00)

being at the rate of _____ per mow; and also that he will pay the Annual Low Rent of Fifteen Hundred Cash per mow Yearly in advance to the Government Banker.

This coming before me, the Intendant, I do hereby arrange and agree that the said Proprietor shall Rent the said quantity of Land to the said Renter upon the following conditions:—

That if the said Renter , his or their Successors or Assigns, shall hereafter make over his or their interest in the Ground now rented to another party, without reporting the same to his or their Consul for his assent and concurrence, and through him to the Intendant for the time being, and for the due registration of the Transaction in their respective Records; or if the said Renter neglect to pay Yearly in advance the said Low Rent of Fifteen Hundred Cash per mow, after being ordered to do so, then, and in each of these several cases, this Deed shall become null and void, and the proprietorship of the said Land, Houses, and Tenements, shall revert to the Lord of the Soil.

A necessary Deed for the Renting of Land.

Kuang-hsü 30th year, | L. S. | *2nd* moon *25th* day.

6th June 1904

LOT No. *1765*

REGISTRATION COMPLETED AT
H.B.M. CONSULATE-GENERAL, SHANGHAI,
this _____ day of _____ 19___

Vice-Consul.

No. 8,04

英册道契 第4768號 (二)

English translation the title deed

greatest benefit from the settlements. The great influx of Chinese necessitated the preparation and adoption of a unique system of land titles.

In buying real estate, foreign residents leased in perpetuity the land from the original Chinese owner. The documents were recorded at the consulate of the foreign lessee. A consular title deed was issued to the foreign lessee by his consul and the Chinese land office in the treaty ports. Actually these transactions were sales of land, but to conform with the treaties they were described as perpetual leases.

The deeds came to have significant value, for they established unimpeachable titles. They were, in fact, easily transferable and the safest collateral for bank or other loans. They came to form the credit foundation of Shanghai, and in the Settlement's one hundred years' history I know of only one fraudulent title transaction. The victim was a prominent American lawyer noted for his cautiousness.[12]

An official, whom I'll name Robb, borrowed ten thousand Chinese dollars from the lawyer, putting up a consular title deed as security. After Robb had left for parts unknown the lawyer presented the deed at the consulate for registration in his name. At that time I was in charge of registering land titles at the consulate. It took me less than five minutes to discover that the deed was forged.

Robb had been clever and had forged not mine but my predecessor's signature. However, he'd made a clumsy slip which was apparent the moment I examined the back of the deed. Robb had cut the seal from an old passport and pasted it onto the deed form which he had obtained through some trickery. The passport seal was embossed, but being pasted on,

---

12   For more on the system of registration of title, see *Gunboat Justice*, Vol 2, p161-163

the embossing hadn't gone through. All I can say is the lawyer should have been smarter.

The consular title deeds brought up an interesting problem. Although the Chinese had moved into the areas that were supposedly for the exclusive use of the foreigners, the consular title deeds could not be issued to the Chinese. But there is always a way around a problem in China. Soon the major part of the land covered by the consular deeds was again owned by Chinese.

The solution was simple. The foreigner who leased the original piece of ground registered the Chinese deed under his own name at his consulate and received the consular title deed, subsequently issuing a declaration of trust to the Chinese friend or associate, who meanwhile had purchased the property. This declaration of trust was merely a document stating that the foreign lessee held the property as trustee for the Chinese buyer and that he agreed, among other things, to transfer or deal with the property thereafter according to the Chinese buyer's instructions. This created two titles to real property in Shanghai and other treaty ports where the same system prevailed: (1) the registered or legal title and (2) the beneficial or equitable title.

In 1930 when we built our home I bought, or rather leased in perpetuity, a plot of ground in a new residential section on Amherst Avenue, then called Fah Wha Road[13]. The Chinese owner, whose family had held title to this paddy field for several hundred years, turned over to me the fangtan, or native deed, which had been issued some two hundred years earlier. To meet the fiction of a lease instead of a sale he also gave me a simple perpetual lease in the Chinese language. I registered both with the American consulate, then filed them at the Chinese Land Office. In return I was given a consular deed.

---

13   Now Xinhua Road. Allman's house was located at 71 Amherst Avenue.

Transaction of this title business was a substantial part of the Shanghai law business. In the early days the British lawyers very nearly monopolized it, but later Americans and other lawyers came in for their share. Not only registrations of titles, but usually all litigation pertaining to the property was handled by the lawyer who held the title. Nice work, too.

Allman's grand house at 71 Amherst Avenue. Courtesy Neal Burnham.

As Shanghai grew and land transfers increased, title companies were formed solely to take over details of such transactions. Still the lawyers kept much of the business in their own hands. In addition to the ones I own personally, numerous consular title deeds are registered in my name and in the name of my firm. What will happen to them now that extrality has been abolished? Just answering that one question will keep lawyers busy for years to come.

In addition to conveyances I, as well as other Shanghai lawyers, was occupied with mortgages and term leases. In drawing up these ordinary leases I usually represented the landlords and had their interests at heart, although I early realized that the customary Shanghai lease contained all the landlord's privileges of feudalistic days.

On one occasion I took keen delight in reversing these privileges. It made me especially happy as the lessor was a wealthy landowner noted for his ruthlessness with tenants. He had constructed a modern office building in the center of the Settlement, and I knew he wanted one of my clients, the branch of a New York bank, as a tenant. I took advantage of this knowledge to reverse the usual covenants of the lease. Wherever it read in favor of the landlord I rewrote it in favor of the tenant. To my surprise, and his later regret, the shrewd landlord signed the lease. Even in the most prosaic legal transaction a lawyer often finds something to amuse him.

X
A Lawyer's Leisure Time

A LAWYER'S LIFE IN SHANGHAI was far from being all work and no play, although the play was never the exciting, all-absorbing kind described in stories about Shanghai. It used to be the thing for tourist writers to make quick trips through the Orient, then hurry home and dash off books which dwelt on Shanghai's gaiety and wickedness, especially the wild night life. It is possible that they may have been right. Before the war Shanghai was a tourist's paradise. The visitor often had an opportunity to see a side of Shanghai that the hard-working resident missed. It isn't my purpose to debunk the tourist's glamorous Shanghai. It may have been there all the time, and I was just too busy to see it.

In all my years in Shanghai I found time to visit the notorious "Blood Alley" only once. "Blood Alley," a short, narrow lane off Avenue Edward VII and officially christened Rue Chu Pao San, for years boasted some twenty cabarets and bars and a reputation for sinful goings-on including knifings, fist fights, and murders. Evidently the participants, mostly soldiers and sailors, found it more convenient to settle their differences without hindrance of legal advice. I must say that the night I made the rounds it was quiet and dull. Perhaps my party timed the visit too early or the right boats were not in. Anyway, we found more excitement in kibitzing a mah-jongg game at the American Club where a much better grade of whisky was served.

Rue Chu-Pao-San "Blood Alley" with police at the standby

Blood Alley by day

Blood Alley at night

Shanghailanders didn't need artificial excitement. Just living in Shanghai provided sufficient stimulation, for it was a place where anything might happen and usually did. However, the social side of life was not neglected. There was always plenty to do. Sometimes too damned much, I thought, but when my work wasn't pressing I enjoyed going out to dinners and official receptions, especially if the gathering included Chinese.

I lived among the Chinese for twenty-five years and from the first I found them likable. In many ways they are much like Americans. Neither wealth nor position affects the innate humor or democratic nature of the Chinese. It is as easy to talk to a Chinese leader as it is to a laborer. The coolie can tell and appreciate a joke even when he may be just one step ahead of starvation. Perhaps one of the reasons why I like the Chinese is because they, too, are individualists.

In Peking and the outports where I had lived I had made many Chinese friends and I had enjoyed their conversation and companionship. When I arrived in Shanghai I was shocked and not a little disappointed to find that Chinese and foreigners did not mix socially. Both my wife, who had spent most of her life in China, and I missed these social contacts and immediately I set about looking up acquaintances of other days and places and soon, through them, I again had acquired a large circle of Chinese friends.

I did all I could to promote Chinese-American friendship. I was among those who worked to open membership in the Shanghai American Club to Chinese and I was instrumental in founding the ABC (American-British-Chinese) Club, later known as the Union Club[1], and with George Fitch[2], C. T. Wang[3], William Yinson Lee[4], and others, organized the Amity Masonic Lodge[5].

It was during this period of increasing Chinese and American social intercourse in Shanghai that I met Mme. Chiang Kai-shek,

---

1   The Union Club was opened in June 1919 for the purpose of "consolidating friendships between Chinese, British and American merchants." It closed at the end of 1934 as other more spacious clubs had opened. "Union Club To Close Doors Here Shortly", *The China Press*, 27 June 1935, p12.

2   George Ashmore Fitch (1883-1979) originally was a missionary in China and then worked for many years in China with the YMCA. He was a member of the Nanjing Safety Zone International Committee during the Rape of Nanking.

3   Wang Zhengting (王正廷) (1882-1961) was minister in the Chinese government from 1924-1931 serving as foreign minister from 1928-1931. He had studied at Yale University. He later became Chinese Ambassador to the United States.

4   William Yinson Lee (1884-1965) (Li Yuanxin 李元信) was a Chinese Australian who had been Deputy Grand Master of the Chinese Free Masons in Australia.

5   The Amity Masonic Lodge was established in 1932 under a charter from the Philippine Grand Lodge.

then Mei-ling Soong[6], and other members of her admirable family. My wife was already well acquainted with her, as they had been at Wellesley at the same time. Mei-ling, one year behind my wife at college, was quite the envy of all the girls when her brother, T. V. Soong[7], then a student at Harvard, came visiting on Sundays accompanied by a dozen or more fellow students who tagged along just to see his pretty and sparkling sister.

Occasionally we dined with the Soongs and often we saw Mei-ling at other social affairs, for she was always popular and had many admirers among the young American bachelors. But even in her butterfly days she was noticeably more serious-minded than her associates. To me she seemed far more interested in politics than in romance. Fortunately the responsibilities and heavy official duties of her marriage have not dulled her ready wit, nor have illness and worry impaired her smart appearance.

My wife and I were among the group of foreigners who attended that history-making wedding ceremony held in the famous old Majestic Hotel in Shanghai in 1926 which united the bright-eyed Mei-ling and the slender, scholarly-looking soldier, Chiang Kai-shek, whose star just then was in the ascendant. I wonder how many of

Chiang Kai-shek and Mei-ling Soong on their marriage

---

6   Soong Mei-Ling (宋美齡) (1898-2003) was the fourth of six children of Charlie Soong a wealthy businessman. She studied at Wesleyan College for 1 year before transferring to Wellesley College. She met Chiang in 1920 and was only allowed by his parents to marry him after Chiang divorced and converted to Christianity. During WWII she toured the US seeking financial support for China. Her sister Ai-Ling married Sun Yatsen.

7   Tse-Ve Soong (宋子文) (1871-1971) was Soong Mei-ling's older brother. He served as Governor of the Bank of China and Minister of Finance in the Kuomintang government. He served as Foreign Minister between 1942 and 1945.

us sensed that this was no ordinary marriage? I, for one, felt that the couple, zealous patriots both, would go a long way and work hard for their country, but I had no way of knowing that as a result of this union China would be more firmly united than ever before in her history.

After their marriage we saw little of Mei-ling and her strong husband with the disarmingly soft voice. Their public duties left them little time for social trivialities, and they attended only the most formal functions. And, too, they soon moved to Nanking, 250 miles from Shanghai; then still further to Hankow, 600 miles distant; and finally to Chungking, 1,600 miles in the interior. Their departure was a great loss. In Shanghai it was well known that China's leader and the first lady of the land liked meeting and talking with Americans.

In my attempts to bring Chinese and Americans together I encouraged the Chinese to play polo, my favorite sport. They made excellent players. One of the keenest teams I've known was composed of Chinese cavalry officers in Peking. They met death, every one of them, fighting the Japanese in 1932.

Horses have played an important part in my life from earliest childhood days spent on a farm near the village of Union Hall, Virginia, in the Piedmont section of the Blue Ridge between Pigg River and Black Water. (I often wondered why one of these streams had such a prosaic name and the other such a poetic one.)

It cuts heavily into one's sleep to get up at daylight and valet a dozen or so horses before going to school, but my seven brothers, one sister, and I thought nothing of doing this and other chores before trudging four miles to a country school which began at 8 a.m. In winters, however, when it snowed we were allowed to ride to school. That is, up until the day Pa caught us galloping the horses into snowdrifts where they stopped short and tumbled us off. That was great sport. In summer weather, out of Pa's sight, we often interrupted our plowing to sneak the horses off and race them against each other.

Aside from the hard work, which left me with the rugged constitution that has enabled me to withstand everything from the overly rich food served at stuffy diplomatic dinners to near-starvation in a Jap internment camp, we had lots of fun. Another game, when Pa wasn't around, was galloping the horses into Black Water and swimming them across. I especially enjoyed breaking and training colts, not to mention a little horse trading on the side, although I considered horse trading a crooked business. Later on when I met automobile dealers I realized that horse traders were mere childish amateurs.

In those days a little jerkwater railroad ran through our farm, but our chief mode of transportation was by horseback or by horse and buggy. It was not unusual to receive visits from elderly relatives who came calling on horseback. One aunt, despite her ninety years, came to see us at least once a month; she always rode sidesaddle, over rough mountain paths.

I remember one horse, Dock, which our whole family loved. He was just my age and very gentle. Frequently my mother rode him sidesaddle with a couple of children perched in front and a couple of others hanging on behind. Dock, named for a favorite uncle, lived to be about twenty- five years old. When he died we all missed him dreadfully. This fondness for horses has never left me. Horses have given me much pleasure and on one or two occasions some trouble. I have been on somewhat strained relations with a sister-in-law ever since a recent visit when to her annoyance I gave all my attention to a six-months-old foal and ignored her six-months-old baby. Indignantly she mentioned my neglect. But I reminded her that although I was the eldest of nine children and the father of three, I still considered a six-months

Allman riding a China pony. Courtesy Neal Burnham

foal far more interesting than a baby of the same age.

When I arrived in Peking, a raw, young student interpreter, I found, to my great delight, that I could ride to my heart's content; it was the thing to do! As soon as I could save enough out of my small salary I purchased a Mongolian pony, known in China as the China pony. I had valeted mules, horses, and cows and thought I knew something about stubborn critters, until I met the China pony.

Someone once characterized the China pony as an animal something like a sheep, yet not unlike a camel; like a pig in disposition, a cat for climbing. The one animal to which he bears the least resemblance is the thoroughbred horse. I'd say that the China pony has all the amiable qualities of a mule.

But my hat is off to the China pony. For size and weight he has more stamina than any beast of burden I have ever met. For instance, an average size, thirteen-hand-high China pony weighing 750 pounds can haul a man weighing 150 to 180 pounds through two chukkars of polo per day, three or four times a week, and not show the slightest sign of strain. Unless watched, a China pony will run his heart out. Bred on the Mongolian plains where their early food is sand, sticks, and dried grass, the China pony when brought to Shanghai has to be conditioned for about four months before it is used to normal food like hay and oats!

Soon after my arrival in Peking I was introduced to polo. In Peking, polo was played on a skinned field, that is, the surface

Major Louis Little who taught Allman polo

was a mixture of broken brick, Peking dust, and clay. Spills usually resulted in considerable loss of skin. Most of my training, especially in the swearing end of the game, I received under the astute tutelage of that master, Major Louis Little[8] of the United States Marine Corps. Anyone who has ever wrestled with mules must of necessity know how to swear. I thought I was an expert until I fouled the major in a game one day, and he ripped into me. He spoke two languages, profane and vulgar. On that day he spoke three, for he mixed the two. His training stood me in good stead later on in Shanghai where I continued to play polo until interrupted by the Japs.

Shanghai polo players took their game seriously. I recall the time when Cornell Franklin[9], another lawyer poloist, was in a

---

8   Louis McCarty Little (1878-1960). Little served with the marines in numerous locations in Asia. He retired in 1942 at the rank of Major General.
9   Cornell Sidney Franklin (1892-1959) had been Allman's law partner at Fleming Franklin and Allman. In 1937, he was elected Chairman of the Shanghai Municipal Council, serving until 1940. His first wife was Estelle Oldham, whom he had courted in Mississippi. She chose Franklin over a struggling author, William Faulkner. In 1926 she divorced Franklin and married Faulkner. Faulkner went on to win the Nobel Prize in literature. Franklin's second wife was Dallas Chesterman Lee. She arrived in Shanghai in 1929 and it is her arrival that is most likely being recounted here.

Allman (front) playing polo

Mrs Franklin presenting a polo trophy to Tony Keswick

dilemma. His bride-to-be was due to arrive on a ship from home on the very afternoon of an important game at the Kiangwan polo field. He knew we'd make life miserable for him if he didn't show up for the game, and he had a pretty good idea of what would happen if he didn't meet the ship. Fortunately it was one of those rare times when the boat arrived on schedule. Franklin met the lady and rushed her straight from the jetty across town to the field just in time to get in the game. Needless to say, Mrs. Franklin became an ardent polo fan.

At home I must have talked a continuous game of polo. When my oldest son William was a small boy he was once asked what his father did for a living. He answered in all seriousness, "He's a polo player." Incidentally Bill, now in the United States Navy, turned out to be no mean player himself and helped me in winning a number of hotly contested matches. Both Bill and I were members of the American Troop of the Shanghai Volunteer

Allman, left, with his son, William, right in SVC uniforms. Steve Clarke is in the centre

Corps, and as I was the captain of the troop and Bill the youngest member it behooved him to put up a good show. But when I saw that he was about to get a polo handicap higher than my own, I sent him to the United States. It was high time, I thought, that he was entering college.

I can't recall a single law suit over a polo pony. This must indicate that the riders really were gentlemen. Or perhaps it was because there wasn't much direct horse trading between individuals. It was the custom to buy in the pony auction which was held weekly throughout the year. From seventy-five to a hundred ponies went on the block each week. In early spring the polo players turned out for every auction. Each one would bid in a half a dozen or so ponies, hoping to get one good one. Usually the buyer was disappointed, and back the ponies would go into the next year's auction. The buyer would purchase new lots until at least one good pony emerged. Eventually he had his string.

Sometimes a really mean pony turned up at auction, and the sucker who had purchased him would hurry him back into auction,

BRITAIN PAYS COSTS
Judge Franklin's Decision

H.D. Rodger, Allman, Du
Riveau and C.S. Franklin in
polo gear

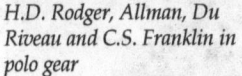

then circulate stories about the mean one's polo potentialities. It was considered great sport to stick a fellow player with such a pony and possibly with a broken collar bone in trying him out.

But H. D. Rodger[10], another polo-playing lawyer, preferred the wild ponies. Rodge, noted for his booming voice, generosity, and athletic prowess, had at one time or another won every athletic event in Shanghai. He was big and powerful, and his idea of a good steady polo pony was a steeplechaser. Well do I remember the time a visiting player got stuck with one of Rodge's wild ponies.

10   Hewitt Douglas Rodger (1891-1948) practiced as a lawyer in Shanghai from the 1910s. He died in Shanghai in 1948.

We discovered this when all of a sudden the pony ran full speed the wrong way round over the steeplechase course adjoining the Kiangwan polo field. By some miracle the player was not thrown, and the pony calmed down sufficiently to return to the game.

H.D. Rodger on horseback before a paper hunt

The paper-hunt and polo seasons always produced a bumper crop of broken arms and collar bones. Shanghai's non-riding doctors always got more business out of the ponies than did the hard-riding lawyers.

Once I very nearly came a cropper. I was in a polo match at the Shanghai Race Club field when my pony got out of hand and jumped over a couple of tennis-court nets near the field. He then committed the unpardonable sin of jumping another fence on to the bowling green and thus upsetting a number of sedate British bowlers. None was injured, but next day I was waited upon by a committee. "Don't you know it's bad form to ride over a bowling green?" the spokesman asked. I admitted that I did but my pony didn't. However, I apologized for both of us.

Not only polo players but all Shanghai was horse-minded. From earliest days horse racing

Allman with his head mafoo, Kanpur Singh, and Dixie Dare. Courtesy Neal Burnham

The Shanghai Race Club in the centre of Shanghai pre 1935

Shanghai Race Club post 1935 with new clock tower

The race track. The Park Hotel and Grand Theatre can be seen on Park Road

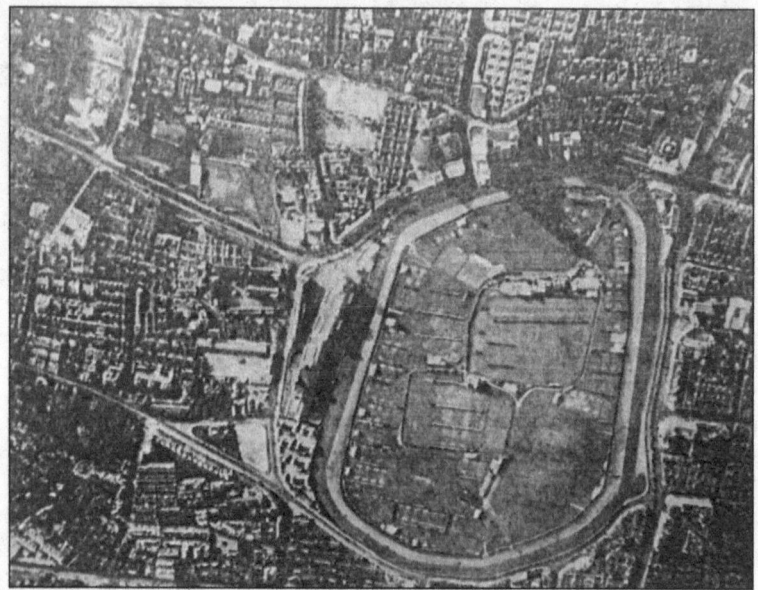

An aerial view of the Shanghai race course showing the polo fields

was an important part of Shanghai life. In fact the first recreation ground laid out back in the 1850's was the race course. Later the city boasted three race courses, The Shanghai Race Club, The Kiangwan Race Club, and The Chinese Jockey Club.

Racing was amateur, and the riders were all gentlemen jockeys. Owners often rode their own ponies, especially in the earlier days when ponies and feed were cheap. In the good old days, and actually up until a few years ago, it was possible to keep a China pony for as little as ten American dollars per month. Small stables were the rule; frequently an owner had only one pony.

My stable usually consisted of four or five polo ponies. If a pony couldn't race I'd use him for polo. If he'd do neither, and in that case he was pretty bad, I sold him. (To keep them from falling into the hands of the Japanese invaders my wife had my stable of ten ponies shot before she left Shanghai; that is, all but one foal which she gave to a Russian friend to keep until I got back.) For many years the Shanghai Race Club encouraged small stables as the stewards, mostly taipans of the bigger companies, thought it more desirable to have their young men out exercising ponies in the fresh air in early morning hours than exercising their elbows in smoke-filled bars late at night.

When Shanghai was young, racing days were traditional holidays. Banks and offices shut up shop, and the entire Chinese and foreign population turned out in full force for the big event.[11] Excitement and betting ran high. When the city grew too big commercially to shut up shop on race days, banks and some business houses kept open. This resulted in the stale Shanghai saying, "Work is the curse of the riding classes."

When the Japanese seized the Kiangwan Race Club in 1937 the members of that club were given club privileges by the Shanghai Race Club. But one Kiangwan member was objectionable to the S.R.C. and was refused privileges. He was barred from the club but got around this by purchasing a ticket for the public enclosure and then crossing over to the clubhouse. I advised the club stewards that it was their right to refuse to sell a ticket for the public enclosure to this man, or to any other man. Furthermore it was their privilege to expel him if he was persistent in attending. The objectionable character was about to bring suit to compel the club to sell him a ticket to the public stands when the declaration of war in 1941 halted his plan.

In no other place in the world was a man's club more important to him than in Shanghai. The American Club, five-story male sanctuary with luxurious fittings and some fifty rooms for members, was the center of social life for Americans. It was always the setting for the Fourth of July, Washington's

---

11   In 1927, during the prosecution of Leonard Husar (see Chapter 7), the former American District Attorney for corruption, the court adjourned for the afternoon on race day.

Carl Crow collecting for the library at the opening of American Club

Birthday, and other community gatherings.

One of my most difficult spare-time jobs was my one-man campaign to have apple pie served at the club at all times. For some obscure reason the cook did not want to provide this traditionally American dish. I fought with obstinate committees continuously for years until finally they all gave in, and apple pie was served at the club at any hour during the twenty-four.

The American Club, which thanks to Carl Crow boasted the best library in the Orient, was built in 1925 at a cost of a million and a quarter Chinese dollars, or at the rate of exchange then, approximately three hundred thousand American dollars. A million-dollar bond issue had been floated, but like most others the American Club found it difficult to pay off this indebtedness. The bond issue was revamped several times. About a year before Pearl Harbor some of the steely-eyed banking members

Shanghai American Club on Foochow Road when it first opened

The club after the Central Police Station was built next door

Cornerstone of the American Club

of the club decided that, although the bonds did not fall due until 1953, in view of the unsettled conditions the club building should be sold, the club reestablished in rented quarters, and the bondholders paid off, thus liquidating one of the Shanghai American community's outstanding obligations.

No doubt this was sound banking practice and proof that bankers are never sentimental. They were determined to sell the club regardless of values, but not even the hard-boiled bankers would consider an offer from the Japanese, who we knew were anxious to acquire the club. But when the bankers and their adherents received, from a bona fide Chinese purchaser, an offer of two million Chinese dollars (then worth only fifty thousand United States dollars) they were ready to sell.[12]

However, the unsentimental bankers soon found strong opposition to this proposed sale from the sentimentalists, of whom I was one. We took the stand that the club was an American

12   The offer was received in early 1941 and effectively voted down by the members. The offer came from Taiping Insurance Company ultimately owned by Chow Tso-Min who had close ties to the Japanese. This led to a headline in the *China Weekly Review*: "Are Japanese Trying to Buy the American Club?" (March 8, 1941, p7)

institution and opposed the sale at any price. In point of fact a three million dollar offer was refused. We realized that the club might be a war casualty at any time, but we preferred to have it go down with its flag flying rather than in any way to alter such an American institution. We all felt that in a sense selling the club would be the same thing as withdrawal from China, a step none of us had the slightest intention of taking voluntarily.

As it turned out the club did go down with the flag flying. The Japanese moved in on December 8, 1941, and bounced the members out. I do not know to what nefarious purpose it has been put.

Japanese flag over American Club

XI

THE BOLSHEVIKS

SHANGHAI'S CONSERVATIVE SET WAS sure that "that rebel Allman" had gone over to the Bolsheviks, lock, stock, and barrel, when in 1927 I represented the Russian government in effecting the release and repatriation of the former Russian military and political advisers to the Chinese government.

The Kuomintang (People's Party) was founded by Sun Yat-sen[1] in Canton in 1911, when China threw off the yoke of the Manchu rulers and became a republic. Although beset at every step by the most discouraging obstacles, the politically inexperienced Chinese patriots comprising the Kuomintang never lost faith in the destiny of their country and continued to work for the ideals of the revolution. Their main objective was a United China, but being inexperienced they stumbled from one idea to another in their attempts to accomplish this objective.

For a time Communism seemed the solution. In 1924 a number of Russian political and military advisers, including Michael

---

1   Sun Yat-sen (1866-1925) known in Chinese as 孫中山 (Sun Zhongshan). Yat sen (逸仙 Yixian) was a name given to him in Hong Kong and the Cantonese transliteration has become his standard English name. Sun had been a revolutionary for many years and became Provisional President of China in January 1912 following the successful overthrow of the Qing Dynasty. He soon ceded the position of the President to the much more militarily powerful Yuan Shikai. Sun founded the Kuomintang in 1912 and it stayed in government until 1915 when Yuan declared himself emperor. The Kuomintang moved its government to Guangzhou. With the assistance of the Soviet Union, the Kuomintang established the Whampoa Military Academy under Chiang Kai-shek. Sun died in 1925 and Chiang then led a Northern Expedition in 1927 to recapture the government of China.

Michael Borodin and General Galens , Russian advisers to the Kuomintang, later expelled by Chiang Kai-shek.

Borodin[2] and General Vasili Bluecher (alias General Galens)[3] were welcomed with open arms. These advisers continucd with the National government until the late summer of 1927.

Vast China with its innumerable dialects, lack of transportation and communication systems, and its strong individualistic or family way of life, had long been a divided country, rife with revolution and civil wars. On the face of it the plan of the Communist advisers for consolidation seemed a good one, but as it turned out, their tactics were wrong. They sought to arouse a strong nationalistic feeling by artificial means, mostly by working the army into a first-class hate against outside enemies.

---

2   Mikhail Markovich Borodin (1884-1951) was the alias of Mikhail Gruzenberg, a promi-
    nent Comintern agent. Borodin was the principal Russian adviser to the Kuomintang
    and helped establish the Whampoa Military Academy and form the alliance between
    the Kuomintang and Communists. Borodin was purged in 1950 and died in a prison
    camp in 1951.

3   Vasily Konstantinovich Blyukher (1889-1938) was a Soviet general. He was a major
    military commander in the Bolshevik revolution and served as the principal military
    adviser to the Kuomintang in China. He was known as General Galens in China. He
    was made a marshal of the Soviet Union in 1935. In 1938 he was purged allegedly for
    spying for Japan and died in prison. He was rehabilitated in 1956.

Ten years later this feeling had a normal birth when the country united in self-protection to fight off the Japanese aggressors. No artificial stimulation was needed. But in this earlier day the Russians seized upon every little grievance, real or fancied, and fanned it high.

The advisers pounced upon "unequal treaties," "extraterritoriality, "concessions," "imperialism," the always popular rallying cries to inflame the hot-headed, and once again the fiery dragon of anti-foreignism was stirred to lead the Eighth Route Army[4] on its march from Canton to Nanking, a march which culminated in the destruction of British and American missionary and commercial property and the murder of a number of foreigners, including half a dozen Americans, in Nanking when that city was invaded by the Nationalist army in February of 1927.[5]

At that almost too late date the cool-headed, saner element of the Nationalists, including Generalissimo Chiang Kai-shek, whose career was almost ruined by the Nanking fiasco, awoke to the fact that this particular advice was getting them nowhere. The country had not gained unity. On the other hand, it was gaining the enmity of friendly powers. For this reason, and perhaps others too, the Chinese con- cluded that they had better get rid of their Russian advisers. In the late summer of 1927 the Russians were dismissed.[6]

The two principals, Michael Borodin and General Galens,

---

4   The army that marched from Canton to Nanking on what was called a "Northern Expedition" was the National Revolutionary Army headed by Chiang Kai-shek. In 1924, Sun Yan-sen had created the Whampoa Military Academy outside Canton where Chinese troops had been trained by Russian advisers. Chiang was its commandant. The Eighth Route Army, a communist battalion, was not formed until 1937.

5   Allman underplays the Nanking incident. There were full-scale battles between foreigners and the Kuomintang with numerous foreign naval ships bombarding Chinese soldiers and rioters over three days.

6   This was part of an anti-Communist purge of the Kuomintang organized by Chiang Kai-shek.

escaped from Hankow, but the others were rounded up all over China, arrested, and concentrated at Shanghai for trial.

The government was undecided what to do with its prisoners. While the government was trying to make up its mind whether to court-martial the advisers or to try them in ordinary civil courts, the prisoners were handed over to the Shanghai district court, then transferred to Soochow. Ultimately they landed in the Nanking jail.[7]

The Chinese government not only made a clean sweep of all the Russian advisers but virtually expelled the Russian diplomatic and consular service from the country. Just before his departure the Russian consul-general at Shanghai asked my law firm, then Fleming and Allman, to represent his government in effecting the release of the advisers and arrange for their return to Russia. Why he chose our firm I really don't know — possibly because Fleming was so highly regarded by the Chinese and other nationals, or perhaps my name was known to him because of my former consular connections. Too, I had met many Russians when I sat as assessor on the Shanghai Mixed Court I was not a Bolshevik and had no deep feelings either one way or the other about the Communist cause. I simply took the advisers on as a legal case, and my job, as I saw it, was to get them out of jail and out of China.

I went to work at once to unravel the legal tangles. It was necessary for me to make numerous trips to Soochow to visit the prisoners. I found the jailer to be a decent but puzzled chap. He was at a loss as to how to treat his twelve Russian prisoners. He explained that he lacked proper facilities for these foreigners and

7   Five of the Russians were Messrs Socal (Zilbert), Kumanine (Zigon), Berg and Mr and Mrs Veger. Zilbert had been a military adviser to the Kuomintang. All five were acquitted by the Chinese courts in Nanking. "Imprisoned Russians Released", *NCH*, Apr 21, 1928, p107. "Nanking Court Finds Not Guilty Russians Accused by French Consul." *The China Weekly Review*, Apr 14, 1928, p194

asked me to purchase some necessary conveniences for them on my return to Shanghai. His list included blankets and Russian food. Of my own accord, I added several bottles of vodka.

The wives of several Russian advisers remained in Shanghai during the negotiations and now and then it was up to me to escort them, singly and in pairs, on visits to their husbands. On one occasion I was waiting on the Soochow station platform with two attractive Russian women when a missionary acquaintance came along. He bowed stiffly. Evidently he thought I had a harem concealed in Soochow, for he lost no time in calling on my wife. He made quite a point of casualness when he asked her, "Who are Mr. Allman's Russian *friends*?"

The prisoners were kept in jail for weeks while I argued with the procurator as to how they should be tried. I went so far as to file a writ of habeas corpus. This is not provided for in the code of criminal procedure but was provided for in the Chinese Provisional Constitution. This writ caused the procurator and judge no little embarrassment as we all knew that the government could, and might at any time, decide to court-martial the prisoners and take them out of the hands of the civil courts. The activities of several probably warranted charges of treason being brought against them. A decision on this touchy point was avoided by a transference of all prisoners to Nanking on the grounds that the court at Soochow had no jurisdiction.

It was toward the end of October that the Russians were incarcerated in Nanking's model prison[8]. Because I had to confer with them frequently, I commuted between Shanghai and Nanking. These overnight train trips were none too pleasant in those unsettled times. I remember once boarding a train almost

---

8   "Model prisons" were established in Republican China as part of the process of legal reform. They were run on Western lines and intended to rehabilitate prisoners. Foreigners were generally only imprisoned in model prisons.

wholly occupied by soldiers who evidently had taken seriously the anti-foreign doctrines advocated by the very prisoners I was defending.

They shouted, "*Yang kwei*" (foreign devil), and reviled me with other unpleasant names. I replied emphatically that I was no more of a devil than they were. When they discovered that I not only spoke their language but was able to curse proficiently in it as well, their hostile attitude changed. We were all pals by the time we reached Nanking.

All Americans and British had left the city after the tragedy of the preceding February and for some time the Russians and I were the only foreigners there. Winter nights and mornings can get damned chilly in China, and Bridge House, then the only modern hotel in the city, had been taken over by a Chinese cavalry regiment and was anything but comfortable for the transient guest. After a couple of freezing visits I asked the prison warden if he'd mind putting me up. He was reasonable about it and gave me a good-sized cell, far more comfortable than any room I could find in the old-fashioned, unheated hotels. Also, conditions being still so unsettled, I felt considerably safer there.

It was during one of these trips, on January 27,1928, while I was occupying a cell in Nanking's prison, that our youngest child, John, was born in Shanghai. I'd always said that there ought to be a law whereby fathers could be retired to solitary confinement or otherwise put out of the way for the birth of their children, for they are almost as useless at births as they are as bridegrooms at the wedding ceremony. This time at least I was out of the way.

There was one difficult moment when the fate of my Russians hung in the balance. A high-ranking Chinese general, whom I had consulted numerous times, accompanied me to the prison one day to see a man who, ironically, had been his former adviser. By this time the prison was a second home and the warden and I were like brothers. Unfortunately the warden had never before seen the general, mention of whose name made strong men quake.[9]

When we entered the warden glared at the general, then motioned me to one side. "Who is this dressed-up fellow with you and what does he think he wants?" he stage-whispered. There was an awkward pause, then I whispered back the general's name. The warden's belligerent manner changed to one of awe. Swiftly he snapped to polite attention and personally escorted the general into his old friend's cell.

My trips to Soochow and Nanking did not go unnoticed in Shanghai. I knew the French municipal police kept a dossier on the Russian prisoners. Many of them had been brought to Shanghai from outports and landed in the French Concession, where they had been received by the French police and then turned over to the Chinese authorities. In fact, two Russians who might have escaped were arrested on landing in the French Concession because a French consul in a south China port had wired the warning that two Russian anarchists were arriving by a certain ship.

It didn't take long for me to catch on to the fact that I was being followed on my out-of-town trips. My shadow was a White Russian in the criminal investigation division of the French municipal police. As my spy and I were about the only two foreigners doing much traveling during these uncertain days, we were thrown together of necessity. We became quite chummy and now and again shared a meal.

One morning in Nanking when I was at breakfast with four Russian women and their children of assorted ages, Pop-up, as I called him, sidled over and asked permission to take our picture.

---

9 The general is likely to have been General Tan Yan-Kai (譚延闓) (1880-1930), who was Chairman of the Nationalist government. Zilbert had been his adviser.

I didn't know if he had a blackmail scheme of his own up his sleeve, nor did I particularly care. There was no use in objecting. I knew he had taken others -surreptitiously, he thought. I assured him that I was only too pleased, indeed flattered, but I insisted that he get in the picture too. I helped him rig up the camera so that this was possible. He didn't like it but he knew it was the only way of getting a picture of Allman and his Bolshevik women and children.

I learned from another member of the French police that they'd built up a good-sized dossier on me. When the case was over, I couldn't resist sending the chief of police a photograph of myself with my compliments. I suggested that he might need a really good picture to complete the dossier and also, in case his detectives had slipped up, he was at perfect liberty to consult my files to ascertain the reason for my many trips to Nanking. Somehow, I don't believe he appreciated my little joke.

Finally, after some months spent in questioning the prisoners about what they were doing, what they had said, where they had been, whom they had seen, I had a complete story which I reported to the Chinese authorities and asked for the release of the prisoners without a court trial. I managed to persuade the government that the best solution for all concerned was the repatriation of the Russian advisers. This course

IMPRISONED RUSSIANS RELEASED

Arrival in Shanghai on Their Way to Russia

The five Russians who had been detained by the Nationalist authorities for about six months on the charge of conspiring to upset the Government, were released on Monday morning in Nanking and arrived in Shanghai on Monday afternoon. They are Messrs. Socal (Zilbert), Kumanino (Zigon), Berg and Veger and Mrs. Veger. They are expected to leave for Russia some time this week.

This case has evoked considerable interest because of the processes of law involved in the case. The five Russians were detained on suspicion and were moved from city to city without due trial or charge until last month when they were given a trial in Nanking and acquitted. They were nevertheless detained to give "interested parties," an opportunity to appeal from the acquittal. The lawyers representing the Russians were Messrs. Fleming and Allman.

Zilbert was the only really important personality among them. He has been the Military Adviser to some of the most important Nationalist militarists, including Generals Tan Yen-kai, Li Tsung-jen and Ho Ying-ching. He was one of the few corps commanders sent to China by Soviet Russia.

Allman's Russian clients released

was adopted, but the Chinese government wanted me to take full responsibility that they would not return to China. This was impossible as I had no control over them.

We compromised. A Chinese government official and I escorted the prisoners from Nanking to Shanghai and personally saw them, their wives, and children safely aboard a ship bound directly for Vladivostok. Thus the case closed.

As a result of this association the law firm of Fleming and Allman was for a time swamped with Russian cases. Among many others I remember defending a Red Russian newspaper man charged with "returning from expulsion from the International Settlement and China."

In the months preceding the Soviet exodus Vladimir Rover[10] had represented the Tass news agency as Shanghai correspondent. At the time of deportation he had accompanied Comrade Koslovsky to Vladivostok to gather news stories of the trip. On his return to his Shanghai office he was arrested.

It was my contention that Rover had not been deported; that, as he was neither a military nor political adviser, nor a diplomat, there had been no order for deportation. He had left voluntarily in the line of duty and, in returning to Shanghai, believed that he had acted legitimately.

Although the Chinese military appeared in court they presented no documents, and Rover was given his freedom on five hundred dollars' bail. His Soviet passport, however, was taken over until all evidence was gathered, and this hampered Rover's news-gathering activities. Tiring of his pseudo freedom, Rover

---

10   Vladimir Aronovitch Rover had had his offices at the Russian Consulate. British re-
     cords record him as an agent for the GPU (a predecessor of the KGB). William Fleming,
     Allman's partner, had met Rover in Harbin and arranged his passage to Shanghai.
     Allman met Rover on arrival in Shanghai and was present when he was arrested by the
     SMP. The Provisional Court ordered that Rover be handed over to a representative of
     the Chinese Garrison Commissioner who then promptly released him. Rover then left
     Shanghai. "The Tass Agency Representative in Court", NCH, May 26, 1928; TNA file
     KV 2/2378. He returned to Shanghai soon after and stayed until 1933.

```
                    SECRET.


        Report by Shanghai Municipal Police dated 18-5-28.
        ------

            Arrest of Soviet Representative of Tass Agency.

                Accompanied by P.C.S. Ovsiannikoff, a
        Japanese Consular Policeman and several representatives
        of the Chinese Authorities, I arrested on a Despatch
        Warrant: Vladimir Aronovitch Rover, Soviet Representative
        of Tass Agency on his arrival here on the s.s. "Sakaki
        Maru" at 7-30 p.m. on May 17.  He was accompanied by his
        wife Elizabeth Rover, who is residing at 6 Carter Road.

                Rover was in possession of a certificate of
        Tass Agency, which certified that he was appointed
        correspondent of Tass Agency in China on March 15, 1928
        and that his term expired on October 1, 1928.  He was also
        in possession of a Soviet passport No. 3560 issued in
        Moscow on March 10, 1928, and a Chinese Registration paper
        No. 1666 issued in Harbin.   Their luggage consisted of
        two trunks which on being searched were found to contain
        only personal effects.

                Rover, on being questioned, stated that he
        had come to Shanghai to take over the local branch of Tass
        Agency from Mr. Strauss, 16 Rue Wantz, French Concession,
        and further stated that he met Mr. Fleming, the lawyer, in
        Harbin who had arranged his arrival here.  Rover was met on
        arrival by Mr. Allman, Mr. Fleming's partner and Mr.
        Soulevich of the Chinese Eastern Railway.

                The prisoner was escorted direct to Central
        Station and will be brought before the Provisional Court
        this morning when a deputy from the Military Headquarters
        of the local Defence Commissioner has promised to attend
        with the proper authority and make application for him to
        be handed over.
```

SMP report of Rover's arrest

eventually gave up and returned to Russia of his own accord.

When in February of 1928 the Chinese Eastern Railway[11] brought criminal action in the French Mixed Court against V. A. Chilikin, editor of the White Russian newspaper *Outre*, for alleged libel, we represented the railway[12]. As neither Fleming

---

11 The China Eastern Railway was a railway built by Imperial Russia across Manchuria. The Russian government had jurisdiction over the railway line and a 60-metre zone next to it. In 1924 the Soviets had taken over the operation of the zone from the defeated White Russian Army. China could not expel the Russians from the railway because of their treaty rights. The flag of the railway from 1925 to 1932 bore the hammer and sickle.

12 "Russian Newspaper sued for libel" NCH Feb 25, 1928, p315 & March 3, 1928, p361

nor I was fluent in French we called in Monsieur J. Barraud[13], noted French advocate, to plead the case for us in court.

On January 5, 1928, the *Outre* had published an article which stated that the Russian Communists, having been ousted from other organizations, had decided to utilize the commercial agencies of the Chinese Eastern Railway as Communist agencies and that for this purpose they had already sent funds and instructions to the commercial agency pending arrival of the qualified Soviet specialists.

In our petition for the plaintiffs we pointed out that the commercial agencies of the C.E.R. acted under strictest control of the Chinese authorities, who would not tolerate any political action by the agencies nor by any Russian members of the agency. Such rumors, our petition claimed, were of a nature to prejudice claims against the C.E.R. and its Russian staff. Branding them as Communists so soon after the 1927 disturbances might result in

The Chinese Eastern Railway flag bearing the hammer and sickle

13   Julien Barraud came to China in the early 1910s to teach law at Peking National University. He moved to Shanghai in 1917 and commenced practice as a lawyer. He was made a Chevalier of the Legion of Honour in 1933.

Allman represents the CER in the French Mixed Court

closing of the offices.

We wanted immediate retraction of the statement and a public apology printed in the defendant's paper and in the leading foreign and Chinese language papers of Shanghai. But Chilikin refused, and our client sought further reparation to include, in addition to a published apology, payment of one thousand taels damages plus costs, suppression of the *Outre* and dismissal of the editor.

But we lost. Chilikin was acquitted. The court found that. Chilikin's remarks were not libelous; that he had merely published a communication from Harbin, which read in part:

The Soviet administration in Harbin are studying counter measures to be taken with regard to the situation existing in the South, particularly at Shanghai, after the closing here of the consulate and other organizations. The solution of this situation has been quickly found by Communists. They have decided to establish, with the least delay possible, special credits for augmenting the commercial activity of the Chinese Eastern Railway.

In handing down his judgment the judge commented, "It has not been established that the facts reported by Chilikin were true or untrue, or if they were false that he knew of their falsity. The article did not injure the personal credit of the plaintiff."

This judgment has always seemed unfair to me, particularly as the editor had not minced words in saying that shippers using the C.E.R. had to pay higher freight than if they had used the Japanese Railway. But at that time assisting the Japanese Railway was not the treasonable offense it would be today. Of course, none of us then had the remarkable knowledge that hindsight brings. It wasn't altogether the fault of the Chinese that they rid themselves of the Red Star instead of building barricades to keep out the rays of the menacing Rising Sun.

Eventually, as a result of the onrush of Japanese armies in 1931 and 1932, all was forgiven insofar as the Soviet Russians were concerned, and on December 12, 1932, an agreement was signed by Dr. W. W. Yen[14] and Maxim Litvinoff[15]. Diplomatic relations were restored. Once again the Russian Embassy on the banks of the yellow Whangpoo[16] became the scene of gay, diplomatic receptions. Once more champagne was served in crystal goblets, and black caviar was brought down from Vladivostok for the especial delight of Shanghai's capitalistic and imperialistic gourmets, as well as for the democratic-minded Chinese.

By this time anti-foreignism and anti-Communism had died natural deaths in Chinese political circles, and Shanghai had forgotten that it had once called Allman a Bolshevik. The stuffed shirts who attended the Soviet receptions didn't even bother

---

14   Yan Huiqing (顏惠慶) or Yen, Wei Ching Williams/W.W. Yen in English (1877–1950) was a Chinese writer, politician, and diplomat from Shanghai. He was China's first ambassador to the Soviet Union and was a delegate to the League of Nations in WWII.
15   Maxim Maximovich Litvinov (1876-1951) was a Russian revolutionary who served in many diplomatic positions for the Soviet Union. He was briefly imprisoned in the United Kingdom in 1918. He died in 1951 in a car accident that many consider to have been an assassination carried out on the orders of Stalin.
16   The building to this day serves as the Russian consulate in Shanghai. For a time when China and Russia had broken off diplomatic relations it was used as a Seaman's Club for foreign seamen.

The Russian Consulate in Shanghai

to blush when I'd heckle them with a loud greeting, "Imagine meeting you here!"

XII
Every Man A Gentleman

THE THREE HAPPIEST DAYS of my life, chronologically speaking, were the day I entered the University of Virginia, the day of my marriage, and the day I said good-by to Stanley internment camp and thumbed my nose at my Japanese jailers.

No one in Virginia, or any other part of the South for that matter, needs to use the full title. Everybody knows what is meant by "the University." I, for one at least, took seriously the legend appearing on the University's entrance gate, "Ye shall know the truth and the truth shall make you free."[1] Ever since those long-ago school days, I have been seeking both truth and freedom. But my truthfulness, most undiplomatic, my best friends tell me, has lost me a number of clients. In the long run, however, I've found that both truth and frankness pay.

I've always followed the policy of telling a client just what I thought about his affairs. I contend that the client, who after all is the one who foots the bill, is entitled to an honest and candid opinion. Because of my truthfulness with one client, I was fired. I considered it a high compliment, as he only wanted a lawyer to find some legal loophole that would protect him in a shady stock-promotion scheme.

The University taught me a number of other things. It has

---

1 This phrase is inscribed on a pediment sculpture in front of Cabell Hall at the University of Virginia. It is from John 8:32.

been a lifelong regret that my university life had to be cut short, but I believe I learned a few things there that have proved more worthwhile than a degree. At the University one of the first things one learns is to assume that every man is a gentleman until he proves himself otherwise; to pursue no man to his undeserved hurt, nor any woman to her tears. For an academic degree what more should anyone know?

Perhaps the idea of dealing with every man as a gentleman is a bit on the idealistic side, but I believe it to be an error, if error it is, in the right direction. I have always followed this policy and it has worked in the main, although I have been badly stung on a few occasions. I have one vivid recollection of a time when I was not only disillusioned but socked squarely in the bank account.

Shanghai was always a hospitable place where almost any presentable person could get around socially, and letters of introduction were accepted without question. One day a well-dressed stranger presented himself at my office with a letter from a Hong Kong acquaintance, a prominent citizen I'd known casually for years. Wilding, which was not his real name, informed me that he was in Shanghai for a few weeks to see about a local agent for his business. One thing led to another, including our having a few drinks and tiffin together. My offer to put him up at my club was accepted.

A day or two later Wilding dropped by my office. Apologetically he asked, "Will you collect a promissory note for me?"

"Glad to," I answered.

He produced the note and I wrote a letter to the maker, a Dmitri Popoff, reminding him of his obligation and requesting payment. Back came a most pathetic letter in which Popoff recited a long hard-luck tale. He offered to pay at the rate of one hundred dollars per month and enclosed his first payment

Trick on American Lawyer

Yang Jen-tang, Fukienese, who recently defrauded Mr. N. F. Allman, American lawyer, of more than $3,000 by raising the amount of a cheque made out by Mr. Allman, and who was arrested by police when he attempted to play a similar trick on another American attorney-at-law, Mr. C. S. Franklin, on Friday was sentenced to three years' imprisonment by Judge Feng in the First Special District Court.

The prisoner, together with a man named Kuo Kiang-pu, called at the office of Mr. Allman, on June 12 and asked the lawyer to send a letter to one Li Chia-ping to pay a debt. This Mr. Allman did and he soon received a cheque for $100 from Li, payable by the East Asia Bank. Mr. Allman cashed the cheque and deposited the amount in the Tatung Bank. At the request of the prisoner, who posed himself as one Mr. Teng, Mr Allman made out another cheque for $100, payable by the Tatung Bank. Through chemical processes, the prisoner and his accomplice changed the amount into one of $3,900 and cashed the cheque at the bank concerned. The prisoner and his accomplice were arrested several days after when they called on the office of Mr. C. S. Franklin and tried to play a similar trick. Mr. Franklin at once recalled Mr. Allman's experience and had the two men placed under arrest.

At the police station, the man Kuo Kiang-pu said he was a Formosan and he was handed over to the Japanese authorities.

The true story of the trick on Allman?

in cash. This I deposited to the firm's account and sent Wilding our check, together with a letter explaining the matter.

Wilding left town soon after and that was the last I thought of him until our bank statement came in the first of the month.

The firm's balance was off to the sum of forty-eight hundred dollars. Investigation disclosed that my gentlemanly client had raised my one hundred dollar check to forty-nine hundred dollars and deposited it in a bank in which he had just opened an account. He waited only long enough for the check to clear, then collected the forty-nine hundred dollars, closed his account, and skipped town. I was left holding a deficit and a handful of club chits he had signed and charged to my club account.[2]

Furthermore it developed that only one man was involved

---

2   Unless Allman was exceedingly gullible (which is unlikely) Allman was, in fact, defrauded in this way by a Chinese, Yang Jen-Tang, in 1933. Yang (posing as a Mr Teng) instructed Allman to collect $100 from Li Chia-ping. Allman sent a demand letter and received a cheque for $100, he then paid Yang the $100 by cheque drawn on his firm. Yang altered the cheque to $3,000 and cashed it. He was caught when he tried the same trick on C.S. Franklin. Yang was sentenced to three years imprisonment by Judge Feng of the First Special District Court. One of Yang's accomplices, Kuo Kiang-pu was Formosan and was handed to the Japanese authorities. "Trick on American Lawyer", *NCH*, Dec 6, 1933, p390. Allman may have invented "Wilding" to make the story more palatable to American readers or may not have wanted to admit being defrauded by a Chinese.

in this entire transaction. That one man was Wilding, who had forged the letter of introduction, prepared the promissory note, rented the office under the name of D. Popoff, and written the heartbreaking letter. All this he had done to gain a check with a legitimate signature. I haven't seen him since, but now I take my time in bestowing hospitality on gentlemanly-appearing strangers.

For some reason the average layman will pay every bill he owes except those owed to his doctor, dentist, or lawyer, in spite of the fact that all three usually render him service when he is in extremis. Unfortunately for his creditors the extremis all too frequently is over or forgotten when time for payment rolls around.

Dealing with a client on the premise that he was a gentleman and that all gentlemen eventually pay their just debts didn't work out to my advantage. I loathed the idea of suing a client over a bill and did this rarely. There was one time, however, when I thoroughly enjoyed such a suit.

The client in the case was a dangerous type, and I wanted to get rid of him when I found out that what he wanted was not a lawyer's honest legal opinion but someone to rubberstamp his off-color transactions.

Shanghai has always had its fair proportion of remittance men. One of these is Leon[3], now a captive of the Japs. Leon is the wastrel brother of a famous American tycoon and, so the story goes, as long as Leon remains outside the United States the brother pays him two hundred and fifty American dollars per month. But this amount was never enough for Leon, who fancied

3   Rudolph William Mayer (1889-1951) the brother of Louis B. Mayer of the Metro Gold-
     wyn Mayer (Allman's client - see Chapter 14). Mayer had fled to Shanghai in 1934
     when he had been charged with fraud in Baltimore. He was in and out of the US Court
     for China during his stay in China. After is repatriation to America, the charges in
     Baltimore were dropped when his brother paid out his victim. He was sued for a stock
     scam in California in 1948 and lost. He died in a hotel fire in 1951.

himself as a great entrepreneuer. Leon, a beachcomber de luxe, adopted Shanghai as his home and immediately set about the development of Big Business.

I learned later that Leon always had some scheme up his sleeve. The scheme usually involved what is known on the China Coast as "the old comprador game." But first what is a comprador? The word itself stems from the Portuguese *compra* which means to buy. The comprador, a China Coast institution since earliest trading days, is the Chinese middleman between foreign enterprise and the Chinese market. It was the custom in many of the smaller businesses for the comprador to finance the firm and its transactions. This gave a crooked promoter the opportunity to play the comprador game which goes something like this:

A promoter first rents and equips an imposing office on the installment plan. After a gullible comprador has been given a

Louis B. Mayer Hollywood movie magnate and brother of Rudolph, "a beachcomber de luxe"

Mayer Sued By Eight Chinese In Stock Deal

Compradores Seek To Recover Newmilks Losses

Mr. Rudolph W. Mayer, former manager of Newmilks (1936) Ltd. and main figure in the long court battle over the dairy company's affairs, appeared in the U. S. court for China yesterday to answer the suit of eight Chinese partners who charge him with bilking them out of $26,000 in a stock deal.

The plaintiffs, compradores doing business as Yu Shing and Partners, seek $26,000 plus interest and costs in return for investments and loans they allegedly made in the company. Attorney Myron Wiener told the court that in April of last year the plaintiffs bought debentures totaling $13,400, and that subsequently money was advanced to Newmilks to the amount of $11,255.40.

Rudolph Mayer sued

peek at the luxurious offices, the promoter's next step is to induce him to make a cash deposit, supposedly to guarantee the faithful performance of himself and staff and out of which, following old custom, he also pays the salary of the foreign manager, or promoter. The comprador pays the firm's bills monthly and recoups later from his employer.

One drawback to Leon's plans was that he had nothing with which to settle his bills. His only assets were the remittance check, which he had no intention of spending in this way, and a remote desire to obtain a good agency at some future time. Leon was a fast talker but not fast enough to talk himself into a good credit rating. To give his transactions a flavor of plausibility he managed to pick up a little local business, mainly buying and selling an occasional used automobile.

Naturally, in time the comprador tired of paying the bills, but Leon, who gave every appearance of having unlimited collateral, usually bluffed him into continuing, at least until the deposit was exhausted. One comprador sued to recover his deposit, but the suit failed because Leon had been just clever enough to stay within the law. Too, Leon anticipated his failures and always had some new plan under way. He was adroit in keeping the outgoing and failing comprador and his staff from meeting the newest victim. I've never been able to figure out just how he managed to work this. But until the Japs took over, Leon had been sharp enough to keep his plans going and himself out of jail. The last I heard Leon was taking the Japanese water cure at Bridge House Prison.[4]

I met Leon soon after his arrival in Shanghai when he came to consult me. I found him out quickly enough, but getting rid of him was another matter. I certainly didn't want to be mixed up in his comprador game, and he wasn't the type to reform. After some thought I hit upon the idea of sending him a good stiff bill. I really did not expect him to pay it but thought it would keep him out of the office.

Upon receipt of the bill he phoned at once. "Your advice was no blankety-blank good and I won't pay!" he screamed. His abusive language made me mad. I made a date to meet him in court, got a judgment against him, and to his surprise and mine too, collected. This was something new to him, as he thought the law was only for other people. Instead of getting rid of him as a client, I had him from then on always around after legal advice. I grew agile in ducking out back entrances and darting into doorways whenever I saw him coming.

Incidentally it isn't easy for a lawyer to avoid unwanted clients. No matter where a lawyer practices, Middletown, U.S.A., or Shanghai, China, there's at least one pest buzzing around to annoy him. My personal affliction was a Mrs. R.,[5] a German woman whom I first encountered back in my consular days

---

4   Bridge House Apartments in Hongkew were converted into a prison by the Japanese Gendarmerie. Mayer was spent some time there before being repatriated. The building still stands at 478 North Sichuan Road.

5   Miss Mary G Rabenow. "Slander Action in the US Court", *NCH*, July 16, 1921, p215 and *Mary G. Rabenow v Pauline A. Grimes and Andrew H. Woods, The Weekly Review*, March 3, 1923, p40 & March 10, 1923, p76. She brought an application in 1925 before a new judge seeking to reinstate the case. It was dismissed.

and who has been trying to sue someone ever since.

In 1916 or 1917, Dr. Andrew Woods[6] of the Peking Union Medical College examined Mrs. R. and diagnosed her a paranoic. This so enraged the good lady that she brought suit against Dr. Woods. The case, heard in the United States Court for China, was dismissed. This angered her further and she transferred her hate from the doctor

Dr Andrew Woods

to the judge. She stormed into the consulate and demanded that I send a cablegram for her to President Wilson denouncing the United States Court in general and the judge in particular. I refused, explaining that she could send her own cablegram to whomever she wished whenever she pleased but not such a one to the President, and certainly not at government expense.

From that point on I bore all the brunt of her delusions of persecution; doctor, judge, and court were forgotten. For a quarter century she dogged my path. But somewhere along the line her attitude toward me changed. It was my bad luck that in later years she pursued me because she wanted me to take her cases into court.

Side-stepping unwanted clients isn't a lawyer's only problem. There's the difficult one of fees. I'd be much happier if I could practice law without ever bothering about them. It embarrasses me to send out bills. Whenever a client indicates that the bill is too low I am happy. Believe it or not, I've enjoyed this pleasant

---

6   Dr Andrew Henry Woods (1872-1956) spent about 20 years in China. He founded the
     medical department of the Canton Christian College. He served in the army in France
     in WWI. In 1919, he was recruited to head the Department of Neurology at the Peking
     Union Medical College.

experience on more than one occasion, and several times I've had clients voluntarily pay me more than I've charged. Once a client more than doubled the bill.

When Chinese clients paid they frequently sent along bolts of silk, elaborate screens, or heirloom vases in addition to their checks. One of my Chinese clients was so pleased with the outcome of his case that in his own calligraphy he wrote a lauditory scroll to hang in my office. This proved more than a little embarrassing as the scroll was large and the client, a famous calligraphist, had let himself go in relating how "Mr. Ah Lo-man"[7] (literal Chinese translation of my name meaning "Full of Pleasure") had done wonders for the writer when he was in trouble and commending me to all and sundry as a sure-fire solution to any legal difficulty. I hung the scroll up for awhile lest I offend the client who came by daily to gaze upon his art, but I blushed whenever I found anyone else reading it. I was afraid the Far Eastern Bar Association would take me to task for personal advertising.

By and large I've found that most men are gentlemen and can be counted on to do the right thing, especially in the matter of paying their just debts — some day. And not all gentlemen are men. Many of them are women. One I discovered shortly after I returned to this country after my repatriation.

I had been in New York City less than two months when I received the following letter:

Dear Mr. Allman:

The enclosed check of fifty dollars I have long planned to send to you. It is from my son on his account. He is now somewhere at sea. Of course there will be more to send you later. The enclosed envelope is one I addressed

---

7   Allman's Chinese name was: "阿樂滿"

to you several years ago to send you a remittance and then saw in the paper that the Japanese were trying to have you and others expelled, so I did not feel you would get it. We are very pleased that you arrived safely and perhaps after all it is best for you to receive these payments over here. I have the statements and accounts all intact. With best regards,

Sincerely,

For a time I couldn't recall what it was all about. Then it all came back to me, and I remembered a case I had closed seven years earlier and marked off my books. This case concerned the mysterious Mr. X, who for a time provided Shanghai with considerable conversation. It also concerned two romantic young Americans who were drawn into it through a spirit of adventure plus the desire to make a little easy money. I'll make a stab at unraveling this highly complicated yarn. Because they've forgotten tall adventure and settled down to serious things, and because they never actually were members of the espionage ring, I'll give fictitious names to the two Americans. The others were found guilty and do not deserve to be shielded.

To begin somewhere near the beginning: On August 24, 1935, after a lengthy trial punctuated by mysterious disappearances and reappearances in first one and then another jail, one Joseph Walden, known also as Mr. X, was convicted on charges of espionage and sentenced by the Hupeh High Court to fifteen years' imprisonment. Walden claimed innocence and maintained that he was not working for the Third Internationale, although he did admit employment by an international group to study political and financial questions in China. He countercharged that he had been framed by the Japanese. In light of more recent events, perhaps he was.

THE "MYSTERY MAN" IN DISTRICT COURT

THE DEFENDANT

THE DEFENDANT'S LAWYER

THE REPRESENTATIVE OF THE CHINESE MILITARY AUTHORITIES

Joseph Walden appears in the Second High Court in Shanghai defended by French Lawyer, M. Paul Premet

To all appearances the case was closed. Then came a series of startling happenings and the case took on an even greater international flavor. First, in Hankow, B. E. Naidis[8], a Shanghai

___

8   Brian Edward Naidis aka Benedict Naidis was Russian but claimed to be Dutch. According to British intelligence reports he was most likely a Russian military intelligence agent.

The Mysterious Mr X

In 1935, a mysterious foreigner, known as Mr X, was arrested by the Shanghai Municipal Police on charges of being a Russian spy. He claimed to be Joseph Walden and that he was French. This led to arguments over whether he should be tried by French or Chinese courts until the French denied any knowledge of him. According to research into Soviet files by Dr. David Chambers, a former British diplomat, Walden was Yakov Bronin, the leader in China of the USSR's military intelligence service, the Razvedyvatel'noe Upravlenie. He had a number of aliases including, Maksim Rivosh. After a hearing in the Shanghai Second High Court (shown above), he was sent to Hankow to trial and sentenced to 15 years in prison by the Hubei High Court, although he only served three. His imprisonment led to an escape plan where Allman's clients pretended to be officers of the Shanghai Municipal Police to try to enter Walden's prison and then substitute one of their number for Walden.

Others have claimed that Walden was Eugene Dennis, who after WWII, was the head of the Communist Party of the USA. Dennis (who had been born Francis Xavier Waldron) was in Shanghai in the early 1930s working as a Russian agent under the pseudonym Paul Eugene Walsh with the code name MILTON. He left Shanghai in 1934 for Moscow via Trieste and Poland. It is possible that he could have returned to Shanghai by late 1934. Dennis and Walden bear a striking resemblance as shown by the photos to the right. Walden and Dennis were both physically very strong; it took 6 policemen to retrain Walden when he was arrested. MI5 described Paul Walsh as having "very wide shoulders giving the impression of great physical strength." The SMP had had Dennis/Walsh under surveillance when he was in Shanghai and it is likely would have identified him if he had been Walden. Perhaps, however, the prison substitution plot, in fact, succeeded and Dennis/Walsh imprisoned in Walden's place.

Yakov Bronin aka Joseph Walden

Allman himself hints that there is more to the case than meets the eye. He refers to "secret instructions" from the US Ambassador, and a trial in Shanghai being "squeezed" into the court calendar with a very light penalty imposed. There does appear to have been something the American authorities were trying to hide. Dennis claimed that he had been working in America's interests while in China. Perhaps he had been.

See further: David Ian Chambers, *Shanghai's "Mysterious Westerner": The Walden Affair And Soviet Military Intelligence Operations In China, 1933–1935*; and "Noulens and Walden Freed from Prison, Now reported to be residing in Shanghai", *China Press*, July 7, 1938, p3.

Eugene Dennis in the 1950s

SUPPLEMENT No. 3 OF 1935

To

THE STRAITS SETTLEMENTS POLICE

SPECIAL BRANCH

POLITICAL INTELLIGENCE JOURNAL

UNIDENTIFIED FOREIGN COMMUNIST
ARRESTED IN SHANGHAI ON 5TH MAY, 1935,
WHO CLAIMS TO BE
"JOSEPH WALDEN", A FRENCH NATIONAL

Information is required by the Shanghai Municipal Police which will help to establish the identity of an unknown communist arrested in Shanghai on 5th May, 1935, whose photograph is given above, and whose description is as follows:—

Age —About 40 years.

Height —5′ 8″.

Build —Powerful. Possesses great physical strength.

Hair —Light brown, turning grey at back and sides. Grown long on left side so that it can be brushed across scalp to hide bald patch.

Eyes —Grey, with red rims. Weak-looking.

Eyebrows —Brown and bushy.

Face —Fleshy and somewhat puffed. Slightly double chin.

Hands —Appear like those of a manual worker, with wrists abnormally thick.

Special marks —Small scar on right index finger. Small perpendicular "half-moon" scar ½ inch long, on left side of chin.

He appears to understand Russian, French, German and English.

After a month's detention he has claimed to be "Joseph Walden", of French nationality, but this is doubtful. He was found in possession of four passports, none of which belonged to him.

He was found in possession of several copies of the right-hand photograph above, (with spectacles), which according to the experts, is a photograph of himself.

The photograph without spectacles was taken after arrest.

Any information about this man's possible identity may be sent to this office, or direct to the Shanghai Municipal Police.

———o———

Singapore,
31st *May*, 1935.   **Special Branch.**

A Singapore Special Branch notice seeking information on Walden

NORWOOD F. ALLMAN

Form 13.
G. Com-10-33

SHANGHAI MUNICIPAL POLICE.
FINGER PRINT RECORD.

No.

Classification

RIGHT HAND. 右 手

1.—Right Thumb 右拇指	2.—R. Fore Finger 右二指	3.—R. Middle Finger 右中指	4.—R. Ring Finger 右四指	5.—R. Little Finger 右小指

[FOLD.] [FOLD.]

Impressions to be so taken that the flexture of the last joint shall be immediately above the black line marked (Fold). If the impression of any digit be defective a second print may be taken in the vacant space above it.
When a digit is missing or so injured that the impression cannot be obtained, or is deformed and yields a bad print, the nature of the injury should be noted in the space provided for that digit and "healed" or "unhealed" specified.

LEFT HAND. 左 手

6.—Left Thumb 左拇指	7.—L. Fore Finger 左二指	8.—L. Middle Finger 左中指	9.—L. Ring Finger 左四指	10.—L. Little Finger 左小指

[FOLD] [FOLD]

LEFT HAND. 左 手
Dabbed Impressions of Four Fingers Taken Simultaneously.

RIGHT HAND. 右 手
Dabbed Impressions of Four Fingers Taken Simultaneously.

IMPORTANT. No prisoner other than the prisoner whose finger prints are being taken should be present while that operation is being done. (1) The Identification Record should first be filled in and the prisoner's left thumb print immediately placed thereon: (2) the finger prints should then be taken on the form provided and (3) the name of the person taking the impressions, the date and Station, should be noted in spaces provided at the foot of the finger print record which, if in order, should be signed by the officer on duty.

Impressions taken by		Date received
Date		Classified by
Where taken		Checked by
Officer on duty		Passed Correct

SMP Fingerprint card for Walden

225

Brian Naidis, Eugene Brinson and Carl Lemcke who tried to free Walden from Chinese prison in Hankow.

motorcar salesman, was arrested on the charge that he had acted as messenger for Walden. Then, on secret instructions from the United States Ambassador, Nelson T. Johnson, the United States district attorney, Felthan Watson[9], flew to Hankow to investigate the arrests of two Americans implicated in the case. The two, Paul Loomis and Fred Johnson[10], also Shanghai motorcar salesmen, were named with Naidis as being involved in a plot to liberate Joseph Walden, alias Mr. X, who, it now developed, was actually a Dr. Maximum Rivosh of Berlin.

The three salesmen were caught because of their too frequent airplane trips to Hankow. The police could not understand why so many automobile salesmen were making so many trips to a place where so few people used automobiles and where scarcely half a dozen were sold from one year's end to another. Shadowing the three suspects, the police found them making

9   Felthan Watson (1902-1987) was from St Louis, Missouri, the same town as judge Milton Helmick and had been appointed on his recommendation. He served as District Attorney for two years from 1934 to 1936 before returning to Washington DC as special Assistant to the Attorney General. He later served in the navy in WWII and was a trial attorney for the Justice Department.

10   Their real names were Carl J. Lemcke (Loomis) and Eugene Brinson (Johnson). Naidis' full name was Brian E. Naidis. Lemcke and Brinson left China soon after the case closed and were living in New York in 1938. "Ex-Shanghai Residents Get together" *China Press*, March 18, 1938

rather clumsy attempts to contact the man in jail. The story went that the three had been offered twenty-five thousand dollars to effect Walden's release and to place him secretly aboard a boat off the Whangpoo. That failing, they were to receive fifteen thousand dollars to take a message to him and carry the reply back to someone in Shanghai.

Naidis, who claimed Netherlands nationality but who was never recognized by that government, was said, with some basis of truth, to be the son of a former chief of the Mongolian Trading Company, in Shanghai, who had returned to Soviet Russia after expulsion of the Soviets in 1927. Therefore Naidis, as a Russian and without extraterritorial rights, was transferred to the Chinese court in Wuchang.

The two Americans, escorted by the United States marshal, were brought to Shanghai for trial in the United States Court for China. And this is where I came in.

Johnson's mother retained me to defend her son, whom she believed innocent of any espionage intrigue. She convinced me and I took the case, primarily out of family friendship, but, too, I thought it would provide amusement. It did.

Young Johnson had achieved some small measure of fame a year or two earlier as the promoter of a whale[11]. Johnson had found the whale washed up on the shore of Hangchow Bay and had hauled it around China exhibiting it to curious Chinese at a few coppers a look. But when whiffs from the malodorous sea monster almost knocked out the Chinese, who supposedly have built up an immunity to all bad smells, the tour ended. Johnson had returned from a visit to the United States only a few weeks

---

11   Brinson has been taking around China a whale that had been preserved in formalde-hyde. Brinson had been employed by its owner, F.W. Fowzer, to take it around China. He slept, with two Chinese, in a special platform about the whale inside the railway boxcar it was on. "Moby Dick Back Aromatically in Shanghai After Big Tour" *China Press*, September 9, 1934, p15

Brinson preceeded by his mother arrives in Shanghai from Wuhan

Lemcke escorted by US Marshall Edward Faupel

before his arrest, and I was certain he had no connection with the Walden group. I was sure that Naidis, a supersalesman, had sold his two colleagues the proposition.

The three were charged with (1) attempt to assist the Communist party to imperil the Chinese government, (2) bribery of officials, and (3) attempt to assist a convict to escape.

My first step was to request the release of Loomis and Johnson on their own recognizance or, failing that, on writ of habeas

Moby Dick Back Aromatically In Shanghai After Big Tour

Trail Of A Whale On Provincial Junket Marked By Drip-Drip Of Fishoil And Formaldehyde: Leviathan Languishes Here In A Box-Car

By ALEX BUCHMAN

When is a 60-ton embalmed whale a white elephant? Aha, 'tis easy to answer: when the huge three-year old mammal is in Shanghai, when its fish-oil and formaldehyde smell wafts gently through the box car in which it is stored, when Shanghai railway officials don't known what to do with the odoriferous box-car, and when, worst of all, the owner sits calmly in the United States with intentions of claiming his sometime money-making pet "is the near future" by coming to Shanghai.

Brinson's whale adventure

corpus.

Bail for the two was fixed at twenty-five hundred dollars each and despite the fact that Johnson refused bail, saying he preferred jail, I posted that amount for him. Loomis, unable to raise the money, spent the weekend in jail.

I next sought reduction in bail on the grounds that the maximum penalty for the crime with, which they were charged was only six months' imprisonment, a fine of one thousand American dollars, or both. Judge Helmick compromised on fifteen hundred dollars. Loomis raised the amount and was released from jail after deposit of his passport with the court and the warning not to leave Shanghai before the case came to trial.

The trial was set for October 25, but in the meantime a bank failure[12] which in some way touched almost every American in Shanghai crowded our little case from the calendar, and one November morning just before tiffin we were squeezed in and

---

12   The collapse of the American-Oriental Banking Corporation. See Chapter 9.

Loomis and Johnson were each fined fifty American dollars and given a six months' suspended sentence.[13]

I haven't the slightest idea what has happened to Rivosh and Naidis, now that China's attitude toward Soviet Russia has changed. Loomis, I hear, is living a workaday existence in New York City. Johnson, adventurous to the end, is dodging torpedoes on an Atlantic convoy. And I, to date, am fifty dollars richer than I ever expected to be and more convinced than ever that everyone — well, almost everyone — is a gentleman at heart.

13 Brinson pleaded guilty and was fined $500 and given a suspended sentence. Lemcke was released due to lack of evidence. In passing sentence Judge Milton Helmick said "It must be thoroughly understood that American citizens in China are to engage in legitimate pursuits only. No one must be allowed to think China is a fair field for American adventurers, or that Americans can with impunity, concern themselves with the affairs of the Chinese government or other governments."

XIII
ABOUT MARRIAGE AND DIVORCE

SHANGHAI WAS NEVER A MECCA for divorce seekers. For one thing it was almost impossible to get a divorce in a British court. The British stick to their mid-Victorian ideas on such matters and for them there's only one ground. Too, most British subjects dislike to admit that they have a domicile anywhere outside of Dear Old England, although they may have lived in Shanghai all their lives.

Most United States Court judges were reasonable in divorce matters. Adultery was a sure ground, but divorces were granted on grounds of desertion, cruelty, and non- support, provided grounds and facts were clearly proved. To obtain a divorce on the usual and most polite grounds, desertion, it was necessary to show that this cause existed two years prior to the granting of the divorce. Also a bona fide China residence of two years had to be proved. However, since 1935, when the District of Columbia divorce law, which applied to Americans in China, was changed, the period of residence also was changed somewhat; that is, the law required the plaintiffs residence in the jurisdiction of the local court for one year when the grounds arose within that jurisdiction; two years when the grounds arose elsewhere. Interlocutory decrees were abolished and absolute decrees were granted for adultery, desertion for two years, voluntary separation for five years, and conviction of a felony in which a sentence of two years was imposed.

This lengthy residence was a big stumbling block for Shanghai divorces. Most Americans in China were transients. Those who wanted hurry-up divorces, or for whom the course of true love required action inside of two years, found it necessary to make quick trips to Nevada, Oklahoma, or Arkansas. Some tried Mexico. I once received a circular letter from a lawyer in El Paso who pointed out the superior facilities across the border in arranging divorces by mail. I never recommended mail-order divorces to any of my clients. I did not believe our own courts would recognize them, not being quite that far advanced in the solution of problems in domestic relations.

Sidney Powell. The British Supreme Court for China refused to recognise his wife's divorce granted in Reno.

I was never what is called a "divorce lawyer." I disliked such cases, especially in a close-knit community like Shanghai where a lawyer invariably knew both parties personally and socially. It is bound to be embarrassing to meet the "other party" in your office, be hard-boiled with him (one's client is always right), and then, perhaps that same night, at dinner or cocktails, run into the man you have just tried to squeeze dry.

Shanghailanders often found that a divorce was not a divorce. The British courts were not inclined to recognize divorces granted in the United States, particularly those, such as Reno divorces, granted after a brief period of residence.[1]

---

1   See *Powell v Powell*. "Mr Powell's Divorce Suit", *NCH*, Feb 17, 1923, p469 where British Judge Sir Skinner Turner refused to recognize a Reno divorce in China. Mr Sidney Powell had married his wife, Catherine Agnes Powell, in Cairo in 1901. She had obtained a divorce in Reno in 1921 and married to Eric Anthony Sykes in San Francisco the same month. Powell did not appear in response to her application. Powell later filed for a divorce on the grounds of her adultery with Mr Sykes and this was granted in 1924. *NCH*, 2 Feb 1924, p181. The former Mrs Powell died the following year in 1925.

There were a number of such cases in China where American women married to British subjects went "home" on holiday and returned with Reno divorces, good under American law and insofar as the women were concerned, but which the British Supreme Court did not recognize as valid. In such cases the only recourse the poor British subject had was patience. All he could do was wait hopefully for his ex-spouse to marry again, whereupon he could sue for divorce in his own court on the one infallible ground, adultery.

A bigamous marriage is as frowned upon in Shanghai as elsewhere. There were a few bigamists in our midst but sooner or later they were found out. An American[2] tried bigamy back in 1923 and was sent to Bilibid prison in the Philippines.[3] His mistake was in thinking that New York and Shanghai were in two different worlds.

This young man married a New York City girl in 1920. Then, tiring of married life with her, he stole the birth certificate of a friend, obtained a passport under his assumed name, and came to Shanghai where almost immediately he married a beautiful Russian girl.

In the United States Court for China

LYDIA SERGIEVSKEY KABELITZ, *Plaintiff*, vs. THOMAS KABELITZ, *Defendant*.	Cause No. 4575 Civil No. 2454 ORDER Filed at Shanghai, China, Feb. 10th, 1941. WILLIAM T. COLLINS Clerk.

The object of this suit is an action for divorce.

WHEREAS, Plaintiff herein, by her attorney, H. D. Rodger, Esq., of Messrs. Rodger & Wiener, has this 10th, day of February, 1941, made application for the substitution of publication for personal service upon the defendant herein; and

WHEREAS, it appears from the files in this case that on the 10th, day of February, 1941, the summons for Defendant was returned by the United States Marshal for China with the following noted thereon: "Defendant cannot be found within the jurisdiction of this Court"; and

WHEREAS, it appears from the files in this case that on the 10th, day of February, 1941, the Plaintiff herein filed an Affidavit to the effect that the Defendant does not reside in China, nor has he resided in China for the past five years, and that defendant's last known address was, c/o Mr. Walter Freeman, 1327 Van Ness Avenue, Los Angeles, California, U.S.A.,

Now, THEREFORE, it is this 10th day of February, 1941, ORDERED that service upon the defendant be made by publication once a week for three consecutive weeks in the "China Weekly Review," a paper of general circulation most likely to reach the defendant.

IT IS FURTHER ORDERED that the defendant cause his appearance to be entered herein on or before the fortieth day, exclusive of Sunday and legal holidays, occurring after the 1st day of March, 1941, the day of last publication of this Order; otherwise the case will be proceeded with as in case of default.

By the Court,
Dated at Shanghai, China,
this 10th day of February, 1941.
MILTON J. HELMICK,
Judge.

A divorce case in the US Court for China

---

2   Charles Carberry aka Bernard Pinder
3   Until the mid-1920s US convicts from China were sent to Bilibid Prison in the Philippines to serve their sentences. After this, they were sent to McNeil Island in Washington State.

Form No. 87—Consular.

TRIPLICATE

CERTIFICATE OF MARRIAGE.

American Consular Service,

Shanghai, China.

February 11 , 19 23.

I, J. B. Sawyer , Vice Consul of the United States of America at Shanghai, China , do hereby certify that on this eleventh day of February A. D. 1923 , at Russian Orthodox Church , in the city of Shanghai, China , Bernard Pinder , a CITIZEN of the United States of America aged twenty-eight years, born in Key West, Fla. , and now residing in Shanghai, China , and Evprasia Zimina , a CITIZEN of Russia , aged thirty years, born in Stretensk, Siberia , and now residing in Shanghai, China. were united in marriage before me, and in my presence, by Father Serhei Borodin, an ordained priest of the Russian Orthodox Church.

In witness whereof I have hereunto subscribed my name and affixed the seal of my office at Shanghai, China , this eleventh day of February , A. D. 1923 , and of the Independence of the United States the one hundred and forty seventh.

[L. S.]

J. B. Sawyer
Vice Consul

Carberry/Pinder's bigamous marriage certificate

Bad news travels fast. The New York wife learned of her husband's whereabouts and wrote to the American consul. The United States district attorney investigated and produced the New York marriage certificate and the bigamist exchanged two wives for two years in jail.[4]

There is too much hypocrisy in divorce actions to suit me. This is brought about by the rule against collusion. Courts will not grant a divorce if it appears at any point in the proceedings. At the same time all judges and lawyers know that in most cases there has been collusion. Usually both sides are anxious for the divorce but care must be taken that no trace of this mutual desire appears in the record.

As in so many other ways, the Chinese are far more sensible

---

4   *United States v. Charles Carberry, The China Weekly Review*, Jan 12 1924, p260, Jan 19, 1924 p296, and Jan 26, 1924, p340. The judge was Charles Lobingier and DA, Leonard Husar. Carberry married in Shanghai under the name Bernard Pinder.

in divorce matters. If a Chinese husband and wife can't agree
to live together they simply agree to disagree. They can obtain
a divorce by a simple written agreement to that effect without
any court action whatsoever. If more formality is desired, they
merely go before the court and explain to the judge that they
both want a divorce. Invariably it is granted for the sole reason
that both parties want it. A reasonable property settlement can be
arranged either in or out of court.

I remember one Chinese divorce suit in the Mixed Court
that did not go through, probably because the plaintiff's lawyer
chose the wrong ground. Mme. Tsu-Tsang-sz asked for a divorce
from her husband, Ping-shung. She charged bigamy and asked
custody of their two children and one hundred thousand dollars
for damages and alimony. Now one hundred thousand dollars
is a good deal of money in any language, and possibly Mr.
Tsu disliked parting with such a large amount plus a son and
daughter. He contested.[5]

Mme. Tsu testified that after the birth of their second child the
husband's affections grew cold, and he sought a new love. He
soon found another sweetheart. And then, said Mme. Tsu, her
husband began to scold and ill-treat her; even her mother-in-law
assaulted her. As time went on the husband grew abusive, called
her an "old hag," and threatened violence if she refused to sign
the agreement which would permit them to separate without
going to court and allow either to marry freely and without
interference of the other.

Mme. Tsu refused to sign. Whereupon the husband gave
a grand dinner at the Great Eastern Hotel to celebrate his
"marriage" to the girl Mme. Tsu claimed was the second wife.

But Mr. Tsu declared that he had not taken unto himself

5   "Chinese Divorce Suit in Mixed Court", *NCH*, March 25, 1922, Magistrate Kuan sitting
     with Mr Blackburn, the British Assessor.

another wife, only a concubine. Now there is a fine line of distinction between a second wife and a concubine. A second wife is no longer accepted by Chinese law. A concubine, or mistress, accepted by "old custom," has no legal rights and insofar as the law is concerned is nonexistent.

Thus, there being no second wife and no bigamy, Mme. Tsu's divorce was denied.

In China it is more troublesome to terminate a betrothal than it is to dissolve a consummated marriage. I recall a case in which I arranged for the dissolution of such a contract. The boy and girl had been betrothed by their respective families since early childhood.

In this case the girl was my client. The family was embarrassed by the daughter's modern ideas. She was a student at The McTyiere School,[6] a swank Chinese girls' finishing school, and preferred a higher education to marriage. She wanted to attend college in the United States. I approached the boy's family and found that they, too, were embarrassed; for their son had the same ideas. A student at St. John's University in Shanghai, he yearned to complete his education at a university in the United States.

With both families mutually agreeable it was easier than usual to prepare the agreement terminating the betrothal and releasing each from all obligations created for them by their families. Then came the real work, the return of the gifts.

It's an old Chinese custom for the prospective bride and groom to exchange presents or have this exchange arranged by their parents; mechanics of the exchange are handled by a go-between.

---

6   McTyeire School for Girls (中西女塾) or Chinese Western Girls' Academy was founded by Dr. Young J. Allen of the American Southern Methodist Mission in 1890. Famous graduates include the Soong sisters: Ai-ling, Ching-ling (Madame Sun Yat-sen) and May-ling (Madame Chiang Kai-shek). It is now the Shanghai No. 3 Girls' High School, at 155 Jiangsu Road.

As both families were enormously wealthy, gifts were numerous and costly. For days my office looked more like a pawnbroker's shop than a law office, for each side had deposited their gifts with me and I had to make the transfer. There was much valuable gold and jade jewelry. But what impressed me most was one of the girl's gifts to her betrothed, a brown derby hat!

The outcome of the broken engagement was that both students went to the United States where they attended the same university. There they met, fell in love and became engaged of their own volition. Now they are happily married. I suppose that, after all, their parents knew best.

Mixed marriage is responsible for some of the marital discontent in China. As a result of the overflow of Chinese labor in construction of the Southern Pacific Railway in California and the Pacific Southwest nearly a half-century ago, great numbers of Chinese moved to Mexico. Since then others have migrated from time to time. Some entered legally, others slipped in, in the hope of some day crossing the border. But no matter; the important fact is that many of the Chinese took unto themselves peon wives. All would go well for a while, but a Chinese always longs for his home village, and trouble came when the Chinese returned to China with the Mexican wife.

In some cases the Mexican woman crossed thousands of miles of ocean only to find that her husband had a Chinese wife by a previous marriage.

Under the Chinese civil law a man can have only one wife, and if previously he had been married to a Chinese wife under Chinese law the Mexican wife had no legal status. In deference to the "old custom" she could be called a concubine, but insofar as Chinese law was concerned, she was nothing at all.

Naturally the situation led to unhappiness and bitterness, and many of the women, although penniless, tried to return to their homes in Mexico. Some years ago the Mexican government arranged for repatriation of a number of the women. This didn't work too well because of the children. In ninety-nine out of a hundred cases there were children to complicate matters; the family averaged not less than six children.

The Chinese father always objected to the children's returning to Mexico with the mother. The problem was solved in one instance by a compromise whereby the male children remained in China with the father, and the female children went back to Mexico with the mother.

While I was honorary Mexican consul, it was one of my duties to handle the cases in Shanghai; but as most Chinese migrated to Mexico from the Canton area, arrangements were made by correspondence. Occasionally a woman came to the consulate. I dreaded these visits. A consul is helpless in such a situation, but the explanation that he can do nothing is cold comfort to a mother who is being separated from her children, perhaps forever, and I much preferred the correspondence method.

Marriages between Chinese and Americans do not always work out as well as many hopeful young lovers expect. These romances often have their beginnings in American universities. As a general rule there is no trickery or deception practiced by the Chinese student who falls in love with an American girl and asks her to marry him. But he forgets that he must take his bride into the Chinese family system, alien to anything in her experience.

When the couple gets out to China, it is easy for the husband to fall back into his native ways, but it is a tremendous shock to the bride when she realizes that they are not to establish their own home; that often she is expected to go into his family, live with them, and submit to the wishes of his mother and all his elder relatives. Naturally this system creates disillusionment and unhappiness. The husband tries to be kind and considerate, but he just can't buck Lao Kwei Chu, or "old custom."

The inharmonious setting is not the worst tragedy of mixed marriage. The children of such unions are the real sufferers. They are the victims of a cruel and perhaps sense- less social ostracism. Rarely are they accepted as equals by either the Chinese or by nationals of the white parent. They are half-castes or Eurasians, names which carry a certain stigma to some insensate residents in the Orient.

This cruel social ostracism often gives the children an inferiority complex they never quite overcome. It is often claimed but never proved that the children of mixed marriages inherit all the bad points of each parent rather than the good. This belief may have arisen from the fact that in the early days most of these children were results of unions between drunken sailors and harlots. This prejudice against Eurasians is really the result of the British caste system. Strange, isn't it, that the majority of Eurasians are part British? Next in number are the Portuguese.

I have known many Eurasians of magnificent courage and ability who have cut through prejudices and risen to the very top in educational work, banking, and nearly every other line of endeavor. But no matter how high they rise or how worth while they are,

Foreign Wife Of Chinese Is Given Divorce

American Girl Unfolds Tale Of Woe In U.S. Court

MARRIED 4 YEARS AGO IN NEW YORK

Husband Of Old School, Insisted She Learn To Speak Chinese

The story of a foreign girl who could not adjust herself to a Chinese husband of the old school was unfolded yesterday in the United States Court for China.

The girl, a naturalized American citizen of German ancestry, told of her husband's mental cruelty and asked for divorce. As the husband, Mr. Te-chih Wang of Chungking, did not put up a defense through his lawyer, Judge Milton J. Helmick granted the decree.

Mrs. Wang married the Chinese youth four years ago in New York, she revealed. In 1935 she proceeded to Chungking to join her husband, who had preceded her there by several months.

Upon her arrival at Chungking she found that her home was situated two hours' distance from the city. The landlady, she said, took in a new tenant, a tubercular patient. Mrs. Wang protested, but her husband refused to move.

Although her husband was tight about her spending money, he continued, in old Chinese style, to help support his brothers and their families.

He also refused to hire an English-speaking servant for her, saying that she was now in China and should become Chinese.

Finding this life unbearable, Mrs. Wang left her husband in September of last year.

there's always some dirty skunk ready to break their hearts with taunts about their mixed ancestry.

Aside from the tragedy of the children, some mixed marriages are successful. Others fail, just as do marriages between men and women of the same race and religion. I know a woman who might have made her marriage to an Eurasian a success if she had known what she wanted before it was too late. Her marriage being somewhat typical I'll change the names and tell it.

Marian Brown married Peter Moore, the only son of a fine old Eurasian family which went back to the very beginning of the Settlement. The Moores were rich, powerful, and much respected in Shanghai. Marian's mother kept a boardinghouse and truthfully the Moores weren't any too pleased about the marriage. They had hoped for a better match.

Marian now had more money to spend than she dreamed existed, and she and Peter were happy until their first child was born. Evidently Marian expected to see something pink and white, but instead a squirming bundle that might have been delivered of Ah-lin, her amah, was put in her arms. And I suppose that it was then that she realized that she was married to a man whose skin was yellow-tinged. She forgot completely the centuries-old culture that had gone into the making of her husband's family and the inherent fineness of Peter himself.

At the time I was called in to draw up a separation agreement Marian and Peter had three children. Afterward they continued to live separate lives in different wings of the great stone mansion; that is, until Peter fell in love with an Eurasian girl. Marian left for a holiday in Europe and returned with a divorce. Peter married his sweetheart.

In the meanwhile Marian had met and fallen in love with Sam, a wealthy taipan in a big foreign firm. Sam sent his wife to Mexico, but there were legal entanglements and the quick divorce fell through. If it hadn't, this story might have been different.

Sam was a lusty, red-headed old *China Hand* who had lived a rough life in outports for a quarter of a century. For my money Peter was a much better bet, either for a quick drink or a long stay on a desert island. But Sam's eyes were blue and Marian overlooked his longshoreman language. Except for his purplish-veined nose, he was *white*!

Some three years after Marian's divorce Sam obtained his in the United States Court for China, but by this time no doubt a little of the keen edge of his desire for Marian had rubbed off. Although now there was nothing to hinder their marriage Marian left in June for a visit with her children, who were at school in Switzerland.

Then, during Marian's absence, the Japs managed the now infamous Marco Polo Bridge and Hungjao incidents. In the midst of bombs over Shanghai, Sam up and married a beautiful tourist stranded by the war in Shanghai. Hostilities eventually simmered down, Sam and his bride went off on a belated honeymoon, and Marian returned home.

She came to see me on some legal business. I was shocked by her appearance. Six months earlier she had been an attractive and young forty; now she was a broken old woman. But here is her story as she told it to me that day:

She was ready to sail from Southampton in August, she said, when news came of the bombing of Shanghai. Her passport was revoked. Sam cabled, "All safe here. Stay there." At first there were cables from Sam. When they stopped coming she wasn't too worried. There were no letters, but letters she knew were often lost or delayed en route to and from China. She kept busy buying clothes and household things. At last the British gave permission and she sailed from Southampton in November. She cabled Sam her plans, and she cabled Peter to have money for her in Hong Kong.

"It was just before we reached Singapore," she said. "We were very merry on that ship, all evacuees returning to Shanghai. Someone was giving a cocktail party for me, the bride, and I was in my cabin dressing for it when the steward brought the cable."

"At first," she said, "I thought it was from Sam, but even before I opened it I knew somehow that the news would be bad." She went on. "The cable was from Peter. He told me of Sam's marriage and advised me to turn back."

I can still see her sitting there in my office staring into space and saying, "I can't believe it. It can't be true. This just can't happen to me."

"I was so sure," she continued, "that Sam would be waiting for me on the jetty. But he wasn't." She barely breathed it. "There was no one there at all, only Peter."

I knew that Peter and his family were the only ones in Shanghai who were being at all nice to her and privately I thought that was more than she deserved. Peter had sent her to me, in fact, to work out a settlement to replace the alimony. He had assured me he wanted her to have as large an amount as possible under the circumstances, although the war had pretty well ruined his business.

It was embarrassing to have her go on. Frankly, I was afraid she'd have hysterics. I thought she'd been a damned fool, but I tried to be sympathetic. "Well," I said, stumbling over the words, "this bombing, you know, it drove a lot of guys haywire. Sam was lonely, and the gal was here. Men can be cruel ..." She snapped out of it then. "Let's see the papers," was all she said, but I knew from the look she gave me that she realized now, too late, that Peter was the best friend she'd ever had.

XIV
In Defense of the Settlement

From the days of Marco polo up to the present time foreigners in China have found themselves involved in the other fellow's scrap.

Shanghai's foreign settlement was only a few months old and numerically insignificant when a handful of British and American residents met on April 8,1853, to devise means of self-protection against bandit groups active in the vicinity. A defense force was the result. A year later in the now historic Battle of Muddy Flat this force had its baptism of fire.

In the early autumn of 1853 a band of Cantonese desperadoes, members of an ancient secret society, the Triads, captured the Native City of Shanghai. This capture brought in its wake a large opposing force of Imperialists who encamped on the western edge of the Settlement.

Battles and skirmishes were of almost daily occurrence. The Settlement residents, however, regarded the fighting more in the nature of a fireworks display than of serious warfare until the afternoon of April 4, 1854, when the Imperialists attacked four separate parties of foreigners in less than two hours. A lady and gentleman walking on the race course were set upon by four or five of these ruffians armed with swords and spears. A small guard of an officer and eight men who came to their rescue found the western face of the Settlement swarming with Imperialists who fired on every foreigner they saw.

When an ultimatum to the Chinese authorities to remove the camps from that neighborhood was refused, the defense force of between three and four hundred men was mobilized. The camps were attacked on the front by the Americans and on the flank by the

Shanghai Volunteer Corps badge

British. "In half an hour," reads one report, "it was manifest that the Imperialists were in full retreat." The whole fight occupied less than two hours. The casuality list was four defense force members killed and thirteen injured.

This defense force formed the nucleus of the Shanghai Volunteer Corps, which was organized in 1870. Control of the corps was vested in the chairmen and members of the Shanghai Municipal Council, who accepted the responsibility and retained it until December 8, 1941.

Whenever trouble threatened Shanghai's International Settlement, the Shanghai Volunteer Corps, better known as the S.V.C., was mobilized. Its main job was to back up the police in case of civil disturbance and riots. And during Chinese civil wars it also isolated the International Settlement and tried to help maintain neutrality. Since its birth a hundred years ago the Shanghai Volunteer Corps has been mobilized twenty-five times in all, beginning with the Battle of Muddy Flat and ending with an "anticipation of trouble" mobilization in 1938 on the first anniversary of the Sino-Japanese outbreak. Some of the more important mobilizations were for the Taiping Menace in 1860[1],

---

1   The Taiping Rebellion was a large-scale civil war in China from 1850-1864 led by Hong
     Xiuquan who believed himself to be the younger brother of Jesus Christ. In 1860, the
     rebels attacked Shanghai but were turned back.

the Tientsin Massacre in 1870[2], the Russo-Japanese War in 1904[3], the Mixed Court Riots in 1905[4], the Chinese Revolution in 1911[5], the Anti-Japanese Riot of 1918[6], the Kiangsu-Chekiang War in 1924[7], the Lungwha Battle in 1925[8], the occupation of Shanghai by the Nationalists in 1927, the Sino-Japanese clash in 1932, and the Sino-Japanese war in 1937.

I joined the Shanghai Volunteer Corps in 1923, soon after my resignation from the United States consular service. I was one of a group of eight or nine enthusiastic horsemen who founded the American Troop, a new mounted unit in the S.V.C. and the American counterpart of the British Shanghai Light Horse which in the early eighties had risen phoenix like from the Mounted Rangers of the Taiping Trouble days.

The American Troop, S.V.C, approved and commissioned by the Shanghai Municipal Council in October, 1923, received American cavalry training and was equipped by the S.V.C. with uniform and saddlery. The balance of the equipment was supplied by the United States government through the efforts of the American consul-general, Mr. E. S. Cunningham. Our motto and device was

American Troop badge

2   In 1870 in Tientsin, Chinese, suspecting foreign missionaries had kidnapped Chinese children, rioted and burnt down the Tientsin Cathedral and British and American churches. Approximately 60 foreigners and Christian Chinese were killed, including 10 French nuns who were raped and brutally murdered. Tensions between foreign powers and the Chinese were very high after this.

3   When Japan took Port Arthur in Manchuria from Russia.

4   Large-scale rioting in Shanghai as a result of a dispute between the Chinese magistrate and British assessor of the imprisonment of women prisoners. Troops from gunboats had to be landed to quell the rioting.

5   When the Qing Dynasty was overthrown and the Republic of China established.

6   In protest against Japan's demands to take over German interests in China.

7   A battle between the warlords in charge of Jiangsu and Zhejiang over who would control the area around Shanghai. Over 130,000 troops were committed by both sides to the battles. Kiangsu won.

8   When the Lunghwa arsenal to the south of the French Concession was taken by troops loyal to one side of a civil war battle.

Allman (centre) as commandant of the American Troop of the SVC

Allman in SVC uniform

"Service Fortiter" in a scroll under eagle and arrows.

When I left Shanghai for Hong Kong in November of 1941 I was the commandant of the American Troop. In the eighteen years I had belonged to the troop, I had acquired considerable valuable military experience, to say nothing of the memories of exciting times.

My first experience in actual warfare came during the Eighth Route Army's[9] march on the Settlement in 1927, when the S.V.C. manned the perimeter. Our main duty was to keep armed soldiers from either entering or leaving the Settlement. I've seen fighting on so much bigger scale since then that the details of this "practice war" have faded into insignificance. One of the few things I do remember is the inconsequential detail that in the midst of terrific shellfire one young volunteer took four hours off to get married.

All of us in the American Troop wondered why another

---

9   In fact, Chiang Kai-shek's National Revolutionary Army. See Chapter 11, footnote 4.

member asked for one hour's leave in every twelve. Many were the conjectures which ranged all the way from an illicit assignation to trading in gold bars. Finally when the mystery got too much for us, a fellow trooper followed him. Then we learned that this mysterious leave gave the trooper just time enough to dash to the Shanghai Club, have his canteen filled with Scotch and soda, and get back to headquarters. The next time he went off I handed him my canteen. "Here," I said, "fill it up with rye and ginger ale."

Japan's undeclared war on Shanghai in the early part of 1932 came as a sequel to the Japanese invasion and conquest of Manchuria. This invasion had led to a nation-wide boycott of Japanese goods, but there were few personal attacks on the Japanese. The first loss of life occurred in a free-for-all fight in front of a Chinese factory in the Chinese area of Shanghai. Two Japanese were wounded, one fatally. A couple of days later a Japanese mob set fire to the factory. In the melee two Japanese were injured and one killed, and a similar number of Chinese police were killed and injured.

At once the Japanese admiral presented General Wu Te-chen[10], Chinese mayor of Greater Shanghai, with five demands. The first three required an apology by the mayor, arrest and punishment of the guilty, and payment of damages and hospital bills. The last two asked that the anti-Japanese movement be controlled and all societies fostering anti-Japanese sentiments be dissolved.

Despite Mayor Wu's acceptance of the Japanese demands and the assurance of the Japanese consul-general that the acceptance was considered satisfactory for the time being, the Japanese marines were landed in Chapei (a Shanghai suburb) in the dark

---

10   Wu Tiecheng (吳鐵城) (1888-1953) served as the mayor of greater Shanghai from 1932 to 1937. He had been a member of the Kuomintang from the early years. In 1937 he transferred to Guangdong as the head of the Guangdong provincial government. He served as foreign minister from 1948 to 1949. He died in Taipei in 1953.

Japanese troops occupy the destroyed North Station

The Commercial Press Building afer the fighting

of the night of January 28. The next day the Japs attacked the city with machine guns and airplane bombing, razing the building which housed the Commercial Press, and almost destroying the North Station[11].

---

11   Located to the east of the current Shanghai Railway Station.

Japanese troops landing in Shanghai

Then the British and American governments intervened and there was a truce, but three days later, on February 2, hostilities broke out again. The truce had merely given the Japs time to bring reinforcements from Japan.[12]

I had been in Manila on a business trip at the outbreak of this war, but my family were all in Shanghai, and I hurried back on the first boat. I arrived the day the truce ended. As my ship steamed up the Whangpoo I watched Jap gunboats shelling Woosung, about twenty miles down river from Shanghai.

The fighting between the Japanese and the Chinese in 1932 was more serious than the Cantonese siege in 1927, but the Volunteer Corps still helped to man the boundary lines, except for the Japanese sector. The Japanese S.V.C. company was founded in 1900 and their sector was Hongkew, which they now took over. The rest of the S.V.C. maintained the neutrality of the Settlement proper.

The volunteers were assigned to what was supposed to

---

12   Sasebo, Japan's major naval base in Western Japan, was only 24 hours sailing from Shanghai.

Yubari firing at Woosung forts

The Woosung guns after shelling

be the hottest sector, the territory from North Station to Tibet Road Bridge. The hottest spot of this sector was a place known as "Windy Corner,"[13] and for protection we had rigged up a

13   The corner of North Henan and Range Roads (Henan North Road and Wujin Road) just south of the North Railway Station. The station was in Chinese territory, but the International Settlement ran just past this intersection.

Maps showing the location of Windy Corner

Shelling near Windy Corner seen from near the Bund. In the foreground is the British Consulate and the British Supreme Court for China

Streets scene near North Station

zigzag system of sandbag tunnels which snaked their way to our blockhouse.

One day during a quiet period in the fighting the then American Minister to China, Mr. Nelson T. Johnson[14], paid us a call. The sentry posted at the entrance failed to recognize him

---

14   A former student interpreter and career diplomat in China. See Chapter 2 Footnote 12

Chinese machine gunner

Japanese marines on a rooftop

and passed him along the tunnel to the blockhouse as he would any casual visitor. The Minister caught us playing cards.

To make some amends for our apparent disregard of duty we escorted Nelson T. to our most dangerous spot, an observation post on the roof of a three-story cigarette factory next door, and where we had an excellent view of both Jap and Chinese front lines just across the wall.

No sooner had we reached the top than we were deafened by the roar of firing and counterfiring. The Minister ducked and so did we. But Nelson T. never knew that all the shooting was merely to impress important visitors.

We were on friendly terms with the Chinese who maintained the machine gun nest across the street. We called him "Charlie Chan" and gave him cigarettes and food. In return, at a signal from us, he would fire off a few rounds to impress visitors whom he could see but the Japs couldn't. The Japs always fired back, much to our amusement and the guests' discomfort.

When the Minister, horrified by the risks his nationals were taking in so exposed and dangerous a position, departed, we made up in some measure for the casual way he had been received by posting sentries at every turn of the tunnel, and stationing a guard of honor at the entrance to present arms as he stepped out. Now Mr. Johnson, as Minister and later Ambassador, has had many guards of honor, but it is doubtful if he has ever had to do so much saluting as he did on that one short trip.

In 1932 the Japs, more or less feeling their way, were not nearly so arrogant as they became later, otherwise a fellow American Trooper and I might not have got off quite so easily.

It was rumored that the Japs were using our Kiangwan polo field as a battery replacement. One Saturday afternoon when we were off duty L. K. Taylor[15], another polo player, wanted to drive out to Kiangwan, on the Shanghai out-skirts, to see what it was all about. It was a dangerous trip, but L. K. was an adventurous soul. As I was determined not to let him get ahead of me, I consented. I was already envious of his trip across The Gobi by automobile long before Roy Chapman Andrews made his scientific expedition and discovered the dinosaur eggs. I had evened the score by making a trip along the upper reaches of the Yellow River. At least Kiangwan was close to home.

Fighting was going on all about us and to avoid bullets and Jap sentries we made the trip by a circuitous route. When we reached the Kiangwan stables we found them burned down; bodies of dead mafoos (trainers) and of ponies littered the ground. Not a human being was in sight. But while we were

15   Lemuel Kennerly "Ken" Taylor (1890-1859), head of L.K. Taylor and Company and engineering firm. He had previously served in the United States Navy.

Charlie Chan

The Chinese machine gunner "Charlie Chan" was named for his resemblance to the very popular fictional character Charlie Chan, a Honolulu detective who featured in over 30 movies in the 1920s and 1930s. "Charlie Chan", a civilian in the Chinese merchant volunteer corps, published his memories of the fighting in the *China Weekly Review* of March 19 1932 under the title "Fighting in the Chapei Hell --- How 'Charlie Chan' Carried On". The following are some extracts:

"I was ordered to look after a lonely nest on high. Our military plan had changed. In addition to front line defence, we were to build as many isolated machine gun posts as possible. These posts were to be on elevated points like housetops, second and third storey windows, so we could better look after the advance of our foes.

My nest was in a dilapidated structure, dirty and ugly. But, because of the filth and damage I could operate unseen and undetected.... The Japanese were facing me in the south. But on my west I could command a good view of the Boundary Road, the intersection line of Chapei and the Settlement. Once the busy thoroughfare of all rail bound passengers and tourists was now the silent path of death. At a junction point further west was a strong redoubt, guarded not by the Japanese nor the Chinese but by the neutrals of the Settlement. I could see the changing of the guards, their buttons and bayonets shining in the winter sun. At first the S.V.C. men, foreign merchant volunteers of the Settlement were stationed there...

It was with the American doughboys that I first cultivated mute comradeship. They watched me operate the machine gun. They saw the enemies fell. When the shooting was over they would clap their hands and wave at me. I waved back. We smiled. The distance between us was only 100 feet [30 metres] but I felt it was infinitely shorter. When the Scots, the Lincolnshires and the S.V.C men came, they all did the same thing. They threw packages of Chesterfield chocolates, candies at me. They shouted at me and nicknamed me "Charlie Chan." I am not Charlie nor Chan, but I like the name. It can be shouted at the top of one's voice. Every morning we waved good morning to each other. We could not converse with each other; the street of death that separated us was the boundary not only between Chapei and the Settlement but between war and peace, perhaps also between east and west."

Allman (left) with L.K. Taylor (right). Dick Harris and Brock Park are in the centre

examining what was left of the stables our number one polo boy emerged from a hiding place.

His entire family in near-by Kiangwan village were dying from injuries, he said. The Japs, passing through, had tossed hand grenades into the dugout where the family had burrowed for safety. We sneaked into the village; the boy's story was true. Two were dead but the others, grandparents, parents, sisters, brothers, about a dozen in all, were badly injured. L. K. and I thought we'd better get them out and to a hospital as quickly as possible.

We could see the battery within firing distance, but, as the fighting had passed through to the other side of the village, our plan might work. Since it was impossible to pile all twelve into our small roadster, we hurried back to Shanghai to borrow a Red Cross truck. This wasn't so easy. All the Red Cross motors were in use, removing the injured from behind the lines.

The hospitals were filled with the wounded and the dying; there was no room for more. But our persistency won out, and

Japanese troops occuypy the Kiangwan racecourse

next morning we drove a Red Cross truck back to Kiangwan village.

Again we entered the village by the back way but thereby consumed so much time that we decided to cut corners and return by the direct road, even though this necessitated our passing the Japanese naval landing party headquarters. All went well until one hundred yards from Jap headquarters our truck broke down.

In 1932 the Japs still recognized the Red Cross and the S.V.C. As we were driving a Red Cross truck and wearing the S.V.C. uniforms the best thing to do, I thought, was to try to brazen it out. I climbed down from the truck and walked into headquarters.

"We've an injured family on our truck out there, and the truck won't go," I explained.

The naval landing officer bared his teeth in what could have been either a smile or a sneer. He ordered a detail to accompany me to the truck. I was certain that the least they would do was shoot the Chinese or remove them to die by the side of the road. I was nervous about the situation, and L. K., I could see, was also a bit on the jittery side. Then, to our amazement, the detail produced a mechanic who repaired the truck in no time, and we

Japanese troops march past the Japanese Naval Landing Party Headquarters

were waved on our way.

But it was as a lawyer and not as a member of the American Troop of the Shanghai Volunteer Corps that I was "captured" by the Japanese during this undeclared war of 1932.

An American citizen, W. S. Hibbard[16], resided in the Hongkew section, which lay just between Chinese and Japanese lines. He refused to leave his house, come bombs or barricades. Whereupon the Japanese arrested him and held him incommunicado in the naval landing headquarters. His family asked me to intercede for him and I consented, although I knew it was ticklish business. The chances were that I, too, would be arrested.

As I spoke no Japanese, headquarters smilingly provided an interpreter, an unusually attractive girl, the daughter of the commandant of the naval landing party. I suppose her job was to blandish me into forgetting the errand at hand. Unfortunately

---

16   Walter Scott Hibbard (1875-1940), an engineer with the public works department of the Shanghai Municipal Council, lived at 41 Kiangwan Road, next to Hongkew Park. He was arrested after fighting between the Chinese and Japanese had ended but immediately following the assassination described in the following paragraphs. Two Chinese photographers fearful of Japanese reprisals had hidden in his home. Hibbard had served in the US Army and was a member of the SVC. He left the SMC later that year. "Hibbard Moves To Settlement After Bombing", *The China Press*, May 3, 1932, p4. "Retiring PWD Official" *NCH*, Oct 12, 1932, p62.

for their sly little trick, I had been allergic to the Japanese for some time. Also I was not interested in romance. My one thought was how to get Hibbard out of the hoosegow.

I asked for his release and was told by a toothy, sibilant officer, "So sorry for you, Mr. Hibbard not here." I knew damned well he was and insisted, loudly, that they turn him loose. As I had expected I was taken into custody. Before leaving the

Walter Hibbard, arrested by the Japanese

safety of the International Settlement and in anticipation of my probable arrest I had taken the precaution of notifying all my friends, including newspaper correspondents and consuls, of my intentions. If I wasn't back in my office within a certain time they were to telephone every Japanese civil, military, and naval official they knew and inquire as to my whereabouts. When, after a lapse of several hours, I had not reappeared each one called the Japanese admiral, the Japanese general, the Japanese consul-general, as well as all the other Japanese bigwigs in the city. The Japanese finally decided that I was too big a nuisance and let me go—Hibbard along with me.

Another legal case of mine in connection with this same fracas concerned Colonel Chang, a Chinese military officer who inadvertently got too close to the Japanese consulate for his own good. For many years the American consulate had been located next door to the Japanese consulate in the Hongkew section of the city, but some months before outbreak of hostilities the old building had been torn down and the consulate had moved into the old Ka Lee Hotel on Kiangse and Hankow Roads[17],

---

17   The Ka Lee Hotel on Kiangse Road (Jiangxi Road) and Hankow Road directly opposite the Trinity Cathedral.

in the Settlement. Chang, unaware or temporarily forgetting this, wandered into Japanese territory one day during a lull in the fighting, "to visit an American official at the American consulate," he said. No doubt his presence in full military regalia did puzzle the Japanese secret service men, who soon spotted him loitering near their precious building. They took after him and Chang ran into the Astor House Hotel in the next block. He might have escaped had it not been for the stupidity of the hotel servants who grabbed him and started an argument which lasted just long enough for the Japanese to catch up with him.

At the time of his arrest the colonel had some highly confidential papers on his person. It was fully expected that he would be executed as a spy. In an attempt to free him alive I jumped into my customary act and pestered every Japanese official available. After much argument I succeeded in obtaining his freedom, but I failed to recover any of his papers. His release did him little good, however, for his own military authorities court-martialed him for his carelessness. Even that was better than torture at the hands of the Japanese.

Shortly after this schemozzle the Japanese, to show their big-hearted friendliness I suppose, celebrated their Emperor's birthday with a party in Hongkew Park to which they invited practically all Shanghai. I had met Admiral Nomura[18] (who later was to go down in infamy as Japanese Ambassador to Washington on that

---

18 Kichisaburo Nomura (野村 吉三郎) (1877-1964) had been commander of the Japanese fighting forces in Shanghai. He later became Japanese Foreign Minister from 1939-40. After the war he worked for the Victor Company and was elected to the Japanese Upper House.

memorable December 7) and consul-general Manoru Shigemitsu[19] on many occasions. I joined the line of handshakers in front of the reviewing stand. When it came my turn to be greeted by Shigemitsu I remarked, jocularly I thought, "This platform doesn't look any too safe." It turned out I was right.

After surviving the receiving line I hurried along with other foreign guests to that trademark of all outdoor parties, the beer kiosk. And none too soon. A minute later a bomb was hurled from the crowd onto the platform. It killed Dr. Kawabata[20], president of the Japanese Residents' Association, injured Shigemitsu, who lost a leg, and partially blinded Admiral Nomura, who lost an eye. Remembering my careless remark, I rather expected to be

The platform with Japanese dignitaries from afar

---

19 Mamoru Shigemitsu (重光 葵 1887–1957) lost his right leg in the attack. He later was Japanese ambassador to the Soviet Union and the Japanese-back reformed government of China. He served as appointed Japanese foreign minister from 1943–1944 and Minister of Greater Asia from 1944 to 1945. He signed the instrument of surrender on behalf of Japan on board the USS Missouri at the end of the war. He was arrested and convicted of "waging an aggressive war" by the Tokyo War Crimes Tribunal and sentenced to seven years in prison. He was paroled in 1950 and entered politics. He was Deputy Prime Minister of Japan from 1954 to 1956 and Foreign Minister from 1956 to 1958.

20 Dr. Teiji Kawabata. General Yoshinori Shirakawa (白川 義則) (1869–1932), Commander-in-Chief of the Japanese forces also died of his injuries in May 1932.

Japanese dignitaries on the platform.

Yun Bong-Gil being led away

arrested as an accomplice at least and lost no time in leaving the party.

The actual assassin, Im Fung Kee[21], a zealous Korean patriot, was seized before he had a chance to follow in my footsteps and leave the park. He was executed without even the slightest delay, and in further reprisal several Koreans were arrested. I was asked by their families to defend them. I managed the release of three, but the others, sent to Japan for trial, were never heard of again.

Yun Bong-Gil before the bombing

Yun honoured on a 2008 Korean stamp

On Saturday afternoon, August 14, 1937, sudden death again descended on Shanghai. Bombs were dropped from planes flying overhead.[22] There was the sharp fire of anti- aircraft. Shanghai was having a second taste of a Japanese undeclared war. Before the end of that day practically all business was suspended and every able-bodied man was in the S.V.C. Those too old to fight were aiding the police in one way or another.

At the beginning of this war, which the Japanese called "the China Incident," I had a number of insurance companies as clients; also some of my clients were insured in other companies.

---

21 Yun Bong-gil (1908-19 December 1932) (윤봉길 or尹奉吉). Im Fung Kee was the Japanese transliteration of his name. Yun was convicted by a Japanese military court in Shanghai and transferred to Japan where he was executed by firing squad on 19 December 1932. His body was exhumed in 1946 and buried in the Korean National Cemetery and in 1960 he was posthumously awarded the Republic of Korea Cordon (the highest honor) of the Order of Merit for National Foundation. Yun is featured on a Korean stamp.

22 The bombs in question were accidentally dropped by Chinese bombers. Later, on October 14, 1937, Japanese bombs were dropped on the International Settlement.

Chinese civilians killed in the bombing of the Great World Amusement Arcade

The scene in front of the Cathay Hotel after it was bombed

Although all business was at a standstill, I found it necessary to take some time off from soldiering and go down into Yangtzepoo (the industrial and warehouse section where much of the fighting had taken place) to investigate fire and bomb damage. Principally I wanted a look at the China Fibre Container Company, a business I had been managing during the owner's absence, and the Nanyang Brothers Tobacco Company building.

Yangtsepoo on Fire

I knew it wouldn't be any too safe a trip. For one thing, the tobacco factory was between Chinese and Jap lines. For company and moral support, too, I took along Bill Painter[23], an architect-engineer and a lieutenant in the American Troop, who was famous for his hearty laugh and fearless disposition. We found the factory, which had once occupied an imposing square block, burned out completely. Even the metal window frames had melted and run down.

It was while we were going through the remains of the factory that I had the fright of my life. Suddenly, out of the quiet of that gutted building, there came the sound of someone moving. It seemed to come from behind one of the charred but still upright walls. We stood still. Again the noise. I don't know about Bill, but I was damned scared. After what seemed like an hour but was probably only a minute or two, we managed to gather enough courage to move. Bill, a little the braver, I guess, shouted out in English, "Who's there?" But no response.

As I wasn't sure who was making the noise, I was afraid to speak in Chinese. Another "couple of hours" went by and I decided that the next move had to be ours. We might as well take a chance than as later. I yelled, "Shemmo jen?" (In Chinese this

---

23   William L. Painter a well known Shanghai architect. He joined US Naval Intelligence in World War II.

means, "What man," but freely translated it's "Who's there?")
Still no response.

With all the courage we possessed and sticking as close to
each other as possible Bill and I crept quietly to the wall and
looked around the corner. Then both of us, tough guys, we'd
always thought, and about as matter-of-fact as they come, were
made horribly and uncontrollably sick by the revolting sight that
met our eyes. Our noisemaker was a half-starved *wonk* (mongrel
dog) gnawing on the remains of burned human flesh and bones.

In the autumn, war or no war, the Shanghai countryside is at
its loveliest. The sky is soft and blue, the leaves of the tallow trees
bright scarlet and gold, and there's an invigorating nip in the
air that calls "Come out" to even the worst old bar fly who ever
tangled foot in a rail. For the horseman there's only one thing to

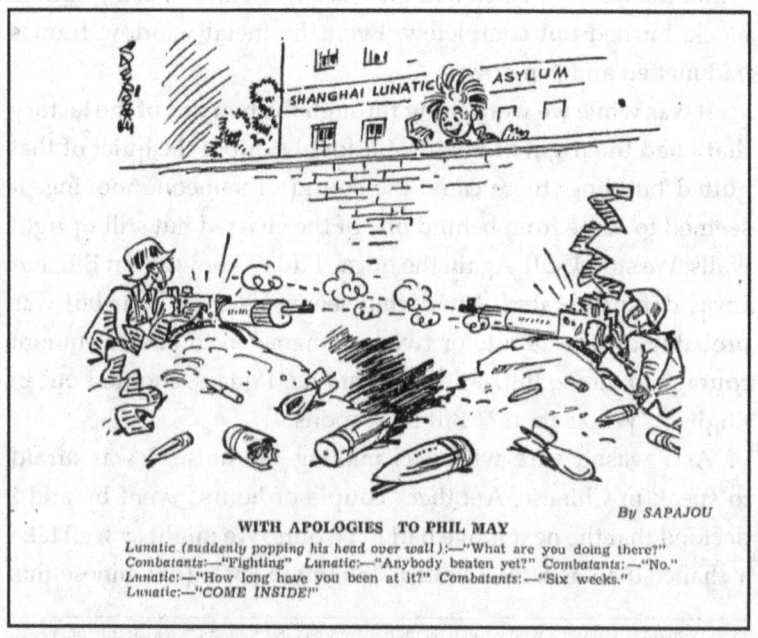

WITH APOLOGIES TO PHIL MAY

By SAPAJOU

Lunatic (suddenly popping his head over wall):—"What are you doing there?"
Combatants:—"Fighting" Lunatic:—"Anybody beaten yet?" Combatants:—"No."
Lunatic:—"How long have you been at it?" Combatants:—"Six weeks."
Lunatic:—"COME INSIDE!"

Sapajou on the Sino-Japanese war

China Press headline on Keswick Road attack

do, ride.

H. D. Rodger[24], another American lawyer and riding fanatic, and I got leave from S.V.C. duties that Sunday afternoon in October, 1937, ostensibly to confer over a law case on which we were collaborating. Naturally, our conference took place astride two China ponies during a cross-country ride.

We completed our business talk in no time at all and joined Chick and Mary Sprague[25], Dick Harris, and several other American friends who were riding along Keswick Road[26] in our defense sector.

Suddenly, and without warning, a Japanese plane swooped low and machine-gunned us, fortunately missing the riders but killing two ponies.[27] A British soldier riding near us was killed. We lost no time in ducking, you may be sure, and went head first into the ditches. We were all too busy burrowing down deep into the ground to watch the flier as he banked sharply and came back to machine-gun us again and again until his ammunition ran out.

---

24   See Chapter 10 foonote 10
25   Mr Sprague worked for Standard Oil. Dick Harris was a young fellow polo player.
26   Kaixuan Road, in the west of Shanghai.
27   The Japanese plane was attacking a British post that it had mistaken for a Chinese post. One British solider and 5 Chinese were killed. One horse was killed and two had to be put down.

I was so damned concerned about the shallowness of that ditch that I've never been able to remember what conclusion, if any, Rodger and I reached. But never will I forget that flier's barbaric delight in machine-gunning us. At that time I was convinced that this topped the torture list, but the Japanese have since let me in on a number of their other methods.

XV
BALLOTS AND BULLETS

AS A RULE LAWYERS CAN'T KEEP out of politics. I was no exception to
that rule. Sooner or later it seems that lawyers the world over get
bitten by the political bug, although I must admit that until the
spring of 1940, it had never occurred to me to run for any office.
Possibly because no one had ever suggested that I do so. Then,
when I was approached to stand as candidate for councilor on
the Shanghai Municipal Council I quickly agreed. And almost
before I knew it, and frankly to my own amazement, I was one
of that dignified governing body of solid citizens in top hats
and morning coats who went about with serious mien, caused, I
found, from trying to dodge taxation issues and Jap bullets and
brickbats.

For almost a hundred years the Shanghai Municipal Council,
functioning somewhat on the order of the modern American city
manager plan of government, continuously guided Shanghai,
from the time it was a scattering of godowns[1] and houses strung
along a muddy waterfront until it became one of the largest and
finest cities in the world. Supposedly the governing authority
of the International Settlement was vested in the consuls
representing the powers which had treaties with China, but in
practice the consuls had little or nothing to say about the way

---

1   A godown is a warehouse.

the place was governed. Almost at once civic affairs were turned over to an unpaid committee, known as the Shanghai Municipal Council but spoken of only by its initials, the S.M.C.

From the first Shanghai was an Anglo-American enterprise. Although British influence predominated, Americans shared in the responsibility of government. The British always composed a majority of the elected council, and prospective British candidates were nominated by a British national society, in recent years The British Residents' Association[2].

The American Association[3] nominated Americans for the council. Any American was entitled to membership in the association by paying dues to the association or to a designated charity, such as the American Civilian Relief. The Japanese members were nominated by the Japanese Residents' Association.

There was an unwritten agreement that the council would consist of five British, two American and two Japanese. This ratio of nationalities was determined by the voters themselves and could have been upset at any election although it never was. The nine nominees receiving the highest number of votes, plus (since 1930) five Chinese nominated and elected by the Chinese Ratepayers Association of the International Settlement constituted the council for one year. With the exception of the Chinese, a ratepayer voted for any councilor he wanted to regardless of nationality. The Japanese always voted a straight Japanese ticket.

A ratepayer's number of votes was determined by the taxes he paid. Shanghai's system of taxation, based on the English, differed from taxation as Americans know it. It worked this way. Landlords paid a small tax on the land they owned, but the bulk

2   Established in 1932.
3   Established in 1938. An American Association of China had been formed in 1898 but in
     1927 it became part of the American Chamber of Commerce.

of the municipal revenue came from the "rates," a tax levied on tenants and based on the rentals they paid.

Under the Land Regulations[4] foreigners eligible to vote had to be owners of land of approximately five hundred Chinese dollars or more or householders paying an assessed rental of a like amount. This was not a property qualification, rather the franchise was given to those who had a real stake in the Settlement. Foreigners voted either as individuals, or members of a firm, or as both; so there was in effect a system of plural voting. The annual municipal elections were only for membership on the council. All other city officials from the mighty secretary-general on down to the lowliest street cleaner were employees of the council.

My preparation for duties as a city father was indeed sketchy. My only previous office-holding experience had been on minor committees in the Shanghai American Club, the American Chamber of Commerce, and the American Association[5]. For as far back as I can remember the American community was run by two organizations, the American Chamber of Commerce and the American Association. They in turn were ruled by a small but powerful clique of stuffed shirts.

This pompous group kept itself in power for years mainly because of the general apathy on the part of the Americans toward community affairs. This indifference was the result of the transient nature of the Americans, most of whom spent only from three to five years in Shanghai then were either transferred by their companies to some other part of the world or sent back home.

---

4   The Land Regulations were the legal foundation of the International Settlement. They had been agreed between the British Consul and Shanghai Taotai in 1853. The Land Regulations provided the basic rules under which Shanghai was governed and established the Municipal Council to be elected by ratepayers.

5   Allman had, in fact, been President of the American Club from 1936-1938 and a director of the American Chamber of Commerce from at least 1935 to 1938. Allman was one of the founding General Committee members of the American Association in 1938.

The American Association had become moribund, and some fifteen years ago, when community problems such as the financing of the Community Church and the Shanghai American School necessitated a more active committee, the association was reorganized and the old fuddy-duddies shoved aside to make room for a younger and more active element.[6] Unfortunately too much of the reorganization work was left in the hands of the elderly and overly conservative directors. They produced a constitution that continued power in a political boss who over a period of years had taken advantage of his countrymen's political inertia and their refusal to give time as councilors. By their default the Boss[7], a dignified, white-haired old taipan with plenty of time for political meddling, had had a free hand in choosing the candidates. The committee always rubberstamped approval of his selections.

I objected to this practice and never hesitated to say so. I was particularly annoyed because the Boss always made certain that at least one of the two American candidates was agreeable to his behind-the-scenes advisers, the public utilities. Personally I had nothing against the utilities and from time to time did legal work for them. But, brought up as I had been in the shadow of Thomas Jefferson, I believed that a man's privilege to vote was sacred and like all Southerners I resented having anyone else do my political thinking for me. I was a thorn in the Boss's flesh for

---

6　The American Association was merged into the American Chamber of Commerce in 1927. The new American Association was only formed in 1938.

7　The Boss was Major Arthur Bassett (1878-1962), born Paris Missouri. B.A., Missouri State University, 1900; LLB Washington University, 1902. In 1903 he move to Manila as assistant District Attorney under the future first judge of the United States Court for China, Lebbeus Wilfley. Bassett came to China in 1906 to serve, at the young age of 28, as the first United States District Attorney for China. He resigned a year after Wilfley in 1910 and then spent some time practicing as a lawyer in Mexico City. He returned to China in 1913 and joined the British American Tobacco Company (BAT). He served as a judge-advocate in Tientsin with the American Expeditionary Force during WWI from 1917 to 1919 and retired with the rank of Major. After the war, he returned to work with BAT serving as a director (hence as a taipan) for many years. He retired and left China in 1941.

Major Arthur Bassett, "The Boss" seen here with Mrs C.S. Franklin and her daughter (See Ch.7 for a photo of Bassett as DA.)

I fought continuously for an election whereby each member of the association would have a direct say in the nomination of a candidate for council.

I made a lot of noise but little progress until the spring of 1940. Then, just before nominations for the election closed, when the political machine had already nominated its two candidates, a group of younger members decided the time had come to toss a monkey wrench into the works.

I was engrossed in office routine one morning when the phone rang. Sid Marco[8], an active member of the new and progressive Junior Chamber of Commerce, asked me to meet him for tiffin at

---

8   Sidney Victor Marco (1912-1986), manager of Bentley's Ltd, Radio Service. Allman's partner Paul Kops was also a member of the chamber, so Marco's call may not have been as unexpected as Allman suggests.

The Junior Chamber of Commerce, Paul Kops, Allman's partner, 5th from right is standing with Sid Marco to his left.

the American Club. "I want to talk over an important proposition," he said.

He didn't wait for the boy to pour out the whisky. He jumped in feet first. "Look here," he asked, "don't you think it's time you did something besides talk?"

I hadn't the slightest idea what he meant. Years of getting other people out of difficulties had taught me the value of being close-mouthed about personal

Sid Marco who encouraged Allman to run for the SMC.

and professional matters, but I was noted for speaking my mind on other subjects. Quickly I tried to figure out what I might have said.

Sid, who noticed my bewilderment, laughed. "Don't worry, old man. You haven't said or done anything—yet, but you're going to. We've decided to put you up for the Shanghai Municipal Council."

Now it was my turn to laugh. Then, when I saw he meant it, I gave that timeworn excuse, "I'm too busy." I explained that I not only had my law practice but several businesses to manage.

Sid said, "It's up to you to put your preachings into action. Anyway, your name's already in."

There wasn't anything for me to do but agree to be a candidate. Besides, I rather enjoyed the whole idea. Even if I weren't elected it was something of an honor just to be a candidate; and it amused me that I was chosen to needle the stuffed shirts.

Evidently I wasn't the only one who was sick and tired of being run by a political machine, for I received more than the necessary number of endorsements for nomination. Naturally,

THE CHINA WEEKLY REVIEW

報論評氏勒密

中華郵政特准掛號認為新聞紙類

Registered at the Chinese Post Office as a newspaper
for transmission with special marks privileges in China

Vol. 92   Shanghai, Saturday, April 13, 1940   No. 7

JAPANESE PACKED VOTING LIST
FAILED TO WIN?

Note:—Results of the election, taking place on

S.M.C. CANDIDATES IN THE
1940 ELECTION

Following are the names of candidates entered in this year's election for the Shanghai Municipal Council. The names marked with an "X" are those of candidates endorsed by the British and American community organizations:

N. F. Allman (American) X
J. W. Carney (American) X
M. Den (Japanese)
G. A. Haley (British) X
Y. Hanawa (Japanese)
W. J. Keswick (British) X
K. Kuroda (Japanese)
Roderick G. MacDonald (British) X
Ranald G. McDonald (British)
G. E. Mitchell (British) X
Issaku Okamoto (Japanese)
Otoichi Okamoto (Japanese)
T. S. Powell (British) X

The candidates for election

the Boss was furious. It was a great blow to his pride, but I wondered why he bothered to show his annoyance. For my money I didn't stand a chance of being elected. By this time I was pretty keen about the whole idea, but I thought the few votes I'd get would be cast more in the nature of a protest than in any expectation of my actual election.

If the Boss had not been more than a little afraid of Sid's group I believe he would have tried to force my withdrawal. Soon after my conversation with Sid the American Association held a special meeting of the committee to add my name to the ballot and present me formally as a candidate.

The Boss, noted for his soft Missourian drawl, was red to the point of apoplexy. He blustered and accused me of trying to disrupt the American Association, the committee, and for that matter the entire American community. He further accused me of being supported by roughnecks, low-brows, and the irresponsible element of the community.

It was all I could do to hold my tongue. I wanted to tell him that some of his own stooges privately had pledged their support to our side. I also wanted to give him a good sock on the jaw. Somehow I managed to hold my temper and as coolly as I

Allman in April 1940 with other member of the SMC.
Front row, left to right: L.T. Yuan, J.W. Carney, W.J. Keswick, Yu Ya-ching and Y. Hanawa. Back row: N.F. Allman, Yulin Hsi, G. Godfrey Phillips,
Secretary-General and Commissioner General, W. Gockson, R.G. MacDonald, E.Y.B. Kiang, G.E. Mitchell, G.A. Haley and T.S. Powell

could under the circumstances I reminded him that he was exaggerating a bit. "All I'm disrupting," I said, "is your damned political machine which should have been smashed to bits fifteen years earlier."

The elections were held on April 10 and 11, and I was elected by the largest number of votes ever received by any councilor in the history of Shanghai. Of course I was flattered, but I realized that merely personal popularity had not garnered the overwhelming vote. It was an endorsement of my revolt against the old guard.

I took my seat on the S.M.C. at a turbulent time. National feeling ran high. There were continual flareups. The Japanese were antagonistic to British and Americans. They wanted increased representation on the council, increased personnel on the police force, more employees in all municipal departments. The British and Americans, on the other hand, were doing all they could to resist further Jap encroachment.

Since their virtual occupation of Shanghai in 1937, it was noticeable that the Japanese voting strength was fast topping the foreign electorate and that, with the constantly increasing Japanese population of the Settlement, Japanese voters would soon outvote all the other voters combined, attain a majority of the council membership, and thus replace the British dominance of the Settlement. As the 1940 elections neared, the Japanese Residents Association announced that it proposed to nominate five Japanese for council seats. This move, if successful, would change the national representation from five British, two Japanese and two Americans to five Japanese, two British and two Americans.

The Japanese Residents Association held numerous pre-election meetings at which Jap firebrands urged taking over the Council. More than one youthful Nipponese patriot wrote

278

A ratepayers meeting at the racecourse

a letter to his councilors in his own blood, urging them to force the issue. The Japanese press carried daily editorials in the same vein, and what's more, falsely charged council and police with inefficiency.

In spite of fears of a Japanese victory the election resulted in their defeat and composition of the council remained the same. This surprising feat was achieved by an intense Anglo-American campaign. British and American residents with large real estate holdings split them into small units, thus registering thousands of new voters. The Japs used the same tactics but without success. Their defeat only added to the agitation and unrest on the part of the Jap nationals.

This tension reached a climax soon after the election.[9] It was the council's custom to introduce the new councilors to the community at the annual ratepayers' meeting which took place a few weeks following the election. Heretofore the meetings had been held either in the Town Hall or the Grand Theater. But this time in anticipation of an unusually large crowd, the meeting was held out-of-doors at the Shanghai Race Club. Hundreds of

---

9   The events described here in fact happened on 23 January 1941, eight months after Allman had been elected. The council had called an extraordinary ratepayers' meeting to seek approval for increasing rates by 40% backdated to January 1, 1940. This had enraged Japanese ratepayers.

ratepayers of all nationalities filled the
public stand. Facing the stand a special
platform had been built for the officials.
We sat at a long table in all our dignity
and various stages of the jitters, just
waiting for anything that might happen.
On a dais behind us sat Paul Scheel[10], the
Danish consul and doyen of the consular
body, who had been asked to preside as
chairman of the meeting.

Yukishi Hayashi, Chairman of the Japanese Ratepayers Association

It was the traditional privilege of any ratepayer to speak out
at this meeting. He could approve or condemn any action of the
council. A number of such speeches had been made by critical
American and British ratepayers when Hayashi[11], a nearsighted
little man who seemed to be hiding behind his huge, horn-
rimmed spectacles, mounted the platform. In a high Hitler-like
voice he harangued in Japanese for almost half an hour.

When he finished, instead of walking down the few steps and
returning to his seat in the stands as the others had done, he turned
and came toward the councilors' table, toward the end where I
was seated. I was already on the Japanese blacklist and I was a
bit qualmish about having an unknown person, especially a Jap,
get behind me. I pointed to the stairs and indicated with my head
that he was to leave that way. But he didn't seem to understand.
Confusedly he continued toward me. I quickly kicked out an
empty chair from the table and pushed it between us, blocking

---

10 Paul Scheel (born 1890) had been appointed Danish Consul-General and Consular
    Judge in 1935. Prior to that he had been at the Danish legation in London. After WWI,
    he served as Danish consul in Chicago for many years.
11 Yukishi Hayashi (born 1891), Chairman of the Japanese Ratepayers' Association and
    Chairman of the Amalgamated Japanese Street Unions. Hayashi was protesting the
    unfairness of imposing extra rates on Japanese when they had been denied a fair elec-
    tion. For further details see: F. Wakeman, *The Shanghai Badlands: Wartime Terrorism and
    Urban Crime*, 1937-1941, pp101-103.

his way. He sat down dazedly and listened to the interpreter translate his bitterly abusive speech. Then he went down the steps and back to his seat.

For some reason I was particularly unnerved by Hayashi's strange behavior and I kept my eye on him. In a minute or two I saw him slip out of his seat I watched his apparently aimless wanderings which brought him back to our platform and up the steps at the end opposite from where I sat. I tried to rationalize his movements. "He

W.J. "Tony" Keswick, Chairman of the SMC

probably has something to tell Mr. Scheel," I told myself, but, still disturbed, I watched him. All the others were intent on the speaker, C.W.J. Keswick[12], the S.M.C.'s youthful new chairman and head of one of the oldest British trading companies in Shanghai. Their eyes were glued to a spot just between his shoulders.

Before I realized what was happening Hayashi made a boxerlike twist, and as he turned, drew his revolver and fired two shots in the speaker's direction. In a split second what had been a dignified meeting was pandemonium, hellish with indistinguishable yells. At the sound of the first shot, which evidently they had been expecting, the Japs, who were sitting in a group, rose as one man with shouts of *"Banzai! Banzai."*

One shot got Keswick in the back and the other accidentally

---

12 William Johnstone "Tony" Keswick (1903–1990) was a member of the Keswick family that owned and ran Jardine Matheson. During the war, he was a member of the British Special Operations Executive.

The Pandemodium on the stage after the shooting

Japanese rush the stage. Major Bourne is at the top of the stairs blocking them

Okamoto with his hand bandaged on the stage

hit the fingers of I. Okamoto[13], a Japanese councilor, who was reaching out for the microphone, presumably to ask his nationals to calm down. The Japs, however, ignored Okamoto's pleas for order and threw bricks, which they had brought in with them, chairs, and anything else throwable they could lay their hands on. Their targets were the councilors, who sat in a stiff row on the elevated platform, too scared to move.

At the revolver's report the Shanghai municipal police had jumped to our aid and pushed us off the platform to safety. Then they took charge of the crazed Japs. How, I don't know, for I didn't wait around to see. We were all upset by this experience but fortunately there were no fatalities insofar as the councilors were concerned.

Keswick soon recovered from a slight flesh wound and was able to preside over council meetings until he was sent by his government to do war work in Washington. I was never sufficiently interested to find out what happened to Okamoto's fingers.[14] Hayashi, the would-be assassin, was arrested, sent to Japan, and sentenced to two years' imprisonment. The sentence, I understand, was suspended and no doubt by now he has been decorated for his brave deed.

Shortly before this meeting an assassin had fired several shots at Godfrey Phillips[15], the secretary-general of the S.M.C., and the police, greatly concerned for the safety of the councilors and senior staff, had asked us to go about the city with bodyguards and in

13   Issaku Okamoto (born 1889), lawyer and former Japanese diplomat who had served as Consul-General in Singapore and Consul in Seattle and Liverpool.

14   Allman continued to serve with Okamoto on the Council. A photo taken a few months later (see below) shows Okamoto's left ring finger still bandaged.

15   George Godfrey Phillips (1900-1965) had come to Shanghai in 1934 as deputy secretary of the council and been promoted to secretary in 1936. In 1939, he was promoted to Secretary-General on the retirement of Stirling Fessenden. On January 6, 1940, 3 gangsters had, in a scene right out of a movie, leapt from commandeered rickshaws and fired multiple shots at Phillips' car on Avenue Haig (Huashan Road) about 100 metres west of Route Ferguson (Wukang Road). He worked for the Special Operations Executive in WWII. He was awarded an CBE on January 1, 1943.

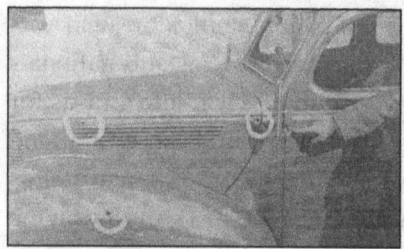

Bullet holes in Phillips' car

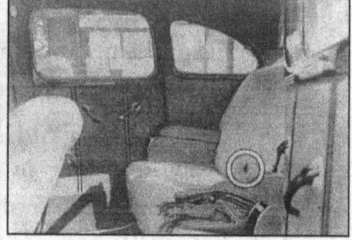

A bullet hole in the seat shows how close
Phillips came to being hit

bulletproof cars. There were not enough such cars in Shanghai
and had there been, they would have been too expensive for us.
Anyway, I was already watched over by two bodyguards and I
considered them encumberance enough. But as councilors none
of us again encountered physical violence from the Japs.

Aside from this exciting incident I found work on the council
interesting. During the first year Dr. R. J. McMullen[16] was my
American colleague. We got along famously. He was willing to
take on the committee work that required the most drudgery and
let me choose the committees that dealt with subjects with which
I was familiar, such as police (called the watch committee), public
utilities, and industrial relations. These committees offered many
legal problems.

The councilors met periodically, at least twice each month,
and oftener if matters of importance required it. We dealt with
policy. The details were handled by the paid and permanent staff,
which was headed by the secretary-general and broken down
into departments such as police, health, finance, public works,
legal, and so forth. The record of the administration of Shanghai
has been particularly honorable. With greater opportunities
for graft than those afforded by the average American city,

---

16   Allman's American colleague for 1940 was J.W. Carney. Carney returned to the USA in
     early 1941 and McMullen was selected in Carney's place in February 1941. Rev Robert
     Johnston McMullen (1884-1962) was a missionary and head of Hangchow Christian
     College as well as head of the American Association at the time.

there was never a scandal of any major proportions. Honesty in the S.M.C. was encouraged by payment of reasonably good salaries coupled with security of employment and eventual retirement pay. The bulk of employees were British, but there was a liberal sprinkling of other nationals. For many years the highly paid jobs of secretary-general and municipal advocate were held by two Americans, Stirling Fessenden[17] and Robert T. Bryan, Jr[18].

Stirling Fessenden, Secretary General of the SMC 1929-1939

The permanent council staff, especially those in the higher brackets, were honest, hard-working, capable British subjects, but, I thought, old-fashioned in their ideas. At first they were fearful that I might propose some shocking measure. Once I did. I horrified them by suggesting, of all things, daylight-saving time.

Another daring councilor had made the same suggestion some years before. His proposal had been snowed under. When I suggested that Shanghai try it

Robert Bryan Municipal Advocate

17   Stirling Fessenden (1875-1943) had come to Shanghai in 1903 and commenced practice of law in 1905. He was elected chairman of the SMC in 1923 and served until 1929 when he was appointed Secretary-General, a position he held until 1939 when he retired due to ill-health. He died in Shanghai during WWII.

18   Robert Thomas Bryan (1892-1974) was born in Shanghai. After studying at the University of North Carolina, he returned to Shanghai in 1917 and practiced for in the firm of Fleming, Davies and Bryan. He became police advocate (later Municipal Advocate) in 1928 and served until WWII. He returned to Shanghai after WWI as a legal adviser with the American embassy. He resigned to enter partnership with Cornell Franklin in November 1946. Following the Communist Revolution in 1951 he was arrested and imprisoned in Ward Road Gaol until 1952 when he was released across the Lowu Bridge to Hong Kong.

Shanghai Adopts Daylight Saving After Persuasion

By a Staff Correspondent of The Christian Science Monitor

SHANGHAI—After extensive debate and deep consideration by the municipal councils of Shanghai's two foreign areas, this city has at last gone over to "daylight saving time" for the present season. Shanghai is traditionally conservative, and the battle was not won without a struggle.

For a time, in fact, it seemed that the project was doomed because of two reasons—first, that a great many persons here had never even heard of the "more daylight" device so popular in many other parts of the world, and second, that Hong Kong refuses to change to "summer time" because it is in the tropics and there is little shift in the hours of daylight throughout the year.

N. F. Allman, newly-elected member of the S. M. C., refused to take "no" for an answer. Chinese members of the Council opposed daylight saving because they had never heard of it, but Mr. Allman told them to investigate among the Chinese community and they would find that all Chinese were natural daylight savers—inclined to fit their work to the sun, not the clock. They inquired and returned full converts.

Shanghai adopts daylight saving after persuasion by Allman

just to see how it worked, most of the staff, and my colleagues too, tried to dissuade me. Patiently they pointed out that they had queried Hong Kong on the subject and Hong Kong thought the idea foolish. I pointed out that New York, London, and even Tientsin were doing very well on daylight-saving time. My opponents advanced the argument that it would be difficult to jibe banking hours between Hong Kong and Shanghai. One prominent banker opposed the measure violently. I suggested that he might circumvent this weighty problem by having one of his junior clerks stay over the extra hours and keep in contact with Hong Kong. Ultimately Shanghai went on daylight-saving time and even staid Hong Kong fell into line by setting the clock ahead half an hour instead of the usual one hour.

Biggest headache of the S.M.C. was the tax question. The tax rate was always decided on at the annual ratepayers' meeting, where all who paid a minimum fixed amount of taxes were represented and had a vote. But in spite of this fact it was largely only by indirect methods that the municipal authorities managed to collect taxes and enforce regulations. With the passage of the years disciplinary measures were used less and less frequently, as a genuine civic spirit developed. Too, the development of public utilities – gas, water, electricity, and the telephone – gave the council a method of meeting tax evasions, for the franchises of these companies provided that they could only serve householders whose taxes were not in arrears. The council could block a householder off from using the public roads, cut off his telephone, his water, and electric power, if he refused to pay taxes. However, there were few tax fights. The refusal to pay was used mostly as a threat, a political weapon against rising taxes.

The councilors did not lack for helpful hints on how to run the Settlement in general and how to reduce the tax rate in particular. These came from all kinds and classes of people, including crackpots. Naturally, the councilors gave consideration to all of them.

One plan I recall was establishment of a lottery. This tax reduction scheme had considerable backing and while it was under discussion by the council a pious, old-style missionary, Dr. Charles W. Rankin[19], apprehensive that the council would approve such a sinful project, rose up in righteous wrath. In his efforts to prevent an S.M.C. legalized lottery

Dr Charles Rankin fearless opponent of gambling

he threatened to bring criminal action against the Chinese, British, and American councilors. Dr. Rankin was not fooling. A lawyer as well as a missionary, he threatened to prosecute each councilor individually and he went so far as to consult with the United States district attorney, the British crown advocate, and the Shanghai municipal advocate.[20]

In my day I've been lawyer, witness, plaintiff, and judge, but this was the closest I ever came to being a defendant in a case. In spite of his threats we gave the proposal every consideration. In the end we voted it down, not because we were intimidated by Dr. Rankin, but because we decided the scheme would not alleviate our tax problem.[21]

---

19   Charles Wright Rankin (1872-1960) was a missionary who established the Soochow University Law School in 1915. He led numerous campaigns against lotteries in China.
20   Respectively at the time, Leighton Shields, John McNeill and Robert T. Bryan. Rankin was not blustering. He successfully brought a private prosecution against the *North China Daily News* for publishing an advertisement for a lottery and then the winning numbers. *C.W. Rankin v. North China Daily News & Herald Ltd, NCH*, May 7, 1941; "An Appeal Withdrawn" *NCH*, Aug 13, 1941, p243
21   This may not be completely true. The council announced that it would not hold a charity lottery on the grounds that it was illegal under British and American law and noted that the council had already received a notice from a ratepayer that he would bring legal action if the lottery was approved. "New Council Bans Charity Lottery on Legal-Moral Grounds", *China Weekly Review*, May 11, 1940, p368

Like taxes, the encroaching Japanese were an ever-present problem. By this time they were beginning to think that the Asiatic world was their oyster and Shanghai their personal pearl. They had been in military occupation of Hongkew since 1937 and had prevented the Shanghai municipal police from operating in this area. They had ousted the Settlement bus and tram lines and put in their own. They had closed several public jettys and roads and by threat of confiscation had forced the council to sell these properties to them. In this way they had gained for themselves more than a mile of continuous stretch of wharf and river frontage.

Now, because of a coal shortage, it was necessary to ration electric power. This was rationed according to the dictates of the Japanese. Against my wishes more and more power was given to industries which favored the Japanese. While I argued against it I knew that there was nothing the S.M.C. could do.

The Japanese had the upper hand; they controlled the coal mines and all transportation. But the one thing we resisted to the bitter end was interference with the police. Demands of Jap councilors to increase their nationals on the police force were refused. Our view was that we had an adequate force, nor would we fire anyone to make room for a Jap. Until Pearl Harbor the Japanese were not in a position to force the issue. The Japanese, though, were determined to increase their representation on the council. In the spring of 1941 they warned the British that they could not guarantee to keep peace and order in the Japanese community if an annual election were held without this increased representation.

Indeed, tension between the Japs and the Anglo-American element was so high that election under any circumstances was fraught with danger. After some months of negotiations, certain parts of the Land Regulations (the governing charter of the

The newly formed Provisional Council. Allman is seated far left. McMullen is seated far right. McDonnell is standing second from left. The Chairman, seated centre, is John Hellyer Liddell (1899-1984) a British businessman

Shanghai Settlement) were suspended by agreement between the powers and a provisional council was set up. Under this Japanese and American representation was increased to three councilors each. Dr. McMullen and I had taken the stand that if Jap representation was increased American representation likewise would have to be increased. In this we were backed fully by the Shanghai American community and our own government. The British representation was decreased from five to three and the Chinese from five to four. Under the provisional council the national basis was broadened to include a German, an Italian, a Netherlander, and a Swiss. The 1941 election was omitted.

Because of conditions that part of the charter requiring the annual election of the councilors was suspended. The various nationalities appointed their own representatives. Dr. McMullen and I were reappointed and R. T. McDonnell[22] was named as the third American member.

Although we are now scattered to the four winds three of us are still members of the S.M.C., at least theoretically. At the war's outbreak all the British and American councilors in Shanghai were forced to resign, but McDonnell was in Chungking at the time and Haley[23], a British councilor, and I were caught in Hong Kong. We were never asked for resignations and I, for one, refuse to give the Japs the satisfaction of resigning voluntarily.[24]

---

22 Richard Timothy McDonnell (1887-1864), general Manager of William Hunt & Co. McDonnell had served on the council in the early part of 1940 as a co-opted member. He had unsuccessfully run for election in 1940. McDonnell had served in the US Army in Tientsin and rejoined after the war started rising to the rank of colonel. See also Chapter 9, footnote 7

23 George Arthur Haley (born 1886) vice-chairman of Imperial Chemical Industries China Ltd, who was appointed to the provisional council in July 1941 when G.E. Mitchell resigned. He had been a member of the council elected in 1940.

24 The council report for 1942 noted that Haley and McDonnell were absent and did not resume their positions. No mention was made of Allman. Mr Katsuo Okasaki (岡崎 勝男)(1897-1965), Counsellor of the Japanese Embassy, and post-war Foreign Minister of Japan, was appointed chairman. The council continued until 1943 with 3 Japanese, 3 Chinese, one German and one Swiss member. It was disbanded in 1943.

XVI
CARRYING ON FOR THE CLIENT

IN CHINA WHERE EXPERT OPINION was very often lacking, or the nearest expert was thousands of miles and weeks of travel away, the lawyer often had to be his own expert, even if it meant making a study of some other profession, or some phase of another profession. I always enjoyed doing that.

One case involving a ship collision required my studying navigation and ship construction. At first my client thought all this amusing. After I'd won him a satisfactory judgment as a result of my special studies his amusement turned to gratitude.[1]

I have always been interested in cases involving some phase of medicine, and during the course of my law practice in China I had occasion to study such subjects as psychiatry, surgery, cancer, the treatment of cancer by surgery and X-ray and radium, the effect of poison on the human system, and a number of minor medical subjects.

In order to handle one client's case I had to study up on the human brain. The client, Smith, a young motorcar salesman, was about to make a sale to his sweetheart, Olga, who had promised to buy a secondhand car from him. He was ready to have her sign on the dotted line when the girl's second-string suitor, Jones, stepped

---

1   Allman is probably referring to the case of the S.S. *Peter Kerr* which his firm had arrested for damage caused to S.S. *Dionyssios Statahos* in a collision on January 14, 1940. "Process Served on American Ship" *NCH*, Jan 24, 1940.

MONITION.

In the United States Court for China

AT SHANGHAI, CHINA

STATHATOS & CO., LTD.	No. Cause 4456 Civil 2335
vi.	IN
SS. PETER KERR	ADMIRALTY.

In obedience to a Warrant of Seizure to me directed, in the above-entitled cause, I have seized and taken into my possession the following-described property to wit: The SS PETER KERR, her boats, tackle, apparel and furniture. For the causes set forth in the libel now pending in the U. S. Court for China, at Shanghai, China, I hereby give notice to all persons claiming the said described SS PETER KERR, her boats, tackle, apparel and furniture, or knowing or having anything to say why the same should not be condemned and forfeited, and the proceeds thereof distributed according to the prayer of the libel, that they be and appear before the said Court, at the United States Court Room, in the City of Shanghai on the 6th day of February, 1940, at 10 o'clock on the forenoon of that day, if the same shall be a day of jurisdiction, otherwise on the next day of jurisdiction thereafter, then and there to interpose a claim for the same, and to make their allegations in that behalf.

GORDON CAMPBELL

Marshal of the United States Court for China.

Monition Notice against SS Peter Kerr

in and queered the deal. "The motorcar's no damned good," he said.[2] This was just one of many clashes between the young men in their battle over the young lady's favors. When Smith learned of Jones's interference he decided that the time had come to beat hell out of his rival. Smith left Olga's flat and stopped by the police station to consult his old friend, the desk sergeant. "How much will it cost to beat up a man?" he asked.[3]

The sergeant ventured that it would mean a twenty-five dollar fine. "That's too expensive for a sock on the jaw. Go home and forget it, he advised. But Smith thought the satisfaction of walloping Jones would be cheap at any price. He left the police station and went looking for Jones. He found him in a "Blood-Alley" bar and called

---

2   Smith was Glenn Mortimer Hargrave, a 25 year old former United States marine employed by Bills Motors as a salesman. Jones was Leslie Malcolm Bell. Bell was a well known Shanghailander who had been a member of the Amateur Dramatic Club and the SVC. His wife worked for the British consulate and he had two children. Despite Bell being married it does appear that the lady in question was "a dear friend to him". *US v Hargrave, NCH*, June 28, 1933, p508.

3   Sergeant Stocks.

Glenn Hargrave, convicted of   *Leslie Bell (right), Hargrave's victim, with his wife*
manslaughter

him outside.[4]

Now, Smith packed a mule's kick in his left hand. He punched Jones squarely on the jaw and knocked him down. Jones's head hit the sidewalk and he received injuries from which he died. Smith was arrested and charged with murder. Jones was British, but as Smith was an American his case was to be tried in the American court. In these extraterritorial matters the nationality of the defendant arbitrarily determined which court had jurisdiction. Smith lacked the money to engage a lawyer but his employer, a good friend of mine, asked me to represent him. I agreed.

Frankly, I was worried. I did not see at first blush how it could be anything but first-degree murder. But after several talks with

---

4   Bell had, in fact, seen Hargrave when he was driving on the Bund and the altercation occurred at the corner of Canton Road and the Bund. Hargrave and a passer-by had taken the unconscious Bell to the offices of Dr. Gardiner at 1 Canton Road. Bell died the next day in hospital of a brain hemorrhage.

my client I learned of his visit to the police station and of the sergeant's advice concerning assault and battery. Smith, clearly, had set out to commit this, not murder. I also learned that the police sergeant was to be the prosecution's star witness.

The United States district attorney[5] was determined to proceed with the charge of murder until I told him that if he did I intended to call his star witness and prove that Smith did not go out after Jones with murder in his mind, that is, with the premeditated idea of killing anyone, but that he had ventured forth to commit assault and battery. I told the D.A., "If you proceed with the charge of murder we will plead not guilty."

While the D.A. was thinking this over I pored over medical books and consulted local doctors. To my mind it was necessary to determine the exact cause of death. Did it result from the blow of the fist, because Jones hit the sidewalk, or from some other cause? Smith, in any case, was responsible for the death, but in order properly and fully to protect his interests it was important for me to know the exact cause of death and be able to explain it to the court. All the doctors agreed that death was due to a counter-coup, that is, when Smith socked Jones on the jaw the wallop was so terrific and so sudden that Jones's brains were jammed up against his skull, rupturing all blood vessels, and he died of internal hemorrhage.

This had no effect on the charge, but the fact that the defendant had not set out to commit a premeditated murder caused the D.A. to change the charge to manslaughter—whereupon we pled guilty. Smith stood up in court and told a straightforward story of the whole occurrence. Much to his own and my relief he was sentenced to two years' imprisonment on McNeil's Island. He might have been condemned to death had he been tried for

---

5   Dr. George Sellett (1898-1988) District Attorney from 1929 to 1934. See footnote 12, below.

murder.

Some time after his trial I found out that Smith had hit at least two other men with his powerful left hand and very nearly killed them. My parting advice to him was, "In future fights use your right hand."[6]

The case requiring the most concentrated study on my part was the revolt of the doctors of the Peking Union Medical College. The Peking Union Medical College of the Rockefeller Foundation, shortened for convenience to the P.U.M.C., was organized as a New York charitable institution and as such was subject to the jurisdiction of the United States Court for China.

From almost the first Percy Kent[7], a British barrister in Tientsin, had been retained as legal adviser, but as the case was to be tried in the United States Court for China he wanted an American associate. I was called in. But to begin at the beginning – Along about 1935 a group of P.U.M.C. doctors decided to reform the institution. It was their idea to oust the old management and

Judge Milton Helmick presiding over one of the PUMC trials at the American legation in Peiplng. Front row: Percy Kent (in his British barrister's robes), Allman, unknown, Robert T Evans, US lawyer from Tienstin.

6   In fact, Dr. Sellett in his submissions on sentence at the trial mentioned three instances when Hargrave had knocked out men. In one case the man assaulted had been married and had been anxious to settle. Sellett decided not to prosecute on the basis Hargrave paid compensation.

7   Percy Horace Braund Kent, O.B.E., M.C. (1876-1963) practiced in Tientsin from 1902. He was Chairman of the China Association, Tientsin.

reorganize with themselves in charge. They went so far in their undermining attempts that the administration feared the institution would be completely wrecked.

On Kent's advice the insurgents were dismissed. The latter sued for wrongful dismissal.[8] Not content with this suit, the leader of the malcontents hinted malpractice in the case of Mrs. Raider, a patient. He led the husband to believe that if he had been allowed to treat Mrs. Raider for cancer she would be alive. This so infuriated Raider that he brought suit for malpractice against the P.U.M.C.[9]

I soon found that to try the case intelligently I needed to know something about gynecology, cancer, X-ray, radium, and surgery. I had to prove that the men who had treated Mrs. Raider for cancer were competent men and had done all they possibly could, medically, scientifically, and humanely. I had flown up from Shanghai to Tientsin for consultations with Kent and now I turned over all other cases to my associates and literally "holed in" for two months of concentrated study. I consulted all the doctors I knew or could find and read all the medical books I could get my hands on, a considerable number since I had access to the P.U.M.C. library.

Having been a judge once myself, I was well aware that if a lawyer wants to win a case he must first make sure that the judge knows what it is all about. It gave me some satisfaction to put my hours of study to good use during the trial, which lasted several weeks and mostly concerned testimony of doctors, nurses, anesthetists, and physiotherapists who appeared for both sides.

One witness in explaining the methods of treatment went on for a half hour in Latin and German medical jargon. I was

8 The dismissed doctors were Chester M. Van Allen, John W. Spies, and John J. Wolfe. "Final Ruling in P.U.M.C. case" *NCH*, Aug 7, 1935, p238.
9 *Harry Raider v P.U.M.C.*, *NCH*, July 17, 1935, p95

watching Judge Helmick and could tell from his expression that he was first puzzled, then annoyed. Finally he could stand it no longer and broke in with a, "See here, this has gone on for days and I don't understand a word of it. Now just what does it all mean in plain English?" It was the doctor's turn to look bewildered. He thought he was speaking in simple language. I knew what he meant, having just read up on the subject; so I interrupted with,

"Your Honor, I believe that what this witness is saying is simply that in this particular case treatment by either radium or X-ray would have produced the same results."

When the long-drawn-out Raider case was dismissed, we won hands down. The doctors and cancer specialists who had treated Mrs. Raider were exonerated.

In the other case insurgent doctors were awarded a compromise judgment which gave them salaries for unexpired terms of their contracts but dismissed their claims for damages. The hospital repeatedly had offered to settle the case on this basis. As far as I could figure out the only one to benefit was N. F. Allman, who acquired an entirely new medical vocabulary most of which he has since forgotten!

Too, I found that a lawyer needs to know something about psychology. At times it comes in handy in dealing with difficult clients and their idiocyncrasies. For instance, a layman will often complain about the archaic verbosity of a legal paper. But let the lawyer prepare a brief document in plain English and he'll balk every time. Perhaps he thinks he isn't getting his money's worth.

It has always been my theory that a will could be drawn up in fifty words or less, but in all my experience I can recall only one client who fell in with my way of thinking and was not shocked by the lack of legal verbiage. This man told me he wanted a will he could thoroughly understand. He wanted it as brief as possible and written in plain English. I wrote his will, which by the way disposed of a million dollar estate, in forty words. No question was ever raised as to its validity. And while I'm mentioning wills, let me say that the foreign lawyer in China was hampered by untold complications in settling estates, particularly when a client died intestate.

I recall a rather discouraging case where a British subject died without leaving a will. Heirs were located in Scotland and in the United States, but while they were squabbling over the appointment of an administrator, the estate, entirely in Chinese dollars and once valued in millions, dwindled with the decreasing value of the currency to practically nothing.

There was the incident of the American consular officer who left a will but little else. In going over his papers and personal belongings I found that his estate consisted mostly of Chinese pornographic paintings, some rare and valuable. I was between the devil and the deep sea as to what to do. If I sold the paintings I might be guilty of dealing in obscene matter. If I destroyed them I might be charged with embezzlement. I submitted my predicament to the judge who, too, was stumped. We went over the list together. Fortunately we found an old top hat and some antiquated photographic equipment. The judge intimated that they might be sold for a high price and the paintings thrown in. I followed his suggestion.

Most important of all, a lawyer must know everything there is to be known about his client and his witnesses before introducing them in court. A reputable lawyer will not tell a witness what he is to say. On the other hand a careful lawyer will not deliberately produce a witness unless he is sure of what the witness knows.

One of my Shanghai colleagues[10] had an unpleasant shock

---

10   Cornell Franklin, Allman's partner at time was the colleague. Franklin and William Fleming were defending the District Attorney Leonard Husar (see Chapter 7).

when without investigation he introduced as a character witness a man who turned out to be a liar. Not only the lawyer but the entire Shanghai American community was shocked to learn that the man they had unqualifiedly accepted as a hero and made a community leader was a downright fake, a megalomaniac with a hero complex.

Unaware of what his grand gesture was going to cost him in prestige, this man, whom I'll call Colonel Riley[11], volunteered to appear as a character witness to bolster the supposedly good standing of another prominent citizen charged with bribery. For years Colonel Riley had boasted in Shanghai clubs and bars of his Congressional Medal of Honor. Proud to have such a hero in their midst, the American community quickly had appointed him to boards and asked him to serve on civic committees. He had accepted all honors. The defense lawyer probably thought that the favorable testimony of a holder of the Congressional Medal of Honor was the equivalent of having an angel from heaven come down to intercede for his client.

The colonel, every inch a hero and pillar of society, went along in fine style during his examination by the defense attorney. The latter made an enthusiastic speech about the witness, and the witness, suffused with delusions of grandeur, elaborated on the story of how he had won his medal and went on to enumerate any number of other heroic

Capt. W.I. Eisler, purported Medal of Honour winner

---

11   Capt. Whitney Irving Eisler (1874-1936) was giving alibi evidence in support of DA Husar. Eisler had served in the US Navy and Philippines Coast Guard. He had been Vice-President of the American Chamber of Commerce. A short summary of his testimony and retraction can be found at *US v Husar, NCH*, May 7, 1927, p257 at 258. Eisler said that he did have a Spanish war decoration but admitted he did not have a Medal of Honour.

deeds.

But unfortunately for the colonel, the district attorney[12], a newcomer to Shanghai, did not take the community hero for granted. To his experienced ear the story did not ring true. He asked for adjournment of the trial and took this opportunity to check with Washington. The day of reckoning for the poseur was swift and sudden.

When the trial reopened the D.A. recalled the witness for cross-examination. He led the colonel into a detailed description of the heroic act that had won him the medal. He asked particulars of the battle. Where was it? What was the date? What did you do? So on and so forth until the colonel was hopelessly enmeshed in dates, names, and places. Then, in reputation-shattering words, the D.A. offered conclusive evidence that Washington had no record of the colonel's medal. Also, the colonel by his own admission had put himself thousands of miles away from the scene at the time of the battle he had described so vividly and so often to admiring listeners.

To brag about honors you have is bad enough, but to claim honors you don't have is unforgivable. The trial resulted in a jail sentence for the accused and complete loss of face for the colonel. He was forced to retire from civic posts and resign from the better clubs. His latter years were spent in obscurity.

While lawyers the world over study other professions, as well as the human frailties and the individual idiosyncrasies of clients and witnesses, it was necessary for the Shanghai lawyer to go a bit further. He had to be prepared at a moment's notice to step in and take over a client's business and run it for him for months or

12   Dr George Sellett (1898-1988). Sellett had just been appointed District Attorney but had arrived in Shanghai 4 years before to take up a professorship in law at Comparative Law School of Soochow University. He had been acting dean in 1924. He also established the firm of Sellett & Blume. Sellett later became a director of CNAC. After the communist revolution he lived in Hong Kong until 1980 but died at the Morrison Community Hospital in the USA.

perhaps even years at a time.

When the owner or manager of a business was called home suddenly for a business conference that stretched into months, or was caught in Europe by war, or died without appointing a successor, the lawyer, already acquainted with some details of the business, seemed the logical one to take over, at least until some qualified person could be sent out to China from the United States, the estate settled, or the business sold.

It simply was taken as a matter of course that the Shanghai business man would call on his lawyer in any emergency. As a result the lawyer led a busy but extremely interesting life.

Time and time again what started out strictly as a legal case turned into a nonlegal job. When a Metro-Goldwyn-Mayer representative consulted me about a number of routine legal matters in connection with the filming of The Good Earth[13] I had no idea I'd end up as a casting director.

It came about in this way: Frank Messenger[14], head of the group that came out to China to film background scenes for the picture, was recalled to Hollywood in the midst of negotiations and I was left holding a bag stuffed full of extraneous nonlegal details. One item was disposition of several carabao purchased for shipment to California.

The carabao, or water buffalo, is the most useful beast of burden the Chinese possess and is almost indispensable in rice

---

13 The Good Earth a novel by Pearl S. Buck (1892-1973) published in 1931 won the Pulitzer Prize in 1932. The novel dramatized the life of a Chinese family before WWI focused on Wang Lung a poor farmer who becomes rich buying the House of Hwang and marrying a slave girl who worked for them, O-Lan. Buck won the Nobel Prize for Literature in 1938 "for her rich and truly epic descriptions of peasant life in China and for her biographical masterpieces".

14 Charles Frank Messenger (1891-1939) was a production manager for MGM.

growing. No doubt one or two of these beasts pictured grazing under a tree would have added much to the film's local color. But two important facts were overlooked. China has a law prohibiting export of carabao, and the United States has a law prohibiting import. As I've already said, anything can happen in China. After some difficulty the Chinese export license was obtained. I was still working on American permission when the studio discarded the whole idea. I was left with the carabao on my hands. As I was anything but expert in the feeding, training, and upkeep of water buffalo, I decided they'd better go back to their farms.

The original plan had been to film the entire picture in China and make it bilingual, with a Chinese girl and a Chinese boy in the leading roles. When Mr. Messenger left Shanghai he nonchalantly dumped the details of casting on my desk. He ignored my protests that I was a busy lawyer. "Easiest thing in the world to pick two stars out of almost five hundred million people," he said.

That's what he thought! Actually it was damned difficult to find two Chinese of any age or sex who could speak both Mandarin and English. Another thing, China had few experienced movie actors to offer. I saw numerous ten-reel Chinese feature films, trying to locate possibilities, but this method failed. I remember sitting through one documentary film of a Chinese famine area, and this cost me money as well as time. Conditions pictured were so horrible that then and there I made a donation, contributing a much larger sum than I otherwise would have.

As a last desperate measure and to avoid seeing any more dreary films, I advertised in the Chinese press in Tientsin, Peking, and Shanghai. For days on end my office was jammed with youthful Chinese movie aspirants. A few could act, some were definitely photogenic, but the bilingual feature eliminated

Sixteen Chinese Biting Nails Waiting For Verdict From MGM

Sixteen would-be Shanghai movie-stars are awaiting with more or less trepidation the outcome of the decision of Hollywood's casting-Agents for the Metro-Goldwyn-Mayer film version of Pearl Buck's best-seller, "The Good Earth," a novel of China.

In March, 1934, the M-G-M China Company arrived with a troup of cameramen, technologists, directors, scene-designers, script-writers, et al and for six months were busy throughout Central and North China making exterior shots for "The Good Earth." During their stay here they also searched for two Chinese actors to play "Olan," the woman, and "Wang Lung," the man, leading characters in the book. But they were unsuccessful in finding just what they wanted and entrusted Allman and Company, American law firm, to find suitable types. Allman and Company inserted advertisements in several vernacular papers. All told, about 200 applicants responded. This number was narrowed down to about 16, eight men and eight women. Screen and voice tests of all 16 were made here and a month ago were sent to Hollywood.

If M-G-M is satisfied with the screen tests they now have, one or two each for the roles of "Olan" and "Wang Lung" will be selected. The lucky actors and actresses will be given trips to Hollywood and will act at rather welcome salaries. But if M-G-M is not satisfied, the search for suitable types will be reopened here by Allman and Company.

"The Good Earth" is one of the most ambitious of M-G-M pictures. The dialogue will be in Mandarin Chinese with superimposed English titles, the second American-made film on a large scale to be produced in such manner. ("Igloo," an Eskimo film, made by M-G-M, was the first). The film is expected to be released early in 1936.

"The Good Earth" is not the only film with China as a background being made in Hollywood. Warner Brothers, according to Hollywood reports, have almost completed the film version of Alice Tisdale Hobart's novel, "Oil For the Lamps of China."

The China Press reports on Allman's search for stars for the Good Earth

Paul Muni and Luise Rainer chosen to act in the Good Earth rather than Chinese actors.

most of them. Then, too, the more conservative Chinese were incensed over the idea of their daughters taking up screen acting as a career, and even the enthusiasm of the daughters could not overcome family conservatism. Anyway, it was all "love's labor lost," because by the time the screen tests were under way MGM had signed up Paul Muni and Louise Rainer for the leading roles.

I think I broke even on this work by taking a mean advantage of one of MGM's ace camera men, Charlie Clark. I induced him to spend all of one bitter cold February day taking moving pictures of Pete Bradford[15] and myself as we practiced shots at the Kiangwan polo field.

The majority of a China lawyer's clients expect him to advise them on all phases of their business undertakings. This advisory business usually drags the lawyer into such deep water he can't swim back, although it may have been that I was more susceptible than most. *Pete Bradford, Shanghai polo star*

15   Peter Bradford was a polo star in Shanghai. He was a manager for American Express and moved to Shanghai in 1931. He left in 1935 to many accolades for his contribution to polo in Shanghai.

At any rate I was probably involved in more nonlegal undertakings than any other practicing lawyer in Shanghai. In handling legal contracts for my client and good friend, T. J. Holt[16], a motion picture exhibitor, I grew interested in the business. By the time war overtook us all, I was one of a group of Shanghailanders who had incorporated to build an additional new modern cinema.

T.J. Holt – Shanghai movie magnate

The war in canceling this venture probably postponed a good many headaches.

The Shanghai exhibitor's problems before the war were more complicated than those of an exhibitor in an average American city, as his clientele was made up of every known nationality. In normal times the exhibitor's first thought in selecting a film was: will this offend the Chinese, the British, the Japanese, the French, the Italians, the Greeks, or the Germans? It was assumed that no film could offend the Americans. The Chinese were particularly fond of musical comedies which they called "singing pictures," but the Europeans favored gangster films. I don't know why.

Then, there was the problem of getting a picture passed by censorship boards of three different municipalities, namely the French Concession, the Shanghai Council, and the mayor's office of the municipality of Greater Shanghai. To justify their existence and show that they were on the job all censors requested cuts. No two ever wanted the same deletion. Our problem was to

---

16 T.J. Holt (He Tinran) (born 1892) was Chinese. He began as a theatre manager working at the Isis Theatre in 1923. By 1937, he owned five of Shanghai's big movie theatres, the Nanking, Grand, Cathay, Metropol and Realto. Allman was a director of the company. After the Chinese revolution in 1949 Holt moved to Hong Kong where he worked for the Hoover Theatre and, later, the Shaw Brothers.

NORWOOD F. ALLMAN

The destroyed projection equipment and badly bruised projectionist at the Isis Theatre

retain enough of the film to amuse the audience. I remember one picture, *The Ghost Goes West*, which was censored in so many spots that it only bewildered the audience, and the run was terminated after one showing.

Sometimes the exhibitors ignored national idiosyncrasies and on more than one occasion Mussolini's countrymen rioted in the theater, destroyed the film, and committed other playful fascist acts.[17] Even a historical picture like Catherine the Great was likely to offend the Russian community, or perhaps the French community, if the slightest aspersion were cast upon a minor French diplomat. Somehow in spite of all difficulties the show went on and Shanghai for a number of years was one of Hollywood's biggest foreign markets.

Another client was responsible for catapulting me into

---

17   In February 1937, Italian sailors from gunboat *Lepanto* attacked the Isis Theatre in Chinese territory on North Szechuan Road. They drive the audience out with ammonia and smashed the projection equipment. They were protesting against the showing of the Soviet film "Absynnia". Similar attacks by Italians had occurred in 1929 and 1930. "Italian Sailors Raid and Burn 'Absynnia' Film" *China Weekly Review*, Feb 27, 1937, p438.

management of the China Fibre Container Company, a paperboard mill. When the Sino-Japanese war started in 1937, A. E. Mandel[18], a client of mine for many years, was in Manila. He cabled me to look after his plant until he was able to return. This I did in a haphazard sort of way between S.V.C. duties until Mandel's return, when the fighting moved away. But he died shortly thereafter of a heart attack. As administrator of the estate it was up to me to run the business until I could find a man to take over.

The company's product was sold mostly in Shanghai, Hong Kong and Manila. All during those war years, 1937- 1941, we were up against shipping difficulties. Also, because of unsettled conditions in the Orient it was impossible to induce a qualified paper-mill man to leave the comparative safety of his home to come out and run things in our war-torn environs. I found myself with a full-time job that was unexciting but required exacting routine attention. For my own convenience I moved the mill office from the factory to a room next door to my law office in Hamilton House. At that the mill took more time from my law practice than I wanted to give and in sheer desperation I engaged as manager a man who swore he knew all about paper mills. Too late I discovered that he was a much better bookkeeper than mill manager.

Knowing nothing whatsoever about the ups and downs of the pulp market, I had to make important decisions blindly. In 1939, as the European crisis neared, the banks suggested that the mill's large supply of pulp be sold and the mill be put in a liquid cash position for protection. But as most of the pulp was imported from Europe it seemed to me that we were better off with pulp than the cash. This proved to be correct, although

18   Albert Edward Mandel (1880-1938). The China Fibre Container Company was established by Mandel in Shanghai in 1922.

it was just a lucky guess on my part. My paper-mill problem came to a sudden end early in 1941 when on behalf of the heirs in America I was able to sell the property to two Europeans. I suppose the Japanese are running the mill now.

XVII
A PRICE ON MY HEAD

THE MOST INTERESTING EXTRALEGAL activity I ever stumbled into was the job of publishing one of the world's largest Chinese language newspapers. This came about through my friendship with Mr. Shih Liang-ts'ai[1], owner of the *Shun Pao*[2].

As a part of my curriculum in the student interpreter corps I had studied modern newspaper Chinese in order to translate political articles in the daily press. Modern newspaper Chinese is almost a separate written

Shih Liang-ts'ai, assassinated publisher of the Shun Pao

language composed of *wen-li* (the classical written Chinese understood by scholars and a very few others) and *pai-hwa* (the vernacuar), plus a generous sprinkling of modern Chinese terms such as "flying boat" (airplane), and the like. Most newspapers have sections in all three languages so that both the erudite scholar and the coolie, barely able to decipher the characters, can find something to read.

In studying modern newspaper Chinese I had become

---

1   Shi Liangcai (史量才) (1880-1935).
2   Shenbao (申报)

interested in the two leading Chinese language dailies, then the *Shih Pao* published in Tientsin, and Shanghai's *Shun Pao*. Both were well written and mostly in the modern newspaper style which I could read. It was during my Mixed Court days that I first met Mr. Shih, who had purchased the latter paper in 1911. It wasn't long before he asked me to contribute articles on legal and international political subjects. A friendship sprang up, and in 1925 Mr. Shih asked me to handle his legal affairs.

The offices of the Shun Pao on Hankow Road in Shanghai

Our friendship continued until 1935 when somewhere between Shanghai and Nanking Mr. Shih was mysteriously murdered. Many thought he had been assassinated by one of the groups or individuals he might have offended in his vigorously independent editorials.[3] Numerous other theories were advanced but to this day the murder remains unsolved. Mr. Shih's eighteen-

Scene of the assassination of Shih

Shih's hearse in the streets of Shanghai

3   Frederick Wakeman shows convincingly that Shih was assassinated on orders of Chiang Kai-shek. See F. Wakeman, *Policing Shanghai, 1927-1937* p257-259.

year-old son, I. K. Shih[4], inherited the paper and took over the management. I continued as legal adviser.

At the onset of the Sino-Japanese war in 1937, young Shih was faced with a desperate problem. The Japanese issued an ultimatum. "Play our game or take the consequences." And the consequences were death.

Since its founding in 1872 by Mr. F. Major, a British tea merchant, the Shun Pao had been free from any propaganda motives and fearless in its editorial policy. Young Shih wanted to keep it that way. He did not want to capitulate to the Japs, nor was he yet ready to die. Diplomatically he hedged by suspending publication for several months.[5] But because his large staff was thrown out of employment by the suspension and also because the *Shun Pao's* 150,000 subscribers were clamoring for its reappearance, young Shih came to me for advice.

I suggested that, since he had no intention of giving way to Japanese pressure and since he and all his staff had been threatened, it would be the better part of valor for him to leave Shanghai until conditions changed.

He was willing to go away if I would take over the management of the paper and continue its independent news and editorial policy. I agreed on condition that I be given absolute control. Both conditions were carried out until December 8,1941.

In order to limit my financial liability I formed an American corporation[6]. My fellow directors were P. M. Anderson[7] and the

---

4   Shi Yonggeng (史泳庚). After WWII. Shi was forced to sell a 51% stake in the paper to the Kuomintang government.
5   For a few months the *Shun Pao* was printed in Hong Kong and distributed into China.
6   The Columbia Publishing Co, Inc. of Delaware.
7   Paul Maxwell Anderson (1892-1966) was in life insurance in Shanghai. He opened the office for Occidental Life Insurance Co of California in Shanghai in 1933. For three years he also was a party in a high end car dealership with Mr Louis Ferrogiarro. He served as a major in the US Army and is buried in Arlington National Cemetery.

 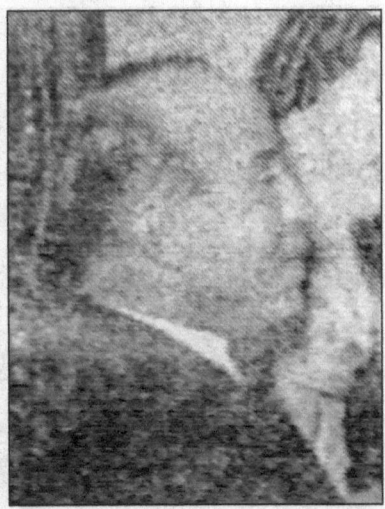

P.M. Anderson and Happy Adams, Allman's partners in Shun Pao

late W. A. Adams[8]. I personally, however, was solely responsible for the editorial and news content. Neither I nor this American company ever advanced any claim to owning the paper, and it was well known to everyone in Shanghai that I was publishing and editing the *Shun Pao* for the Chinese owner, but on my own responsibility.

I was as proud as any member of the Shih family of the *Shun Pao's* traditions, and I would sooner have cut off my right arm than give in to Japanese "cooperation." One of my prized possessions is a telegram from the Generalissimo commending the paper's stand.

The *Shun Pao* boasted the most modern newspaper plant in the entire Far East. It had three Hoe presses and an average daily paid circulation of 150,000. Due to a Chinese publishing peculiarity the circulation was deliberately kept down to this

8   William Alexander "Happy" Adams (1883-1941) was president of the China Realty Company. He also served as an officer of the American Troop of the SVC and secretary of the American Club. He died in Shanghai in November 1941.

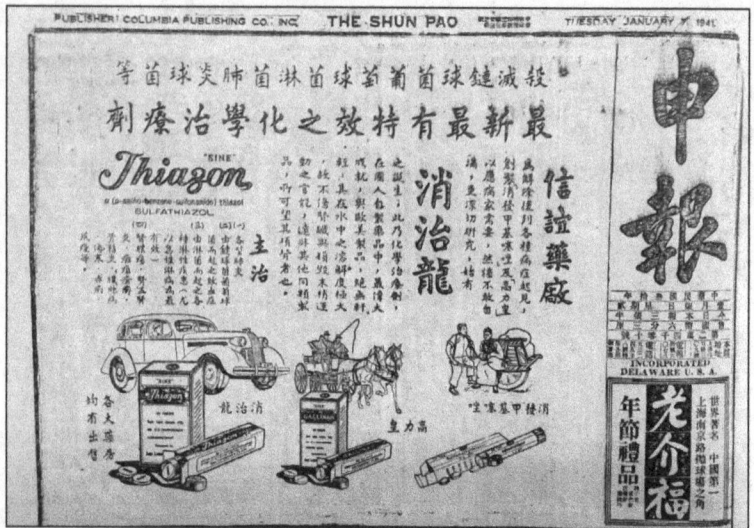

The Shun Pao masthead. Published by the Columbia Publishing Co, Inc. of Delaware

figure. Chinese advertising rates were based solely on space and not on circulation. Therefore a Chinese advertiser paid no more to reach 150,000 subscribers than he did to reach 50,000.

The *Shun Pao* was jealous of its independence and literary merits. It catered to the home and school, to the intellectual and the man in the street. Contrary to the usual custom of the Chinese press, it neither sought nor accepted subsidies from any source. Nor was it to be confused with any of the China Coast propaganda rags and blackmailing or "mosquito papers." The latter publications, usually weeklies or biweeklies with a few hundred circulation, were generally printed for one or two issues at the most just to embarrass some wealthy or political figure.

Except for its Chinese characters and pagination the *Shun Pao* was much like any up-and-coming American paper. I must admit the *Shun Pao's* page numbering presented a real Chinese puzzle to the Western reader. If, say, he picked up the first two sheets which were folded together, and read from right to left in the true Chinese fashion, he was likely to find that the page sequence went 2, 3, 6, 7, 8, 4, 1. If he took the sheets three and four, again folded together, he might possibly be confronted by the sequence 10, 11, 14, 15, 16, 13, 12, 9. The theory was that each sheet should be read by itself, and as each sheet was given a number, there should be no difficulty in following the proper sequence of pages. Actually the method followed by the average Chinese reader was to run through the entire paper until he eventually hit upon the page he wanted.

There were daily features such as the editorial, a woman's page with learned discourses on woman's rights and duties 'at home, a children's page with its "small stories," and a column headed "Fifty Years Ago Today." Further to intrigue our readers there were translations from leading" American publications. We lifted these bodily from such magazines as *Time*, *Life*, *Collier's*, and *Cosmopolitan*, without permission or payment, as was our right under the Sino-American treaties. Unlike other China publications, we were punctilious in giving due credit lines to the periodicals.

From 1937 until December 8, 1941, the *Shun Pao* was the only unbiased Chinese newspaper of any consequence to which the 250,000,000 Chinese in occupied areas had access. The *Sin Wan Pao*[9] followed our lead in the treatment of news but lacked editorials.

Often it was necessary to smuggle the circulation into Free China as well as into many of the occupied ports, not to mention Hong Kong, where the Chinese press also was censored to death.

Japanese kept a twenty-four-hour vigil in the Chinese post office and automatically confiscated any copy of the *Shun Pao*

---

9 *Sin Wan Pao*(新聞報) was established by an American, John C. Ferguson in 1896. It had been taken over by Chinese interests and initially after the Japanese invasion limited its reporting. Later, it was published by an American company leading to great freedom in its reporting.

The Chinese Post Office on North Szechuan Road

that came their way. We found numerous methods of outwitting them. One was to send a truckload of fictitiously addressed copies to the usual mailing platform. Then, while the Japs were busy seizing and destroying those, other trucks drew up at the back of the building, and with the connivance of friendly Chinese postal employees our men speedily and quietly unloaded the papers and put them in the mails. Due to a queer Japanese myopia, back doors were never guarded.

We also made good use of Japanese steamers to smuggle the *Shun Pao* upriver to such occupied cities as Hankow and Nanking. Practically every steamer employee innocently carried a copy on board with him. Their copies were wrapped around packages, and still others were shipped in bundles as wastepaper.

The *Shun Pao* maintained a news-gathering force of twenty-five reporters in Shanghai alone, plus string correspondents in every large Chinese city. It carried releases of all the world-wide news agencies, and its own communication system picked up news from Free China. We didn't have to wait for the news to go to London, New York, Berlin, or Tokyo and come back to us propagandized.

And this seems a good place to say a little something about propaganda.

Decent American news never had adequate coverage in the Chinese language press, and no one seemed to care much or even take the Chinese press seriously except the Japanese and the Germans. Until recent years American news reached the Chinese press through translations from Reuters, Havas, Tass, Domei, Transocean and the Italian Stafani agency. This Europeanized American news was confined largely to the seamy side of American life, as most of these agencies had national axes to grind and were only too happy to black-guard and belittle Americans.

For years all these agencies maintained excellent Chinese translation and most of them supplied complete translations to the Chinese press free or for a nominal charge. When the few ethical Chinese newspapers began throwing this propagandized news into the wastebaskets, both the Germans and the Japanese established their own Chinese-language newspapers to publish the stuff. And now there is not one "free" and independent Chinese-language newspaper in all Chinese-occupied territory. The Japanese-controlled Chinese press has for years been violently preaching hatred of the whites, particularly of Americans and British. The German-controlled press has also done and is doing its part in urging the extirpation of American and British interests from the Far East. The cumulative effect of all this hatred bodes ill for American interests in China, whether missionary, cultural, or commercial.

American news agencies cannot be expected to do much to correct this situation, since their business is the collection and dissemination of news on a commercial rather than a propaganda basis. Due to the practice of most of the European agencies and the Japanese agency Domei in giving away their services, the Chinese press has not been educated to pay for news services. This situation will require serious attention in the postwar era.

In Shanghai, Kuomin, the Chinese news agency, distributed translations of foreign news to the Chinese press for years. Even when the national government established the Central News Agency it allowed Kuomin to carry on as a sort of orphan stepchild.

Later the puppet government of Wang Ching-wei[10] in Nanking also had a news agency, Domei-controlled, which accepted occasional translations from Kuomin and published some of them, especially bad news for the Allies or something that could be construed with an unfavorable slant toward the white man and his ways.

In connection with his news agency, Wang Ching-wei established the

Wang Ching-wei: Head of the Japanese controlled puppet government of China

10 Wang Ching-wei (汪精衞 Wang Jingwei) (1883–1944) was a senior Kuomintang leader who the Japanese convinced to head the Reformed Government of China which was controlled by the Japanese. Wang died in Japan in 1944 when receiving medical treatment.

Nanking *Central China Daily News* in Shanghai about a block from us. The *Shun Pao* staff was none too happy about this but joined all Shanghai in chuckling over a typographical error. A patriotic typesetter had inserted, "Down with the traitor — Wang Ching-wei" in a half-page ad, and intentionally or otherwise the proofreader had not caught it. The error wasn't noticed until all copies were on the streets. Then everybody saw it, and in Wang's own paper, too.[11]

I took over the *Shun Pao* just at the time the Japanese were beginning their insidious needling of the Shanghai Municipal Council to force a strict censorship of the International Settlement press. The council called a meeting of all publishers of both foreign and Chinese-language newspapers, explained its predicament and requested our cooperation. The press flatly refused to accept any censorship but agreed to delete editorials or news items that would tend to provoke violence in the Settlement.

The *Shun Pao's* stand was that it never printed inflammatory news, although it was well known that in the quarter-century of Shih Family ownership and management it had never hesitated to criticize any individual, institution, or government. I made it plain to the council that the *Shun Pao* hadn't the slightest intention of submitting to even the mildest form of censorship. The *Shun Pao*, I advised, would continue to publish news as news and not as propaganda.

This, coupled with the fact that editorially we continued to condemn Japanese action in China, angered the Japanese, of course. They charged us with being a pro-Chungking newspaper. I knew that before too long something would break, but just

---

11   The words were included in an advertisement for the Dah Sen Gambling House in Nantao in December 1941. This resulted in a raid on the premises by Chinese police who smashed furniture and arrested the manager and several of his assistants. The paper apologized. "Gambling Den Smashed by Chinese Police", *NCH*, Dec 11, 1940, p416.

Journalists Threatened

Nanking Authorities Demand That One British And Six American Pressmen Should Be Banished

Shanghai, July 16.

DEMANDS that seven foreign newspapermen, including a member of the Shanghai Municipal Council, Mr. N. F. Allman, publisher of the "Shun Pao," should be banished from Shanghai, were reported last night to have been made by Mr. Wang Ching-wei to Mayor Fu Siao-en, following previous orders for the arrest, of four prominent Chinese newspapermen.

The complete manifesto, which was to have been released by a news agency in today's editions of all newspapers, came over the air last night, when one of the foreign newsmen named in the "order," Mr. C. D. Alcott, broadcast the intimation that they might be required to leave Shanghai.

In addition to Mr. Allman and Mr. Alcott, the order requesting that these foreign journalists should be asked to leave Shanghai named:

Mr. C. V. Starr, Director of American Asiatic Underwriters and President of the "Shanghai Evening Post and Mercury";

Mr. Randall Gould, Editor of the "Shanghai Evening Post and Mercury," and correspondent in Shanghai for a number of American newspapers:

Mr. J. B. Powell, Editor and Publisher of the "China Weekly Review," and Secretary and Executive Editor of the "China Press."

Mr. H. P. Mills, publisher of the "Hwa Mei Pao"..

Mr. J. A. E. Sanders-Bates, Managing Director of the University Press, Ltd., publishers of the "British Evening News."

Allman finds out he is on the black list

what would happen and when, I wasn't sure.

It was early morning of July 16, 1940, and the beginning of what promised to be one of those horrendously hot Shanghai days. I was sitting at the breakfast table reading the British-owned English language paper, *The North China Daily News*. As usual there was little that the *Shun Pao* hadn't printed the day before, anyway nothing to excite one on so sticky a morning. It was time for my first cigar, and I was about to shout, "Boy!" when a news head, buried at the bottom of an inside page, according to the best tradition of "the old lady of the bund," caught my eye. "Newspaper Men on Black List," I read. Then I went further and found that eighty-seven Chinese and seven foreign newspaper men had been ordered by the Wang Ching-wei (Japanese) government, to leave Shanghai. I was one of them. That was the first I knew that I was on any Japanese black list.

I can't say that I was particularly surprised. It was a bit of a shock and I admit I was worried; I had no way of knowing how far they would go in trying to enforce their order.

The other foreigners were C. V. Starr, publisher, and Randall Gould, editor of the *Shanghai Evening Post and Mercury*; J.B. Powell, editor and publisher of the *China Weekly Review*; Carroll Alcott, news commentator for radio station XMHA (owned by U. S. Harkson[12], another American, whom the Japs evidently had lost in the shuffle); Hal P. Mills, editor of the *Hwa Mei Wan Pao*; all Americans; and J. A. E. Sanderson Bates, a British subject and manager of the *University Press*. About fifteen of the eighty-seven Chinese were *Shun Pao* men. Both Powell and I also were directors of the Chinese-owned *China Press*.

---

12 Ulysses Severin Harkson (1893-1969) head of the Henningsen Produce Company that had a large share of the ice cream and candy bar business in Shanghai. Harkson worked with Allman in the OSS during WWII.

Others on the Black List

Cornelius Vander Starr (1892-1968) founded the insurance company AIG in China. He set up his first insurance venture in China in 1919. In 1943, Starr set up the OSS' Insurance unit in New York as a way to identify German and Japanese properties to attack. Insurance companies were given by their clients detailed lists of plant and equipment. Starr had through AIG been providing such intelligence and more through AIG from at leat the late 1930s when in China.

Randall Chase Gould (1895-1975) had been a journalist in Asia from 1923. He continued to edit the Shanghai Post and Mercury while back in America during the war and returned to China after the war. From 1949 he worked for the Denver Post in Denver. In 1941 and 1946 respectively, he published the books, *Chungking* and *China in the Sun*.

John Benjamin Powell (1886-1947) first came to China in 1917 to co-found *Millard's Review of the Far East*. In 1922 he took over the paper and later renamed it the *China Weekly Review*. When WWII started, Powell was arrested by the Japanese, accused of espionage and held at Bridge House for many months. He was forced to sit on a concrete floor in the cold and hardly fed. On his repatriation in August 1942, he weighed only 75 pounds (30 kilograms) and suffered gangrene. Both his feet needed to be amputated. He died in 1947, not having fully recovered from his injuries. His son, Bill Powell, was tried for sedition in 1959 for alleging the US had used chemical weapons in Korea. The case ended in a mistrial.

	**Carroll Duard Alcott** (1901-1965) came to Asia as a journalist in 1927 and moved to Shanghai soon afterwards where he worked for a time for C.V. Starr's *Shanghai Mercury*. He broadcast every evening from 8.00pm to 8.15pm and was a must-listen for English speaker. The Japanese tried to jam his broadcasts. He left Shanghai in September 1941 and was in America when the Pacific War started. He was seeking funds to finance an American radio station in the Far East. He worked for the Office of War Information and OSS as a broadcaster from 1942 to 1943. He published a book in 1943, "*My War with Japan*".
	**Harold Peck "Hal" Mills** (1896-1956) had come to China as a journalist and wrote extensively for the *China Press* particularly on boxing. Mills had been the subject of numerous attacks since 1938 and lived in a hotel with 24-hour police protection. In August 1940 he was sent a package containing 2 heads of Chinese. Mills was questioned for 25 days but the treatment given him was much better than that meted out to Powell.
	Joseph Albert E. Sanders-Bates (born 1887) first came to China in 1915 and was involved in advertising, publishing and radio broadcasting. The University Press published the *Morning Leader*, *News Digest* and *British Evening News*. Sanders-Bates was interned in the Haiphong Road camp during WWII.

Carroll Alcott in a bullet proof vest

I telephoned at once to Carroll, J. B., and Randall. "What do you intend to do?" I asked each one. Their answers were the same, "Nothing." And not a one of us budged. Luckily all but three foreigners on the list happened to be out of China on December 8, and those who were out had left in the normal course of their business. Of the three in China, Powell was imprisoned in Shanghai and given inhuman treatment. Hal Mills was interned in Shanghai and I was interned in Hong Kong where I received the same general bad treatment accorded to all internees there. Many of the Chinese have been liquidated. All of us had our offices bombed and were trailed for months and shot at by assassins.

Not one of us on the black list was a propagandist for the American or any other government, but publishing independent news and truthful editorials proved more poisonous to Axis ideologists than any amount of propaganda.

After conferring with Gould and Powell I lost no time in hurrying down to the *Shun Pao* offices on Hankow and Shantung roads. I found the building intact. The Shanghai municipal police had already stationed armed guards around it.

Major Kenneth Bourne[13], commissioner of the police, was upset by the deportation order, and took the black fist more seriously

---

13   Kenneth Morrison Bourne, MC, CBE, (1892-1968) was the son of Sir Frederick Bourne Assistant Judge of the British Supreme Court for China from 1898 to 1916. Bourne was appointed Commissioner of Police in 1938. He had served in the British Army in WWI earning the rank of major. He had been working with the British Special Operations Executive since 1939 in Shanghai. Bourne left Shanghai in August 1941 on leave but in fact to take up a post with the British Army Intelligence Corps. He retired in 1946 with the rank of Lt. Colonel. He then joined MI5 where he was stationed in Delhi before and after Indian independence.

than did any of the black-listed. He provided two armed guards for each of the foreigners on the list. For the next year and a half I was constantly attended by my "nurses." One sat in my car all day and the other accompanied me in and out of all buildings. At first I thought this all a lot of foolishness. Even when I did realize their value I never could get used to having the guards around.

Kenneth Bourne, Commissioner of the SMP. Later an MI5 agent

My first concern was for the Shun Pao staff. I arranged for the Chinese clerical and editorial staff to live in the building. Outside reporters were to phone in their stories from secretly designated places, and no one, except myself and chit coolies, was to enter or leave the building.

But before we could get our protection system in good working order we were bombed. That very afternoon of July 16 six thugs chucked six hand grenades in through the open windows. A printer was killed and nineteen others injured.

Nothing more happened for a month or so. We carried on our independent news policy as usual. Then in September, one of the clerks, in shifting a section of the reference library into another room, discovered a bomb which contained enough explosives to blow out an entire floor. Thanks to a defective battery the bomb had failed to go off. This bomb had been cleverly executed. It was in the form of a large Chinese book and had been placed on the reference library shelf with other books of similar size. The dud bomb was discovered on Friday the thirteenth, which thereafter was considered a lucky day around the Shun Pao office.

It was about this time that one of our editorial writers, tiring of the monotony of his imprisonment in the Shun Pao building, went

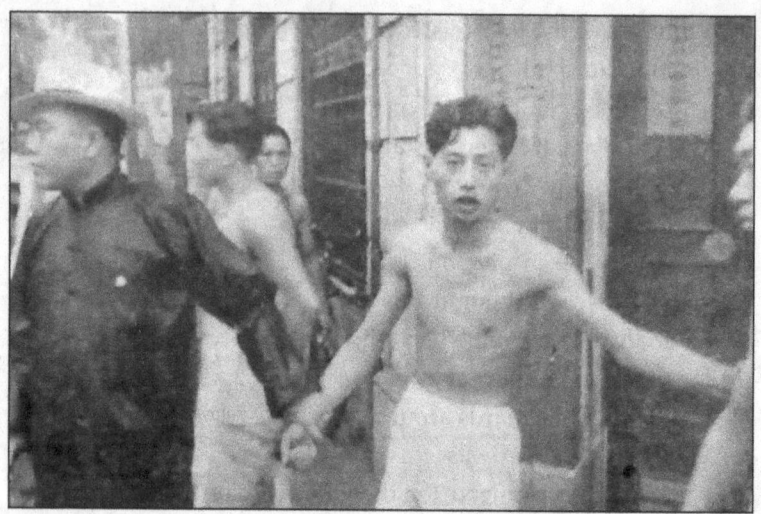

Arrest of a Shun Pao bombing suspect

outside in search of a little recreation. As he was sitting in a neighborhood tea shop, sipping tea and eating watermelon seeds, assassins who had followed him there shot and killed him.[14]

King Hua-ting, assassinated Chinese editor of the Shun Pao

Nominally the Wang Ching-wei regime in Nanking had issued the black list, but none of us had any doubts as to its real sponsor. Fu Hsiao-an[15], then mayor of Greater Shanghai, was supposed to execute the order and expel or otherwise dispose of us.

Shortly after publication of the list Mayor Fu and I

---

14   The story is not exactly as Allman described it. King Hua-ting (金华亭), a Chinese editor of the *Shun Pao* was killed in February 1941 outside a ballroom at 4.30am in the morning by an assassin posing as King's body guard.

15   Fu Xiaoan (傅筱庵) (1872–1940) was a successful businessman in Shanghai who had been appointed mayor of Shanghai by Wang Ching-wei's puppet government in 1938 replacing Wu Tiecheng.

inadvertently met at a cocktail party in the Settlement. The host and hostess couldn't conceal their nervousness when they realized what had happened. The mayor's bodyguards, some dozen cutthroats armed to the teeth, had been left outside. I, too, had left my plain-clothes men in my car or there might have been a shooting in that dignified drawing room.

As it was, I was armed, and so was the mayor. When he came in I backed up against the wall and waited for him to make the first move. He came over to shake hands but I most conveniently had mine filled with sandwiches and a glass. That was the last time we were invited to the same party, accidentally or otherwise. Our combined army of bodyguards was too much for even a Shanghai hostess. Too, Mayor Fu didn't last long. On October 10, 1940, he was assassinated by one of his servants.[16]

Fu Hsiao-an, mayor of Shanghai Assassinated by his chef.

Ch'en Kung-po, new mayor of Shanghai and later, puppet President of China. He was executed for treason in 1946.

Fu was succeeded by Ch'en Kung-po[17], who held a master's degree from Columbia University and had been president of

---

16   He was slashed to death by his chef while he slept in his bed at his house on Scott Road (Shanyin Road) near Hongkew Park. Some reports say he was beheaded.

17   Chen Gong Bo (陳公博) (1892-1946) was the president of the Legislative Yuan of the puppet government. He had been a member of the Kuomintang in Canton and accompanied the Northern Expedition in 1927. In 1944, he became President of the Reformed government on Wang Jingwei's death. In 1946 he was tried for treason—described as the "No. 1 Living Traitor". He was convicted and executed by firing squad on June 3, 1946.

the Wang Ching-wei Japanese-sponsored Legislative Yuan at Nanking. The *Shun Pao* continually referred to him as the puppet mayor when it referred to him at all. At the time of his installation, November 20, 1940, I was a member of the Shanghai Municipal Council. Soon Ch'en let it be known that he wanted to see me about municipal matters.

Here again the bodyguard question was an embarrassing one. Ch'en lived out in the badlands[18] and had hundreds of armed adherents in addition to his regular bodyguards. To tell the truth I was afraid to visit his estate. Finally Ch'en assured me safe conduct if I would come, leaving my guards at the nearest police station. I decided to take a chance. To my surprise he really did want to talk about municipal matters, particularly about the dwindling rice supplies. Major Bourne had warned me against these visits and a near incident convinced me that he was right and' put a stop to these nocturnal calls. I was sitting talking to Mr. Ch'en in his parlor, and all unconsciously in reaching in my vest pocket for a cigar, I exposed my shoulder holster and gun. Ch'en's eyes bugged out in fright. I had visions of hot lead all over the place, but nothing happened. That, however, was my last visit to the Japanese-sponsored Mr. Ch'en.

The black-listed men and the *Shun Pao* staff weren't the only ones to bear the brunt of Japanese displeasure. Sammy Chang[19], the smiling business manager of the *Shanghai Evening Post and Mercury*, was assassinated a few days after our building was the target for hand grenades and the Post was bombed numerous

18   The badlands were the area of west Shanghai outside the International Settlement where, due to overlapping jurisdictions, crime was rampant.
19   Samuel H. Chang (1900-1940) had studied at the Anglo-Chinese School in Swatow (Shantou) and then high school in Seattle before attending Haverford College and the Pulitzer School of Journalism at Columbia University. He returned to China in 1924 as a journalist with the *North China Star*. He worked for the Kuomintang government for some time. He was at the time of his death working for the Post-Mercury Company owned by Cornelius Starr.

Samuel H. Chang, murdered journalist   *Hallett Abend, New York Times*
correspondent beaten and robbed by Japanese

times. Once the terrorists over-powered and killed the guards,
then went inside and hurled their bombs. But it was so early in the
morning the building was empty. The *China Press* was bombed,
and J. B. Powell had the interesting experience of having a hand
grenade bounce off his shoulder — and fail to explode. Hallet
Abend[20], the *New York Times* correspondent, was attacked and
beaten by Japanese who entered his apartment and destroyed the
manuscript of a book he was writing which they said was anti-
Japanese.

A further attempt was made to throw hand grenades into our
building, but the hired assassin was caught by the police guards.
Asked who he was looking for, the man answered, "Ah Lo-man"
(my Chinese name). Questioned further, the man admitted that
he had been paid twenty dollars and had been promised another
twenty dollars if he got me. As forty dollars in Chinese currency
was then worth about two dollars American money I was

20   Hallett Abend (1884-1955) moved to China in 1925 as a reporter for the *New York Times*.
He wrote a number of books on China and reported in depth on the Rape of Nanking.
His apartment on the 16th Floor of Broadway Mansions was raided by Japanese on
midnight of July 19, 1940, hours after Samuel Chang was shot. Abend left China soon
after in October 1940. For more see: "NY Times Correspondent Attacked by Japanese
Thugs", *China Weekly Review*, July 27, 1940, p310.

somewhat annoyed. I was even madder a few days later when I learned that thugs had been paid fifty dollars to get Carroll Alcott!

Carroll was a perpetual thorn to the Axis. He often had Italian and Japanese thugs following him around. The Japs frequently jammed his radio station. For a while he announced, "This broadcast comes to you through the courtesy of Bakerite bread and the jam comes to you through the discourtesy of the Japanese navy." By sheer good luck alone all the Americans escaped physical injury, except J. B. Powell, and his injuries were the result of deliberate cruel treatment in prison.

I escaped torture in Stanley internment camp because the Jap gendarmerie there didn't catch up with my identity until it was too late for them to do anything. When the Japanese in Shanghai had made inquiries as to my whereabouts my family, partners, and associates answered, "Chungking." Once on the repatriation list, it was too late for the Japs to take me off. Our government had insisted that all Americans detained by the Japanese be repatriated on the first trip. My claim to fame is that I'm the only newspaperman who didn't go through the inquisition. At that the *Shun Pao* printed more anti-Japanese editorials than all the other papers combined; we published at least one a day. Perhaps this is why the Japanese language press and the puppet Chinese language press tried for a while to intimidate me further by constantly headlining articles about the foreign black-listed men as "Allman and others" or "Allman and six others."

XVIII
WAR TRAPS ME IN HONG KONG

I LEFT SHANGHAI ON november 15, 1941, for Hong Kong to buy newsprint for the *Shun Pao*, and for a number of other local newspapers and paper dealers who had commissioned me to represent them.

At the time I realized the war situation in the Pacific was rapidly becoming critical, but like most everyone else I was lulled into a temporary sense of security by the knowledge that Japan's special peace ambassador, Kurusu[1], was already en route to Washington. This fact, I thought, would give me ample time to make a two weeks' business trip and get back to my family before anything happened. Like many others I already had devised a plan of escape from Shanghai should war come.

Early in 1940, when trouble with Japan seemed imminent, Jack Doughty[2], another American, and I, under guise of cross-country rides, had made a minute survey of the Shanghai countryside and had drawn up detailed maps to use in escape. We knew every pig path in and out of Shanghai, as well as all the creeks, villages, bridges, and wooded temple patches. If war came, our plan was to sneak beyond the barbed-wire boundary to a place

---

1   Saburo Kurusu (1886-1954), Japan's special envoy to the United States. Kurusu also claimed to have been surprised by the attack. He said the military had not told him about it.

2   Jack Doughty (born 1896) undertook officer training with the US Navy in WWI. He moved to Shanghai where he joined the SVC and American Legion. In 1933 he was elected sergeant-at-arms of the legion.

where I had stabled ponies for my family and for Jack and his fiancee, Ella Jacobsen. We planned to hide by day then ride for four or five nights, shoot the ponies and continue the short distance into Free China on foot or by wheelbarrow. (Note to inquisitive Japanese: all maps were destroyed by my wife the day you struck at Pearl Harbor.)

Jack Doughty

Business in Hong Kong seemed to be going on about as usual, but with an air of tenseness. I had completed my mission and was scheduled to return to Shanghai eight hundred miles north, aboard the S. S. *Mingsang* on November 30 when I was informed, the day before, that its sailing had been postponed. On that day the British government ordered all ships to stay out of northern China waters. Our last real hope of getting back faded when two ships that had sailed for Shanghai and other northern ports returned to Hong Kong, bringing back many Shanghai-bound passengers, including the late Russ Engdahl[3] of the consular staff at Shanghai and F. L. Davidson of du Pont.

Like many other Shanghailanders whose only means of getting back home had been cut off, I kept hoping that the British would find some way to get us out. They never did. Eight hectic days of alternate hope and despair passed and then about 8 a.m. on December 8, when I was having breakfast with a group of friends in the Hong Kong Hotel, the Jap bombs began to fall.

After the first shock of war passed, I decided that since I was caught a long way from home without even means to

---

3   Felix Russell Engdahl (1907-1842) was a consul with the US Consulate in Shanghai having worked there from 1935. He died in internment at the St Stephens Prep School in Hong Kong after falling down some steps. He is buried in Hong Kong at the Stanley Military Cemetery.

Japanese bombing of Hong Kong on 8 December 1941

communicate with my family a volunteer job would be the best cure for worry.

I first called on the American consul-general, Mr. A. E. Southard[4]. He said he had nothing for me to do and sent me to Dr. P. Selwyn-Clark[5], the very efficient director of medical services for Hong Kong. Dr. Selwyn-Clark put me to work at once organizing a dispersal camp for the Chinese population in Kowloon, on the

Percy Selywyn-Clarke

mainland a mile or so opposite Hong Kong. With such camps he hoped to cut down casualties and control feeding.

The Shumshuipo barracks, later the Jap military prison, had been bombed by the Japs and evacuated by the Canadian troops. Dr. Selwyn-Clark thought this would be an excellent place to set up a dispersal camp. He gave me the necessary military and other passes and the authority to do anything necessary to establish the camp which was to care for about fifteen thousand civilians. I had some trouble in getting to the barracks as there were four or five bombing raids just before I started out for Kowloon. I finally borrowed a private car at the ferry which took me there with my one Chinese assistant.

---

4   See Chapter 1, Footnote 10
5   Sir Percy Selwyn Selwyn-Clarke KBE, CMG, MC, MD, FRCP, DPH, DTM&H, CStJ (1893-1976) was the director of medical services in Hong Kong. He, at his own request, remained in post and continued working as Director of Medical Services until May 1943 when he was arrested by the Japanese Kempeitai on suspicion of being a spy. He was imprisoned and tortured in the Supreme Court building for 19 months. After the war, he, however, refused to give evidence in the war crimes trials in Hong Kong. He later served as the governor of the Seychelles. "A hard-boiled saint: Selwyn-Clarke in Hong Kong" BMJ, Vol 11, 19 Aug 1995.

We were faced with many difficulties in getting the camp organized. I could locate neither transportation nor any form of communication, but I managed to collect several tons of rice to feed the dispersed persons due to arrive the following day. The sergeant of the Shumshuipo police station agreed to guard our camp entrance but after he and I watched Jap planes bomb a not far distant spot I suspected that his guardianship wouldn't last long. My hunch proved a good one.

It was no time at all before my Chinese assistant called my attention to the fact that our police guards were no longer at the gate. I pushed through the milling crowd outside and forced my way into the nearby police station. I found it being looted by a mob and the police gone. I tried the phones; all were dead. Hurrying back to camp I shut the gates and then started out to get police help from somewhere. The crowd outside the camp had swelled considerably, and I was fearful that they would get out of hand. I warned my Chinese assistant to keep the gates closed but not to resist if the crowd broke in. I told him to take care of himself in any case. Then I commandeered a truck and made the rounds of Kowloon police stations. I found them all abandoned and in the process of being looted.

Zigzagging from police station to station I picked up a number of European women and children who were out on the streets hoping for rescue. Our last stop was the ferry which ran from the mainland to Hong Kong. I saw my passengers safely aboard and then went to the police station which guarded the ferry. The men there were on the point of leaving, certain that the Japs were right at their heels.

It took some time to convince the sergeant in charge that I had just covered Kowloon and hadn't seen a single Jap. At that he refused to send any of his men back to the dispersal camp with me. He said he had orders to abandon the station at once. He

Japanese troops in Tsimshatsui

also suggested that I accompany him on the last police launch to leave. By this time I needed little persuading.

While we were talking he suddenly remembered that he had the previous night's crop of prisoners under lock and key, some twenty in all, and that the keys had disappeared with one of his men. I suggested that he shoot the locks off. He tried, but his service revolver was too light. He scouted around and located two soldiers waiting for the ferry and they shot off the locks with their rifles. We all pitched in then and dismantled the radio apparatus and wrecked a dozen or so automobiles in the station courtyard.

We piled all arms and ammunition from the station on the launch and everyone, civilians included, was armed with a rifle. One excited chap began loading the fixed gun on the prow. I grabbed him just in time to remind him that our own pole extending up from the prow stood just four feet from the muzzle and under the circumstances a shot would be far more dangerous to us than to any possible enemy.

I notified Dr. Selwyn-Clark at once about my Shumshuipo experiences. He agreed that there was no point in trying to operate without police protection. Anyway, he said he wanted me for another job, that of deputy chief medical transport officer. This was a fancy title but when boiled down it meant that my job was to keep the ambulances and trucks repaired and available for moving the wounded into first-aid stations and hospitals. Most of the vehicles were driven by Chinese chauffeurs. Some fifth columnists had slipped in among them and wrecked their machines, but others, like the Loh brothers, did a grand job. These two boys, Stanley and James, thought nothing of patching up an ambulance under fire. Time after time they drove into fighting areas to pick up casualties.

All British civilians were in the Hong Kong Volunteer Corps[6]. As the war went on there was a dearth of ambulance and truck drivers and men to operate the food control, so the Americans volunteered for these services. I recall one brave group in particular, Eugene Pawley[7], Carl Neprud[8], Albert Fitch[9], John Norton, Charles Shafer[10], Charles Winter[11] and Robert Henry[12], who joined the medical corps and drove throughout the war under shell and machine-gun fire and continued as drivers up to the time of repatriation.

---

6   The Hong Kong Volunteer Defence Corps was formed in 1854. At the time of the Japanese attack it had 2,200 members.
7   Eugene ("Gene") Pawley (1915-1988) was the brother of China National Air Corporation (CNAC) President, William Pawley. With his brother he had helped set up the Flying Tigers the US volunteer pilot corps established in China to help fight the Japanese.
8   Carl Alvin Neprud (1889-1976) worked for the Chinese Maritime Customs as a Commissioner of Customs. From 1940-1941 he had been assigned to special duties.
9   Albert C. Fitch (1916-1997)
10   Charles Louis ("Chuck") Schafer (1916-1995) was a traffic manager for CNAC and had remained in Hong Kong to wind up the affairs of the company, missing the last transport plane out. In later life he published with his wife Violet a number of books including Teacraft, Wokcraft and Breadcraft.
11   Charles ("Chuck") Winter was a Seventh Day Adventist Missionary and teacher. He ran a school in Clearwater Bay.
12   Dr. Robert Timmons Henry (1894-1971) was a doctor of divinity and missionary based in Shanghai.

Hong Kong Bank Building with the Supreme Court and HQ of the Kempeitai to the left

To expedite the badly needed repair work we commandeered a truck and fitted it up as a mobile repair unit. Eric Shekery[13] and Paul Dietz[14], both of Shanghai, offered to help out.

We lost so many cars by accident and shellfire that soon we were beating the bushes for anything that would run. William P. Hunt[15], another Shanghai American, phoned me excitedly one morning. "I've located a number one motorcar out near the Happy Valley Race Course," he said and asked me to drive him out to get it. The first-rate auto turned out to be a broken-down Ford which we had to repair before we could get it back to headquarters.

On the way in we learned that the wife of the chief transport officer had been hit by a shell splinter and that the chief censor of Hong Kong had been blown to bits by the same shell.

---

13   Eric Hay Shekury (1905-1981) was at the time British. He later naturalised to be American. He had been an employee of the Office Equipment Department of Messrs Dodwell & Co.
14   See Chapter 1 Footnote 1
15   See Chapter 1 Footnote 5

The sympathy of the various stranded Shanghailanders over this tragedy was tempered by the fact that this same censor had held up all their mail for the past several months.

We all had some pretty close calls. On December 17 I was in our headquarters in the Hong Kong Bank Building when the Japs started shelling a British artillery battery which was blasting back a short distance from us. The Japs' aim was none too good. A couple of rounds fell on the plaza in front of our office, and a third landed on a window ledge just outside, wrecking the office completely. Those of us on duty dodged behind a wall and got off with only a few scratches from flying debris. The rest of the day we spent moving to the back of the building, which was safer.

Charles Winter, one of our drivers, was captured. One morning as he was delivering bread to the French hospital in the Happy Valley area he was suddenly surrounded by a platoon of Jap soldiers who informed him politely, "You are captured; prease stay here." Then in a hurry to join their advance they did not stop to tie him up, just left him sitting in the truck with the threat, "We come back." Winter waited just long enough for them to march out of sight beyond a bend in the road, then turned and drove like a bat out of Hades back to town.

I don't pretend to possess psychic powers or any well-defined extrasensory perception but there have been a few times in my life when I have had distinct forewarnings of danger. One of these occurred during the Hong Kong fracas, when, I admit, all our nerves were sharpened to a keen edge.

John Raymond, an American shipowner who had been caught in Hong Kong, came to bunk with me. He volunteered for service at once and was put in charge of the motor transport's gasoline dump. This was in a dangerous spot and exposed to direct Japanese fire. Each daybreak when he left I said good-by, fully expecting that would be the last time I'd ever see him alive.

But each night he returned, weary but uninjured.

Two mornings before Hong Kong's surrender I awoke with the strong feeling that at all costs Raymond must be kept away from the dump that day. I knew he would ignore any casual request I might make, so I told him a barefaced lie. "We have another dump on the other side of the island," I said, "and we want you to inspect it." He agreed to come, somewhat reluctantly, and when, after hours of ambulance inspection, there was no sign of a second dump Raymond could not hide his annoyance.

But this annoyance turned into relief when we returned to headquarters and learned that his gasoline dump had been bombed out of existence that very afternoon.

A day or two earlier I had borrowed a brand-new Chrysler Imperial from Chris Livingston, American manager of the Texas Oil Company, for our service and had driven it down to headquarters. While I was on my way upstairs a shell landed on the car and blew out the whole rear end. This was sheer luck for me; my sixth sense wasn't on the job that day.

At Dr. Selwyn-Clark's request I turned detective about this time to solve the mystery of a looted motor lorry. A truck loaded with army stores had disappeared, but the commandant of the food depot had traced the empty truck to our headquarters. He accused us of stealing his supplies. Dr. Selwyn-Clark, much perturbed, asked me to find out what it was all about.

The entire medical-headquarters staff ate together in the American Club, which was in the same building, but the club soon ran short of food. We persuaded Dr. Selwyn-Clark to get us some of the food which was spoiling in the refrigeration plants for want of power. He had done this. It was Shafer's job to seek out and open up the godowns. This he did, frequently under shell and machine-gun fire. I questioned him but he knew nothing of the missing lorry.

Knowing them to be practical jokers and hungry men I next sought out Neprud, Pawley, and Hunt. At first they denied any knowledge of the lost food. But when they saw that all of us, especially Dr. Selwyn-Clark, were due for trouble with the commandant, they confessed. They had taken our director's permission to get food literally and when they found a military truck abandoned by the road-side and loaded with stores they had simply driven it in and unloaded the provisions in the American Club commissary. Peace between the medical transport and the food depot was restored by return of the truck and what food we hadn't eaten.

On Christmas morning the officer in command of the Hong Kong forces recommended to the governor that we surrender on the grounds that he had not more than four and a half hours' ammunition left and that civilian morale had gone for lack of water and light. The Japs had captured the source of both three days earlier. I don't know about the ammunition but I am positive that civilian morale was much higher than the governor thought.

Dr. Selwyn-Clark phoned medical headquarters at four o'clock on Christmas afternoon that the Colonial government had surrendered Hong Kong and ordered us to demobilize. About six o'clock Bill Hunt and I left the office and walked to the hotel, fortunately dodging Japanese patrols who were all over the city. The Japs required everyone to tip his hat to them. I wasn't bothered by that because, except for polo and paper hunts, I've never worn a hat. Just the same it made me damned sore.

That evening all the hotels destroyed their liquor stocks to avoid having drunken Japanese around. Bill and I managed to annex a case of beer and with it we managed a forlorn sort of Christmas party with four friends, Alice Dobbs[16], W. H. Taylor[17],

---

16 See Chapter 1, Footnote 13. Most likely unbeknownst to Alice, her husband had died that day.
17 See Chapter 1, Footnote 8

Roy Pharis[18], and Walter Frese[19].

Next day I went over to the medical service headquarters in the Hong Kong Bank Building to wind up some work but found the Japs in possession of the building. The front entrance had a sign on it, "Military Headquarters." I went around to the back of the building. There were no sentries there, but the door was locked. Then, just on a hunch, I telephoned the office and much to

William H. Taylor

my astonishment got a connection and learned that several of my colleagues had been in the office when the Japs took over and couldn't get out. I rounded up the building manager and obtained a key to the unguarded back door. It was a simple matter then to get up to the office on an upper floor and free the temporary prisoners. The Japs had only occupied the first two floors.

The Japanese sent a sound truck around on the twenty-seventh, and a voice announced in English and Chinese that the people were to go about their affairs but stay off the streets at night. Loiterers, the voice said, would be shot. In spite of this announcement looting went on all over the city. People frequently were held up and robbed in broad daylight. Food was becoming scarce. It was impossible to get more than two small meals a day in the hotel.

Hawkers, however, were selling canned goods and other

---

18   Leroy Masters Pharis (1884-1966), vice-president of the Shanghai Power Company.
19   Walter Frederick Frese (1906-1987) was an assistant chief accountant of the Treasury's Bureau of Accounts. He worked was an assistant to Mr Taylor and A. Manuel Fox a member of the Chinese Currency Stabilization Committee. He was a professor at the Harvard Business School from 1956 to 1972.

edibles which undoubtedly they had stolen. Some of us decided to buy up a supply of this stuff to have as a reserve if we were interned. And it was a good thing we did. One of the war's comical characters was George Chen, a sort of purchasing agent for medical headquarters. No job was too tough for him if he could smell a little profit. We utilized his services in buying or looting odds and ends for us, and were quite happy to let him do a little profiteering on the side.

Hunt and I discovered that prisoners of war were being collected at North Point; so we went there several times. It was probably a foolish thing to do but we wanted to make as complete a list as possible of the prisoners of war, especially the civilian volunteers. While I was in the enclosure I ran across a friend who had represented a big paper company in Hong Kong and with whom I had had some business dealings. He was a member of the Hong Kong Volunteer Corps and had come through uninjured.

He asked me to get some of his private papers out of his office in the same bank building that housed the medical headquarters. I also had some papers in this office together with several thousand dollars which I planned to use in escaping from Hong Kong. I agreed to try.

After leaving the prisoners I tried to find his secretary to get the keys to his safe but had no luck. Then I asked a friend of mine who had been an official in the local police force to put me in touch with a good safe-cracker. This he did in no time at all. And that's how I met Chun An-ping, whose name means "Peaceful Spring." To look at Chun no one would dream that he was a burglar by profession. He was a mild-mannered, soft-voiced, inoffensive little runt, but he'd been a safe-cracker for more years than I had practiced law. About two-thirds of this time had been spent in jail, but he had been free often enough to keep his hand in. In fact he was serving a jail term when the police lent him to me.

Chun and I conferred in my hotel room and then set out for the bank building. By this time I had become adept at sneaking in through the back door.

We reached my friend's office on the sixth floor and agreed that I would watch in the hall for any wandering Jap sentries or competitive burglars while my new partner opened the safe. If we were interrupted he was to sit in the office and act like one of the regular employees. Nothing happened and he had the safe open and the papers out within half an hour.

The news of our success soon got around and a number of other friends who were prisoners commissioned me to get things out of their safes. I hadn't much to do right then; so I made a deal with my tame burglar to open up a safe-cracking business at ten dollars per job.

We did such a good business that my partner raised his fee to twenty-five dollars per safe. Luck attended us wherever we operated, and we actually had only one bad scare. That time a Jap sentry came clumping down the hall and entered the office where we were at work. I had just time to grab a newspaper and pretend to be reading while my burglar went through the motions of dusting some furniture. The Jap grunted and I grunted back at him. That seemed to convince him that everything was all right and he went on about his duties, while we finished cracking the safe in peace.

Early in the morning of the twenty-ninth the Japanese notified the manager of my hotel that all guests must be out by eight o'clock as the Japanese were taking over. Bill Hunt, who had an office in the Gloucester Building, next door to the Hong Kong Hotel, invited me to join a group there and set up housekeeping. The hotel was more than willing to give us enough blankets, towels, and so forth, to make ourselves reasonably comfortable. We slept on desks and on the floor and ate the canned food we had bought from time to time from the street hawkers.

By the end of December the Japs had about completely taken over the city. They had seized all the main office buildings and the principal hotels. Most of the Chinese and many of the Europeans were still milling about the streets like frightened sheep. There were rumors of internment in Formosa or Japan. I had an idea that I was likely to be sent back to Shanghai, since I was on the Japanese black list there and had a price on my head. It wasn't too happy a picture. I considered plans for escape but gave them all up as I was uncertain of the effect it would have on my wife and son, John, in Shanghai.

Thus the year 1941 came to a close. On New Year's Eve Mr. Southard managed to get into the American Club with a case of champagne. Where he found it remains a diplomatic secret. A few Americans slipped in and drank a melancholy toast with him. I was there for a while and then took one of the bottles back to our quarters in the office. The gang there celebrated the New Year with a strictly canned dinner topped off by the wine.

Hong Kong was a dead city by this time, cut off from the world. Our radios were useless without power. I attempted to get into the new Domei office to send a message to Shanghai but was refused entrance. I sent the manager, Yamamoto, a note asking him to cable my family in Shanghai that I was safe, but I never heard from him, nor did he transmit any message I had known this scoundrel well in Shanghai and once, the good Lord forgive me, had gone so far as to do him a small favor.[20]

The city was full of rumors about what the fate of the civilian

---

20 Yamamoto may have been doing Allman a favour. If he had telegraphed Shanghai that Allman was in Hong Kong, the Japanese authorities there may have asked for him to be sent to Shanghai.

Japanese victory parade in Central. The Supreme Court is on the left and Murray Parade Ground to the right

foreigners was to be, but we could learn nothing direct. Our only news was supplied by a few of the local newspapers which had sprung up under Japanese supervision and the four or five Chinese puppet papers, all of which took great pains to denounce the British and Americans.

Rumors came to a head on January 4. That evening when I visited the office of the *South China Morning Post* to try and get some definite information I found them in the process of printing an internment notice. All civilians from Japanese enemy countries, British, American, Dutch, were ordered to assemble at the Murray Parade Ground[21] the next morning.

We had only a few short hours to decide whether to turn up or make a dash for freedom. Those of us with families at Jap mercy decided to sit tight and take what came. The last evening

---

21   Located just south of the cricket ground. The Hilton Hotel occupied the site from the 1960s to 1990s. The Cheung Kong Center now stands there.

before my internment I worked with my burglar on our final job, cracking Bill Hunt's safes. I hated to bring our useful and exciting partnership to a close and I bade Chun, of whom I'd grown quite fond, a sorrowful farewell. I reminded him in parting that he was now on his own and God help him if he got caught by the Japs.

XIX
I'm Going Back

WHEN THIS WAR IS OVER I'm going back to China and try to pick up the life I was pushed out of so unwillingly when the Japanese walked in. I know it won't be just like "those good old days" but I'm prepared to make the necessary adjustments. Most of my adult life was spent in China. Returning to Shanghai will be just like going home.

I'm making all my plans, of course, on the assumption that the Chinese government will permit foreign lawyers to return to practice as they did before abolition of extraterritoriality. As I foresee it, the chief, and about the only, difference will be that law practice will be confined to Chinese courts and to office or out-of-court practice.

This won't bother me. Close to seventy per cent of my firm's cases were tried in Chinese courts. When you come right down to it there were not so many cases tried in the United States Court for China. At the time declaration of war closed our court in Shanghai, the calendar was so clean there were few civil cases and not one criminal case pending. As I understand the treaties abolishing extraterritoriality, all pending cases will be tried in accordance with the laws involved, whether American, British, or French.

Now that consular jurisdiction is a thing of the past, American nationals and businesses in Chinese territory will be under the protection of the modern Chinese laws drawn up by China's best jurists and most experienced lawyers. The United States Court and the courts of other former extraterritorial nations no longer exist.

The lawyers who do not speak Chinese will have to learn the language or do their work through interpreters or through Chinese associates. The majority of foreign lawyers in Shanghai did not speak, read, or write Chinese to any appreciable extent and appeared in court with interpreters.

I already have a leg up on this because I not only know the language, but (and I don't want to sound too boastful) I've been considered somewhat of an expert in Chinese law. I was exposed to it so many times I suppose a little of it had to take.

Too, I had the interesting experience of teaching for about four years in Soochow University's Comparative Law School of China. While I taught insurance, evidence, and other phases of American law, I had to familiarize myself with Chinese law. Many of my hard-working and serious-minded students later wrote books on various legal subjects and asked me to write forewords for them. In spite of myself I had to keep up with Chinese law.

It is possible for an American lawyer to practice in a country where we do not have extrality rights, as witness the number of American lawyers in Paris and other European cities before the present war. Only a few weeks ago in Washington I lunched with William B. Spencer[1], an old friend who had been practicing law in Yokohama for twenty-five years, right up to Pearl Harbor, as a matter of fact. And we gave up extrality in Japan as long ago as 1899. Strangely enough he longs to return to Japan. Even though I have no love for "the little people" I see his point. It

---

1   William Boyd Spencer (1888-1948).

isn't easy for a lawyer who has spent over a quarter-century in one country to be forced to pull up stakes suddenly and start all over again in an unfamiliar place, even if it is his own native land.

But actual practice under Chinese law is not what bothers me. I'm used to it. When I get back to Shanghai to resume my practice there will be untold problems. I have no way of knowing just what changes the war will force. Whatever changes there are I am prepared to meet and I'm ready to adapt myself to them, although like most men my age I'd much prefer going on from just where I left off. No, the problems that worry me are the numberless ones for which the present Japanese regime is responsible.

Some of my dreams of my return to Shanghai are nightmares. Are my partners alive? Have they been interned? Are they getting enough to eat? What about my law office staff, business associates, and the huge staff of the *Shun Pao*—how are they faring? I do know that if I were in Shanghai now I'd be no help to any of them. I haven't a doubt that had I been where the local Jap authorities could have put their hands on me I would have been one of the first Americans interned—and tortured.

I wonder about my Chinese friends and if they have survived the Jap occupation. I shall not soon forget the help they gave me while I was interned in Hong Kong, and my wife and son in Shanghai during that same period, all at great personal risk.

I wonder what's happened to my office equipment, the files of hundreds of cases, some closed and others pending. And what has become of the registration records of thousands of trade-marks? The latter can be reconstructed from the records of the Trade-Mark Bureau in Chungking, but it will be a tedious, laborious job that will take months if not years.

I shudder when I dare let myself think of what has become

of our law library, the largest and one of the most complete law libraries outside the United States. My first partner, Mr. Fleming, spent years collecting many of the books. I constantly added volumes. There were Federal Court Reports, United States Supreme Court Reports, State Court Reports, and several of the reporter systems as well as encyclopedias and collections on all branches of law, including a valuable and extensive Chinese law library.

I can't be sure where the books are today, but I do know that a few days after December 8, 1941, the Japanese gendarmerie moved in and took over our five-room suite in Shanghai's most modern office building, Hamilton House. I can't blame them for appropriating such a comfortable place so conveniently located, but I wonder what they've done with the books, a number of which dealt with the sanctity of private property under international law. I doubt if these had any influence on the gendarmerie. I wouldn't be surprised if the library is now in Tokyo.

At home I had a large library on the Far East. When my wife left Shanghai on the repatriation ship in June of 1942 she turned our house over to a British family, but I've since heard from British friends, repatriated two months later, that a large sign was posted on our front door which read:

"This is the property of the Imperial Japanese Army. Trespassers will be dealt with according to military law" — a polite Japanese way of saying, "Trespassers will be shot."

I'm not fooling myself the slightest. It will be an expensive, time-consuming job to reestablish the firm of Allman, Kops and Davies. When the gendarmerie notified the staff to move out they moved fast, taking time only to box and store the files in a godown which I hope the Japanese haven't found and looted. I can't conceive of what possible use the files would be to anyone.

SHANGHAI LAWYER

In the United States Court for China

UNITED STATES OF AMERICA, vs. KARATZAS BRO- THERS, FEDERAL INC., U. S. A., George D. Happer, Roy G. Allman and Emil S. Fis- cher, Trustees, Defendants.	Cause No. 4470 Civil No. 2349 Filed at Shanghai, China, June 11, 1940. WILLIAM T. COLLINS Clerk.

The object of this suit is to recover a judgment against the defendants for Federal income and excess profit taxes for the calendar years 1937 and 1938, aggregating $5,102.16, United States Currency, together with interest thereon at 6% from November 2, 1939, and to have judgment of condemnation of certain property of the defendant, Roy G. Allman, levied on under attachment issued in this suit to satisfy the plaintiff's claim.

IT IS THEREFORE, on this 11th day of June 1940, ordered that the defendant, Roy G. Allman, appear in this Court on or before the fortieth day, exclusive of Sundays and legal holidays, after the day of the first publication of this order, to defend this suit and show cause why said condemnation should not be had; otherwise the suit will be proceeded with as in case of default.

By the Court:
Milton J. Helmick,
Judge.
United States Court for China.

United States v Karatzas

A first step in getting back to work again will be to find the files of unfinished cases, locate the parties and witnesses, now scattered to the four winds, and conclude the cases.

One pending case that I recall is the *United States Government versus the Karatzas Brothers Company*. The United States government claims an income tax is due from them. In defending the brothers we claimed no tax was due. When last heard of one brother was in Greece, the other in Tientsin. If the government wants to collect the money it will have to help us find the Karatzas boys because only the good Lord knows where they will be when the shooting is over.[2]

Thousands of firms and individuals in China have lost property — another problem for the lawyer who will have hundreds of diplomatic claims to prepare for clients. These claims will range all the way from loss of automobiles seized by the Japanese to destruction of personal property, homes, and factories. Proving these claims will be difficult, as the Japs have seized or destroyed practically all records and evidence of ownership and cost and value of property.

---

2   In fact, the United States Government was also suing Allman's brother, Roy. Allman had been a director of the company that had claimed to be American. It had been de-registered on the basis it was not American owned by order of the United States Court for China in 1938, but the court kept jurisdiction over it to recover taxes. *US v The Karatzas Brothers Company*, NCH, March 30 1938, p524

352

The cases for the Americans will be prepared by the owners with the assistance of their lawyers and then filed with the American government, which will recover from the Japanese or set them off against counterclaims. The only trouble with these diplomatic claims is that you must have grandchildren if you want to receive any benefit. With my three children I have some prospective beneficiaries.

As I see it, the American lawyer in China will have more work to do than ever before. For, in addition to all the jobs he had before the war and the abolition of extrality, there will be additional details. One big job, certainly, will be the reorganization of American companies.

It is not clear from the treaties just what will happen to foreign corporations; whether or not they will be recognized by the Chinese courts as legal entities. If not, and because Chinese corporation laws are based on the continental system, there will be radical readjustment for American and British firms already incorporated in China under the laws of their own countries. Unless, of course, some provision is made in the treaty or in Chinese law permitting these American and British corporations to continue as legal entities and carry on their management in accordance with the principles of American and British law.

Many of the larger public utilities in China are owned and operated by either British or American corporations. It is not clear whether these utilities will be allowed to continue as private companies or whether the Chinese government will take them over as government-owned institutions. Either way there will be endless paper work involved. There are many contracts now outstanding with the provision that in case of dispute the contracts will be adjudicated according to American, British, or French law. Assuming that the Chinese courts recognize these provisions of these numerous contracts, foreign lawyers will be kept busy

353

helping their Chinese colleagues interpret such foreign laws.

I see no reason why American and Chinese cannot continue to work together. I say, "continue," because we've been working together harmoniously now for nearly two decades.

In recent years a group of young, non-imperialistic men have taken over the control and developed American business in China. This group is entirely sympathetic with China's national aspirations, and none has been engaged in business that would in any way injure China politically, economically, or socially. In no sense of the word can they be called imperialistic old China Hands in thought or deed. This little group with which I am proud to be identified (I consider myself a business man as well as a lawyer) had, at the outbreak of the war, more Chinese than American associates and employees. C. V. Starr[3], for instance, developed an extraordinarily successful insurance business by close cooperation with the Chinese. His associates are still carrying on for him in Free China. Max Polin[4], another of the group, helped organize the China National Aviation Corporation, one of the smaller but one of the most efficient aviation services in the world. This company was formed with joint American-Chinese capital. The businesses in which I was interested, cinemas and manufacturing of various types, were also backed by Chinese money.

Whatever benefits these businesses and industries have obtained in China and whatever money the Americans, as individuals, have made, it should be borne in mind that the Chinese have benefited to an even greater extent. There have been a great number of them employed, for one thing, and for

---

3   See Chapter 17, box showing others on Japanese black list.
4   Max Polin (1888-1958) migrated to the United States as a young child from the Ukraine. He moved to Shanghai in the 1920s. He helped established the CNAC. He was repatriated to the US on the *Gripsholm* and recruited by the CIA as an agent for the rest of the war. He returned to Shanghai in 1946 and moved to Hong in 1949. He died there 1958 but his remains were returned to the US for burial.

another the American businesses consistently have paid higher wages than have the Chinese themselves. We have contributed no little in raising China's low standard of living.

After this war there will be even more opportunities for Americans in China than ever before. When American trade with China started a couple of centuries ago, the Chinese were opposed to trade and all other intercourse with the foreign devil, but China, like all of us, has moved forward. It doesn't take a soothsayer with a crystal ball to predict that transportation, industries, and communication systems are now necessities to the people of the Middle Kingdom. China needs both technical and financial help from the Americans. They know they will be safe in accepting such assistance. They know we hold no unnecessary political strings in our hands, such as, for example, Japan's "Greater East Asia Co-prosperity Sphere " nonsense.

I, for one, want to be in on the ground floor in the reconstruction of Shanghai. I hope to be the first American back there. It may be quite a different Shanghai from the one I left over a year ago. The Japs, when they see they are on the losing side, may burn to the ground this city they have saved for themselves, but Shanghai is a resilient place. It was born out of the wars of 1842 and it survived the Taiping rebellion, the Revolution of 1911 and its resulting civil wars; it was attacked by the Japs in 1932 and again in 1937. No matter what happens, Shanghai will rise again. It is impossible to destroy its tradition and perfect geographical location. No matter what happens, I want to return to Shanghai.

EPILOGUE
by Douglas Clark

ALLMAN DID GO BACK to Shanghai. He returned in early 1946 after an eventful war – three and a half years as a spymaster overseeing secret intelligence and counter-intelligence efforts in China for the Office of Strategic Services ("OSS"). The OSS had had been established as the United States first intelligence service during the war and was later replaced by the Central Intelligence Agency.

Allman had turned 49 while in Lourenco Marques after arriving there from Hong Kong on the *Asama Maru*. His wife, Mary Louise, and his thirteen-year-old son, John, met him there having been repatriated from Shanghai. After four weeks sailing on the MS *Gripsholm* via Rio de Janiero, the Allman clan arrived back in New York and they took

The Gripsholm on arrival in Rio de Janiero

up residence in an apartment at 88 Morningside Drive in New York.

Judge Milton Helmick of the United States Court for China and his wife were also aboard the *Gripsholm* as the first group of Americans to be repatriated from the Far East. Other Shanghai American lawyers were not so lucky. Allman's partner, Jim Davies was interned throughout the war while Allman's former partner and fellow polo player, Cornell Franklin, had to wait another sixteen months before being repatriated. About half of that time was spent in internment in the Haiphong Road Internment Camp. The doyen of the American legal community, Stirling Fessenden, died in Shanghai in February 1944 after he turned down a place on a repatriation trip. Due to poor health, he had not been interned. Robert Bryan, the Municipal Advocate, was due to be repatriated at the same time as Franklin but at the last minute the Japanese authorities took him off the list[1]. He remained in internment with Jim Davies in the Chapei Civilian Internment Camp until August 1945.

Allman's draft card showing him working for the OSS

1   Flight From China, p206

Allman had kept himself busy on the long trip through the western Pacific Ocean and across the Indian and Atlantic oceans. He finished an outline of this book, *Shanghai Lawyer,* and also prepared a report, most likely for the US Government, explaining the Chinese and Japanese governments' propaganda tactics. Allman's coverage of Japanese propaganda related not only to China, but also to Hong Kong and Latin America.

An advertisement for Shanghai Lawyer

Soon after arrival in New York, he gave a talk to a New York community club where he said, "We've got to destroy the Japs or they'll destroy us." Good to his word, almost immediately after his arrival, he took up a job where he could strive to do just that. He started working for the OSS as the head of secret intelligence in charge of operations in China. His good friend, Cornelius Starr, the head of the insurance company AIG had recommended him to the head of the OSS, William Donovan. AIG under Starr's control had worked with the British secret services for many years gathering intelligence in China. Insurance companies were seen as an invaluable source of intelligence as to a country's

Allman speaks in New York

E-3

industrial capabilities. When applying for insurance, companies have to state what equipment they have and insurance claims also provided very useful information on the current state of equipment. Insurance agents have good reason to be snooping around war areas and could and often did collect valuable information. Insurance intelligence was so valuable that the British government specifically allowed Lloyds of London to continue to underwrite risks in enemy territories throughout World War II.

Allman in a promotional photo for Shanghai Lawyer

Allman was later to tell a US federal court that he "developed a highly sophisticated intelligence organization in China."[2] This network which he built in close cooperation with Starr, who at the time was also working for OSS, included John King Fairbank a young history professor from Harvard who later became one of America's most prominent historians of China. Not surprisingly, and almost certainly with relish, Allman found himself in the middle of a turf war. Both the State Department and the United States military did not want the OSS to be gathering intelligence covertly in China. China was an ally and both the State Department and the military had developed close ties with the Kuomintang and its head of intelligence, Dai Li (written Tai Li at the time). The chief US representative on Sino American Cooperative Organisation (SACO), US Navy Captain Milton Miles had agreed with Dai Li that all secret intelligence (SI) gathering, was to go through SACO. In one memo, Miles wrote:

2   Shvetz v Commissioner 38 T.C.M. 1163 (1979). Allman gave evidence in the United States Tax Court to assist Mr Shvetz in a tax case.

"No SI man is wanted here... The job of SI in China is one of TAI LI's worries, and we can not step in here and expect to do any SI work anymore than we would knowingly let the Mexicans send SI men to operate in the USA."[3]

Allman was ordered to turn over control of his senior SI operative Alghan Lusey and his team to Miles. Starr found this unacceptable and left the OSS to work directly with British intelligence rather than deal with American turf wars. The British Special Operations Executive ("SOE") included a number of their former colleagues from Shanghai. Tony Keswick, former Chairman of the Municipal Council, led a team of commandos into China. Kenneth Bourne, former head of the Shanghai Municipal Police, ran an intelligence network aimed at China from India (he later joined MI5) and former Secretary General of the Municipal Council Godfrey Phillips was also with the SOE.

Allman also found handing over his operatives unacceptable. He personally disliked Dai Li, blaming him for the assassination in 1937 of Shi Liangcai, the proprietor of the *Shun Pao*. Allman, however, remained with OSS and became the head of counter-intelligence in the Far East. This was certainly a ploy to allow Allman to continue to do exactly what he was doing. Counter intelligence requires spying just as much as secret intelligence. While formally in charge of counter intelligence operations, he could continue to run his own operations in China without reference to the military or the State Department. One attempt Allman made with the assistance of Starr was to use Starr's newspaper the *Shanghai Evening Post and Mercury* as a front to operate in Chongqing and New York. Randall Gould, a newspaper man from Shanghai who had also been on the Japanese black list, was dispatched to Chongqing. This met with little success as it was

---

3   Maochun Yu, "OSS in China", p88 for this quote and information on the war years.

THE SHANGHAI EVENING POST AND MERCURY

Correspondents Get Sailing Orders

C.V. Starr dispatches Randall Gould and Fritz Opper to Chungking

seen as too transparent an attempt by Starr (and Allman) to continue intelligence gathering in China.

However, this may well have been a diversionary tactic. By early 1944, Allman had dispatched perhaps up to fifteen to twenty agents to China. The presence of some was detected by Dai Li which led to a witch hunt within the US intelligence community seeking to identify the agents and even to an investigation of Starr himself. Allman was furious, writing:

> "I further understand that Major Hoffman and associates are tracing down some 12 to 15 other American citizens in the Far East ... It occurred to me that the OSS organization in the Far East should spend more time chasing Japs and less time chasing Americans."

Allman and his colleagues back in the US did not stop. From almost as soon as he had been working for the OSS, Allman had been looking for a way to place agents in Communist-controlled areas of China in order to cooperate with the communists in the war against Japan. As can be seen from *Shanghai Lawyer*, Allman had an ambivalent view of communism and was more than willing to act for Bolsheviks. Allman had met Mao Zedong in 1917 when he was a student interpreter in Peking when Mao was working as an assistant librarian at Peking University. Allman later fondly recalled Mao's sense of humour.

In a visit to China in 1943, Donovan, the head of OSS had obtained Dai Li's consent for Donovan to lead a mission to Communist-controlled areas in China. When Donovan was unable to return to China, the leadership of the team was turned over to OSS operative Ilya Andreyevich Tolstoy (grandson of the writer Lev Tolstoy), and an elite team commenced training. Problems arose because the Army was also planning a mission to communist areas that was later dubbed the Dixie Mission. Eventually, the Army's mission went ahead but with a number of OSS operatives as part of the team.

The Dixie mission grew to be full-scale cooperation between the US and the communists, with the US and particularly the OSS providing

Members of the Dixie Mission pose in Mao suits in Yanan

much-needed funding and material for the communists. The mission generated much goodwill with the Chinese communists and member of the mission were feted when they returned to China in 1972 when the US restored diplomatic relations. Through the Dixie mission, Allman arranged a number of covert operations (without reference to Dai Li) and was very happy with the intelligence the Communists could provide not only from across China where they had established cells but even from Japan, Korea and Manchuria through the Japanese Communist Party.

Almost as soon World War II finished, Allman returned to Shanghai arriving in early 1946. He first re-started his practice in Washington DC before returning to Shanghai. The OSS had been abolished but he continued to work with the War Department and

Allied flags in Shanghai following the Japanese surrender

The Bund from the air just before the Japanese surrender

American Internees released from Chapei camp

clearly remained involved in intelligence activities while in Shanghai.

Allman's partner, Jim Davies, as soon as he and his wife, Jean, had been released from internment, set about re-establishing their practice in Shanghai. The Japanese gendarmerie had taken over his offices in Hamilton House after the war started. Davies had hoped to return to those offices and obtained permission to do so, when the US Army requisitioned the building. He opened a temporary office with James Lee in the Sun Sun Company Building and then moved to the China Realty Building on 290 Szechuan Road. Davies wrote to Allman in October 1945 that he had not yet been able to find a trace of the books, files or furniture.[4] A later employee, Denis Jen, wrote that his James Lee, Allman's Chinese partner, had been able to move during the war to a new office in the Ta Shing Department Store Building on Nanking Road taking all the files with him.[5]

It seems that Davies, who was by then 65, decided to retire and return to the United States. However, Paul Kops, Allman's other American partner did return to Shanghai. Kops had stayed in

---

4   "Among Those Liberated", the *Shanghai Post and Mercury* (New York edition), October 26, 1945, p6
5   Denis Jen, One Thousand Ounces of Gold, Chapter 6.

Among Those Liberated

James B Davies wrote from Shanghai to N. F Allman, on Oct 5 that Jean and he stood the two and one-half years in camp quite well although they both lost considerable weight.

"I opened up a temporary office with James Lee in the Sun Sun Co. building," he continued, "as I have been unable to get back any of our old space in the Hamilton House I got the necessary permission to reoccupy our old office but the U. S. Army requisitioned the building. We have now moved to the China Realty Building, 290 Szechuen Rd You will recall that the Jap gendarmes kicked us out of the Hamilton House and I have not up to date been able to find trace of any of our books, files, records or furniture."

Mrs. Elsie H. Hollett of New York City, Mrs. Hollett is now in Minneapolis awaiting her sister's return.

* * *

Jeanne Perkins von Hengel and her husband, Bert von Hengel, are back in their home on Edinburgh Rd, Shanghai, according to word received this week in Philadelphia by her sister-in-law Mrs von Hengel was with the YWCA in Shanghai.

* * *

Laurence Dowdall, mining engineer formerly with the George McBain Co. in Shanghai and Indo-China, has cabled from Colombo to his sister, Nois, in Vancouver, B. C "Arrived safely British hands. Hope to be home soon."

* * *

A report on Jim Davies' letter to Allman

The Teia Maru in Goa

The Gripsholm docked in Goa

Shanghai when war started and had been interned in early 1943 in an internment camp in Pudong. While in internment, Kops had been appointed to the camp court to try other internees for crimes committed in the camp. Kops had been separated from his wife and young boys who had left Shanghai for the Philippines shortly before the war started and were interned at the St Tomas Camp in Manila. They were all repatriated on the *Teia Maru* in late 1943, and after transferring at Goa to the MS *Gripsholm* they arrived in New York in early December 1943. Mrs Kops recalled later the difficulties in feeding 4,000 internees in the camp and the monotony of the food.[6]

The firm was renamed Allman, Kops and Lee with James Lee becoming a name partner. With American extraterritoriality now abolished, all civilian Americans in China were now subject to local laws[7]. This made James Lee a very important member of the firm because only Chinese were allowed to try cases in the Chinese courts, although Allman did appear at times with Lee. They were also joined by Paul Hoffman, a stateless Jew originally from Austria who had graduated from Aurora University in Shanghai just after the war. In all, the firm had about ten other male staff and ten secretaries.

Two other American lawyers who returned to work in China were Cornell Franklin, the former Chairman of the Shanghai Municipal Council and Robert Bryan, the Chinese speaking former Municipal Advocate. Bryan, who had also been interned until 1945, after a short break at home in America returned to Shanghai with the State Department. He worked on issues around the liquidation of the Shanghai International Settlement including the conversion of consular title deeds to new Chinese title deeds. He left the consulate in 1946 and formed a partnership with Cornell Franklin. Other US lawyers, including Judge Milton Helmick H.D. Rodger and Thomas

---

6   Gripsholm arrival record, Dec 1, 1943; Flight from China, p176 and 206; "Your Wartime Food Problems", The Portsmouth N.H. Herald, Jan 15, 1944, p5
7   US military personnel were covered by separate agreement reached when extraterritoriality ended exempting them from Chinese criminal (but not civil) jurisdiction.

EPILOGUE

Sellett also returned to act as lawyers for different US companies.

Instead of reducing foreign lawyers' work, the end of extraterritoriality increased it. All foreign companies seeking to re-establish themselves in China now needed to comply with Chinese laws and regulations. The incoming government enacted a string of laws that continually changed the legal landscape.

One employee of Allman Kops and Lee at the time, Denis Jen, recalls working long hours keeping up with the demands of the job. One very lucrative practice was helping foreign companies to suspend their business in China. The firm charged at least US$200 for this service, a very sizeable sum at the time. The Chinese officials who issue the approvals looked for their share of the pie and asked Jen for $15 to process each application. He was told by his immediate supervisor that the firm could not pay this. Jen took the problem directly to Allman who, as Jen recounts, was ever practical:

> "I went to Judge Allman. He asked me how much
> it would cost if I took a taxi to do the job. I never took
> taxis, but I quickly answered, 'Maybe $5 for a couple
> of times.' 'Then charge your fare, but include it as
> additional transportation or lunch costs,' he said."[8]

Allman did not give up his career as a newspaperman on his return to Shanghai although this was also likely to be part of his intelligence work. He took over the English language *China Press* which took a virulently pro-Kuomintang line – so much so that even the US Consulate in Shanghai noted an article that was not as fully supportive of the Kuomintang when Allman was out of town. In 1948, CIA files show Allman being requested to arrange a US$600,000 loan

---

8   Denis Jen, "One Thousand Pieces of Gold", Chapter 6 for this and quotes below. This is a solution to an age old problem in China that may possibly still be found in foreign law offices.

● CONFIRMATION ●

DATE   March 19, 1948
FROM: Shanghai
TO   Washington
METHOD: Private Code.

S-271 FOR CHENNAULT WE CONSULTED CHANG KIANGAU WHO SHOWED US TSUYEE PEIS

CABLE QUOTING OUR REQUESTING PEI ASK CHANG FOR FOREIGN EXCHANGE FIFTEEN PLANES

AT FIFTEEN THOUSAND DOLLARS EACH STOP APPARENTLY PEI EITHER MISUNDERSTOOD

COST OR DID NOT UNDERSTAND FOREIGN EXCHANGE TWENTY FIVE THOUSAND EXTRA MAKE READY

DELIVERY PLANES STOP PRESENT STATE OF RECORD EMBARRASSING TO REQUEST SIX HUNDRED

THOUSAND STOP UNLESS PEI GOES FURTHER PERSONALLY ENDORSING PROJECT AND INCREASING

FIGURES BELIEVE VERY DESIRABLE ABANDON THIS AVENUE PARTICULARLY IN VIEW PEI

AND CHANG DIFFERENT POLITICAL CAMPS STOP CONSULT ALLMAN POSSIBLE "EX-IM" LOAN

THIS PURPOSE

CIA cable about consulting Allman to arrange an export import loan to purchase planes for China

Allman partying with members of the Flying Tigers in Shanghai

E-13

to a Chinese warlord on behalf of General Claire Chennault, formerly the head of the Flying Tigers who was supporting the Kuomintang war effort against the communists.

In April 1949, Communist troops were outside Shanghai and Allman lost both of his partners. Paul Kops had left Shanghai on vacation in early 1949 and simply never returned. James Lee, Allman's partner, moved to Hong Kong just before the Communist troops arrived in the city. Lee did not return because of his connections with the former Kuomintang government. He later moved to Taiwan where he re-established Allman Kops and Lee there. (When, in 1965, Lee was joined by another lawyer, C.N. Li, the firm changed its name to Lee & Li.)

Allman was in the United States on a speaking tour supporting the Kuomintang government in early April 1949 but returned despite the threatened Communist takeover. He continued to run the firm with Paul Hoffman as his office manager and two Chinese lawyers Jerry Liu and Denis Jen handling the bulk of the cases. As Jen recalls, Allman remained because "some highly confidential work had come up." The firm was kept busy for a long time helping foreign corporations with the new legal system and, in particular, new labour relations as workers organized in unions. Workers sought to blackmail and extort money from their employers and Allman, Kops and Lee became "the respectable third-party negotiator" to resolve many disputes. The firm was even able to continue enforcing trademarks that had been registered under the old system.

Allman was also handling some highly sensitive and lucrative cases. Jen recalled being called into Allman's office in 1949 and being sworn to secrecy to assist with the translation of documents relating to a banking transaction worth $30 million dollars. As, Jen described, this was an "absolute fortune" in those days. Even more than 50 years later, he declined to disclose what this work involved.

Allman was also able to re-establish his contact with Mao Zedong,

"I came back from a Red death cell"

Brutal arrest

Here's Robert T. Bryan, Jr.'s own story of his escape from operation. Read how an innocent American was railroaded into a Chinese jail without evidence, without trial, without hope of freedom.

Nightmare prison

What trumped-up charges sent him to the death cell? What is it like to spend 16 months in a Red jail? What special "treatment" is reserved for Americans? What is the untold torture of the 1,000 suis?

Miraculous release

What incredible bargain did he make with the Reds to gain freedom? What is "brainwashing"? Read this true story of Communist "justice" in action, I Came Back from a Red Death Cell, by Robert T. Bryan, Jr.

Now on Sale

The Saturday Evening POST
January 11, 1957

Robert Bryan: Back from the dead

meeting him on a number of occasions during his rise to and after he came to power.

In 1950, Allman left what he called "the workers paradise of Shanghai [...] and resided in New York City [...] — of necessity, not choice."[9] He put Allman Kops and Lee in liquidation. Allman's contacts and influence – perhaps even his personal relationship with Mao – appear to have allowed him to leave China with little trouble. The other American lawyers in Shanghai had a much more difficult time. Cornell Franklin was only granted an exit visa in late 1951 and Robert Bryan was imprisoned by the communists in Ward Road Gaol for sixteen months where he was accused of being a spy and attempted to brainwash him. He was freed across the border into Hong Kong in mid-1952. The Communists may have been right about Bryan being a spy. Allman wrote to Bryan at one point asking for assistance in formally joining the CIA.

His work with the CIA was both as a propagandist and a coordinator of operations. His cover was to work in Manhattan as "an editor" for Business International Corporation, a publishing and advisory company that also provided cover for CIA operatives. (Barack Obama worked there for a year in the 1980s, and it is now owned by the Economist Group). In 1950 and 1951, Allman appeared on a television show called The Court of Current Issues which pitted two lawyers and their so-called clients

---

9   Cited in Laura Moorhead, "Norwood Allman and the Third Force: From a Movement of Moderation to An Anti-Communist Crusade", Stanford University thesis, 2010. Much of the information in this epilogue is drawn from that work.

ON TELEVISION

Channel 2   V
Channel 4
Channel 5

7:15-7:30—**Going Places:** Teen-Age Show, With Betty Betz—(7)—
(Première).
8-9—**"Sure As Fate"**—Play: "The Rabbit," With Martin Brooks and
Marie Riva—(2).
8-9—**Star Theatre:** With Milton Berle; Ralph Edwards, Andy Russell,
Janis Paige, Artini and Consuelo, Guests—(4).
8-8:30—**Court of Current Issues:** "Should We Give Aid to Chiang Kai-
shek?"—John Osborne, Judge Norwood F. Allman, Prof. Randolph
Sailer, Dr. Derk Bodde, Francis D. Wells—(5).
8-8:30—**"Drill Call":** Navy Training Program—(9).
8:25—**Basketball:** N. Y. U. vs. St. John's; Manhattan vs. La Salle, at
Madison Square Garden—(11).
8:30-9—**Johns Hopkins Science Review:** "Seventy-Five Years of
Science"—Dr. Detlev W. Bronk—(5).
9-9:30—**Fireside Theatre**—Film: "Going Home," Dabbs Greer—(4).
9-10—**Cavalcade of Bands:** Guy Lombardo Orchestra; Jackie Gleason,
Kitty Kallen, Rolly Rolls—(5).
9:30-10—**"Suspense"**—Play: "The Victim," With Stanley Ridges—(2).
9:30-10—**Circle Theatre:** "That Simmons Girl," With Bonita Granville,
Robert Pastene—(4).
10-10:30—**"Danger"**—Play: "The Corpse and Tighe O'Kane," With Pat
O'Malley, Don Hanmer—(2).
10-11—**Original Amateur Hour,** With Ted Mack—(4).
10-11—**Star Time:** With Frances Langford, Lew Parker; Harry Belafonte
and Singers; Jimmy Nelson, Guests—(5).

Allman appeared on TV in 1951 to discuss if aid should be given to Chiang Kai-shek

against each other on various topics. One 1951 episode of the show discussed "Should We Give Aid to Chiang Kai-shek?"

With the CIA, Allman was also involved in China with "in a number of covert operations [the U.S. government] would rather the Nationalists not know about," most notably organizing "on the mainland anti-Communist forces who were [...] covertly known as the 'Third Force.'" During 1953, Allman was part of the CIA operation that overthrew the democratically-elected president of Guatemala, and he went on to push a similar coup d'état in Iran during 1954.[10]

In 1953, Allman joined a group that sought to extend the Marshall Plan to China. This brought him back to Taiwan and Hong Kong, but not to the Mainland of China. Throughout the 1950s and 1960s, he continued to interview Chinese and others with knowledge of as they

10   Moorhead: Citing Jack Samson. *The Flying Tiger* (New York: First Lyons Press, 2005) 313-314.

Allman in New York. In town in body, perhaps out of town in spirit

arrived in America, often flying to San Francisco of Los Angeles on the West Coast to conduct the interviews.

Allman became fiercely anti-communist, joining and supporting a number of Free China groups. In 1965, he interviewed Chiang Kai-shek in Taiwan in a widely-published interview. Allman asked Chiang who would succeed Mao, to which Chiang replied: "I do not think the Mao regime will last much longer. I therefore prefer not to speculate about Mao's successor."[11]

Allman's beloved wife, Mary Louise, died on New Year's Eve 1970. Allman re-married to Dorothy "Dottie" Dennis, who was twenty years his junior. Dottie was from the town of Carlisle in Pennsylvania, where Allman settled down with trips to Florida in winter.

From time to time, Allman was called upon to give evidence in support of those with financial claims involving China. In 1979, he acted as a witness for a Mr Shvetz regarding the value of properties he had bought in Shanghai.[12] That year, Allman and other former

11   "Chiang Scoffs at China's Might: Asks 'Moral Support" For Mainland Invasion", the Lima News, May 9, 1965, pA-13.
12   Shvetz v Commissioner 38 T.C.M. 1163 (1979).

members of the American Club filed claims for compensation for the seizure of the American Club building in Shanghai in 1953 by the new Communist Government. In 1979, as part of the restoration of diplomatic relations the Chinese had agreed to contribute to a fund to compensate members. The total claim was valued at US$392,230. Allman, as former president of the club, agreed to act as trustee for the moneys. He also gave evidence for some former members to support their claims.[13]

At 75 and still not quite retired, Allman was "working on a series of five-minute radio commentaries on Far East subjects" for national radio. In 1982, Allman was awarded a Blue Ribbon Distinguished Service Medal by the Chinese-American Academic and Professional Association "in recognition of his past achievements and outstanding service to improve Sino-American cultural relations." Allman, in response to the award, said: "China, the country — I do love China, that much is true. [...] Who thought it would go like this?"[14]

On 28 Feburary 1987, Allman died at the age of 93 at the Forest Park Health Centre, Carlisle, Pennsylvania. He was buried at the Lincoln-Noyes Cemetery in Greensboro, Vermont, next to his one true love, Mary Louise.

Allman is gone, but not completely forgotten. The American Club building still stands in Shanghai. It was used for many years as the Higher People's Court and Intermediate People's Court in Shanghai. In 1989, I was taken there to watch a show trial of an alleged thief put on for foreign students. The courts all moved in the early 2000s and the building has stood empty since then. Hamilton House remains on the corner of Fuzhou Road and Jiangxi Middle Road (now called the Fuzhou Building). Allman's offices at Rooms 206 -208 are now occupied by two state-owned companies, the Chinese Medicine

13 Comptroller General of the United States, Claims to the Proceeds of Foreign Claims Settlement Award to American Club, Inc. decision B-201150, May 13, 1981
14 Moorhead, citing: "Biographical File, 1940–1987." Norwood F. Allman Papers, Box 1, File 2, Hoover Institution Archives. Notes and various articles.

Hamilton House in 2016   *Dilapidated corridor leading to Allman's old office*

Industry Association (Room 206) and the China Electronic Appliances (E-China) Company (Rooms 207 and 208). The building looks like it has not been renovated since Allman last occupied it with electrical wiring in the corridors poking out from ancient fuse boxes. The paint in the ill-lit corridors is long faded.

On a brighter note, his firm Allman, Kops and Lee continues, albeit under the name Lee & Li, as one of the largest law firms in Taiwan with a thriving intellectual property practice. The firm occupies many floors of an unpretentious office building near Songshan Airport in Taipei and has partially returned to Shanghai by establishing a relationship with a local Shanghai firm.

But, this book, *Shanghai Lawyer*, with its invaluable insights into a long forgotten time will continue for years to come to serve as a testament to the long fascinating life in China of Judge Norwood Francis Allman.

NORWOOD F. ALLMAN

REVIEW IN THE NEW YORK TIMES, OCTOBER 31, 1943

A Lawyer's Story of War in the East

SHANGHAI LAWYER, By Norwood F. Allman, 283 pp.
Whittlesey House. $2.50.

AFTER NUMBERLESS war-time books on the Orient which have been compounded of "the stuff to feed the troops," "Shanghai Lawyer" is refreshing. It is honest. Its author has not bothered to edit history for our supposed benefit. He tells his story of twenty-seven years in China with good nature, humor and a matter-of-factness which is far more palatable than all the wishful-thinking-in-retrospect to which we have been treated.

Norwood F. Allman - "a green hillbilly from the Blue Ridge Mountains of Virginia" — went to Peking in 1915 as a consular corps student interpreter. After he had learned to speak Mandarin Chinese - and there are so many Chinese dialects that every expert who counts them emerges with a new total - he served in Antung (on the Korea-Manchuria border), Nanking, Tientsin, Tsinan, Tsingtao, Chungking and Shanghai. Made a full consul on his appointment to Shanghai, he was assigned to sit on the International Mixed Court. This strengthened his already well-developed bent for the law and, in 1922, he resigned from the American consular service and entered private practice.

The years bridged by his Shanghai practice were active. Something was always happening. At the outset the Yangtze Valley was overrun with rival warlords who fought every Spring. In 1927 Chiang Kai-shek emerged with the aid of Soviet Russia and the Canton business men. In 1932, and again in 1937, the Japs and Chinese fought around Shanghai. Through it all ran the threads of Chiang's ambition to unite

375

China and Tokyo's grasping for increased influence.

In much of this Mr. Allman played a part. When Chiang arrested the Russian military and political advisers who had helped him to power, the author was retained to effect their release and repatriation. In 1932 and in 1937 he served in the Shanghai Volunteer Corps when the Japanese attacked and was the commandant of the American troop when he left Shanghai for Hongkong at the end of 1941. The outbreak of war between America and Japan caught him in the latter city and he was interned there in the first half of 1942, returning to this country on the *Gripsholm*.

In any book about the Orient background is important. Mr. Allman sketches it in sharply but economically, using each explanation as a setting for a number of amusing anecdotes, many of them unimportant but all worth the telling. "Shanghai Lawyer" gives a better picture of what life was like in the Orient in the days before this war than has appeared in any other Pearl Harbor-inspired book.

The story begins and ends in Hongkong, in the Stanley Prison — and again the writing is colorful but restrained. You know what it was like to be there, with the scarcity of food, the worry about wife and children in Shanghai, the brutal guards. Mr. Allman has brought all this to life and has made it believable with the minutiae of prison organization. The story of discipline in the American camp, of the escapes, abortive as well as successful, of the school for 400 children, of the birth of a baby girl and the labor of making her a crib - all these are rich and rewarding moments.

The strangest chapter in the book is the next to last, which covers that period between Dec. 8 and Jan. 5, during the defense and fall of Hongkong. The island fell on Christmas day, but for eleven days the Japanese did not perfect their prison arrangements. Americans and British were allowed some freedom of movement, and Mr. Allman - taking advantage of the fact that the Japs never guard a back door

- was able to rescue business papers from office buildings occupied by the invaders. In this he was helped by a "tame" Chinese burglar, Chun An-ping, who cheerfully opened safes at $25 the job.

REVIEW IN CHINA WEEKLY REVIEW, OCTOBER 26, 1946

That Rebel Allman!
Reviewed by A.L. Meyer

AMONG WELCOME WARTIME volumes to come to China since the end of the war is this strictly non-technical "Shanghai Lawyer" of "Judge" Allman's, a delightful rambling account of that onetime youthful Virginian student interpreter's 26 busy years in China, starting with his arrival in Peking as a language student and ending with his repatriation aboard the Gripsholm in 1942 following six months as a prisoner of the Japs in Stanley Prison, Hongkong.

That quarter of a century of the Judge's in China saw something doing each and every day after what he himself describes as a slow start. To one of long residence in this country, the book is a series of milestones, each turning back the years to some well-remembered happening or a half-forgotten one. And in addition to events there are names and places and people, all recalled with a whimsical humor which makes Judge Allman's book light, appealing reading throughout.

Dedication of Shanghai Lawyer, incidentally, is "To the Generalissimo and Madame Chiang Kai-shek, The Two Outstanding People of History," in Judge Allman's own words. His collaborator in producing the book was Frances Russell Kay, whom Shanghailanders may recall was on the staff of the North-China Daily News 10 years ago.

Writing his book upon his return to the United States in 1942, the Judge, with good news sense and judgment, devoted his opening chapter to his experiences in Hongkong after its capture by the Japs on Christmas Day, 1941. A week later he joined the other 315 American, 2481 British and 70 Netherlands civilians behind the barbed wire which ringed the former British prison on Stanley Peninsula. It was, he says, an unhappy home.

Even in internment camp, however, Lawyer Allman found plenty of law business. His first client paid with two pancakes and a cup of coffee which were "more welcome than any banquet I can recall or any fee I ever collected." Fortunately for Internee Allman, the Hongkong Japs never caught up with the fact that he was a "wanted man" as far as their compatriots in Shanghai were concerned and he was able to depart, unharmed but minus weight, on the *Asama Maru* for Lorenco Marques. There he was reunited with his wife and family, who had been repatriated from Shanghai on the Conte Verde.

The Judge was lucky because as editor of the *Shun Pao* he had been placed on the Jap blacklist announced by Wang Chingwei & Co. in July 1940, an honor he shared with 86 others, including J. B. Powell of *The Review*; Owner C. V. Starr and Editor Randall Gould of the *Evening Post*; Carroll D. Alcott, Hal P. Mills and L. Z. Yuan, all newsmen once associated with the *Post*. Sammy Chang, editor of the Post's *Ta Mei Wan Pao*, also on the list, was assassinated at Kiessling's tearooms. The *Ta Mei, Post, Shun Pao* and other newspaper plants were bombed. Yet the Japs let Allman slip through their fingers — some joss!

For the newcomer to China as well as the oldtimer, there are great gobs of information, background, color in Shanghai Lawyer. The greenhorn, reading the Judge's tales of "the good old days" and grand old customs, perhaps will sigh over what he missed. But he would best forget all that and buckle down, as the Judge announced he intended, to do his bit in the reconstruction of Shanghai, of whose rise to its former glory he was confident. "No matter what happens," said this Old China Hand in 1943, "I want to return to Shanghai."

Judge Allman did return, of course, for he foresaw, he says in his book, more opportunities than ever before; the need for transportation and communication systems, for industries, for technical and financial help from the Americans to China. He saw no reason why Americans and Chinese could not continue to work together as they had for two decades before Pearl Harbor.

For the oldtimer there is real pleasure in Allman's reminiscenses of Peiping, Tsinan, Peitaiho, Tsingtao, Nanking, Hankow, Chungking and Shanghai, mainly the last-mentioned city, naturally, as it was here that he spent almost 20 years. His recollections of people and events are amazingly clear considering he did not have his files — they were in Jap hands in his Hamilton House offices. The Judge charitably resorted to fictitious names in several instances in which the characters concerned are still alive.

His chapters on the International Mixed Court, where, he sat as American assessor; Americans in this country; the U.S. Court for China; his "Chih Fan" and other cases; his "Bolshevik" clients and his dossier in municipal police files; his *Shun Pao* editorship and other extra-legal activities and his sweeping triumph in the last Shanghai Municipal Council elections as the American "non-machine" or rebel candidate — all will be found of more than passing interest by foreigners and Chinese alike.

ACKNOWLEDGEMENTS
by Douglas Clark

I WOULD LIKE to thank Graham Earnshaw of Earnshaw Books for commissioning this work and Jason Wong for his hard work on putting the various parts together.

Norwood Allman's grandsons, Richard Allman and Neal Burnham, both provided photographs and useful information about the grandparents, Norwood and Mary Louise Allman. Thank you to both of them. Laura Moorhead, who wrote her masters thesis at Stanford on Allman kindly shared her thesis and spoke to me at length about her research. I am very grateful to her for this. Thanks also to David Ian Chambers who provided much useful information on the case of the mysterious Mr X.

Dominique Wadley and Laura de Crescenzo both helped me with research at the Bibliotheca Siccawei in Shanghai. My sister, Nicola, visited the National Library in Australia to retrieve some hard to find archive materials. Thank you to all three of them as well as to the staff at Bibliotheca Siccawei who provided much useful assistance during my research there. I am also grateful to David Allison who lent me his copy of Allman's trade mark text as well as a text book on Shanghainese that included many court forms from the International Mixed Court. Thank you also to Alicia Mayer Beverly for her prompt responses in regards Rudolph Mayer together with my apologies for uncovering a black sheep in the family.

My thanks also to Daisy Wang of Lee & Li in Taiwan for sharing a photo of James Lee and providing me with a very interesting history of the firm.

SHANGHAI LAWYER

Simon Drakeford (author of the wonderful It's a Rough Game but Good Sport) located the very hard to find picture of the US Court for China sitting in Peiping and he and Dr James Ginther, Senior Archivist of the Archives Branch, Marine Corps History Division helped me track down a high resolution copy. Col Mary Reinwald (USMC (Ret.)) was very helpful and responsive in providing me that copy. My thanks to all three.

I was also able in preparing this work to rely on research that I had done for my history of British and American court in China and Japan, Gunboat Justice. I thank, once again, those who provided assistance with that book.

As always, thank you my wife Tomoko and children, Leila, Kai, Ray and India for your patience and support.

INDEX

As an autobiography, almost all events described involved Norwood Allman. Norwood Allman is, therefore, only indexed where there is no other reference to a person or event in the index.

n = footnote; i=illustration; p=photograph; t=textbox; E= Epilogue

Antung (Andong/Dandong)   40-41,
41p

Appeals 69-70 (Mixed court), 99n, 100,
112, 118, 120n,

Arnold, Julean   65, 65p

Asama Maru   18, 19p, E1

Assassinations (or attempts)
vii-viii, 170n, 210n, 258n, 260-3, 283-4,
310-11, 324-30, E5

Assessors (Mixed Court)   vi, 1, 26t,
27n, 69-84, 99, 201, 235n, 245n

B

Barraud, J.   207, 208i

Bassett, Arthur 125p, 126, 271-2, 272p,
275-8

Beidaihe   See Peitaiho

Bell, Leslie Malcolm   292-6, 294p

Berg (accused Russian)   201n

Bigamy   233-4

Blood Alley   179, 180p, 293-4

Bluecher, Vasili See: Galens (General)

Bolsheviks   198-211, E7

Borodin, Michael   198-201

Bourne, Kenneth Morison   282p,
324-5, 325i, 328, E5

Bradford, Peter   305

Brewer, Andrew Jackson   25-27, 26p

Bridge House Prison   218, 322t

Brinson, Eugene (real name for Fred
Johnson)   See: Johnson, Fred

British American Tobacco   56, 272n

British Bar Association   127-128

British lawyers   13, 98, 177, 288, 296

British Residents' Association   270

British Supreme Court for China
127n, 136n, 137i, 144, 231, 232-3, 232n,
252p, 324n

British Intelligence   15, E3

Bronin, Yakov   See: Walden, Joseph

Bronski (aka Jones)   155-57

Brown, Marian   240-242

Bryan, Robert T.   119i, 132p, 147t, 285,
288n, E2, E11, E15, E15i

Bucknell, Howard 62, 62p, 64, 75p, 99i

Business International Corporation
E15

C

Carberry, Charles (aka Bernard
Pinder)   233-4, 233i

Carl, Kate   35, 35p

Carney, J.W.   277p, 284n

Censorship   306-7, 319, 338-9

Central Intelligence Agency   viii,
E12-4, E13i, E15-6

Century of Humiliation   viii

Chang, Samuel H.   328-9, 329p

Chang Yao-tsen (Zhang Yaozeng)   82

Chapin, Albert Clark   25-27, 26p

Chapman, William Alden   138, 140p

Charlie Chan (Chinese machine
gunner)   253-4, 255n

Cheloo University   45-47, 47p

Chang (Colonel)   259-60

TABLE OF CASES